SUPERVISION &
MANAGEMENT

SUPERVISION & MANAGEMENT

A Guide to Modifying Work Behavior

JOHN N. MARR

AND

RICHARD T. ROESSLER

The University of Arkansas Press • Fayetteville • 1994

98 97 96 95 94   5 4 3 2 1

Designed by Gail Carter

The paper used in this publication meets the minimum requirements of the American National Standard for Permanence of
Paper for Printed Library Materials Z39.48-1984. ∞

Library of Congress Cataloging-in-Publication Data

Marr, John N.
   Supervision and management : a guide to modifying work
behavior / John N. Marr and Richard T. Roessler.
      p. cm.
   Includes bibliographical references and index.
   ISBN 1-55728-306-0 (pbk. : alk. paper)
   1. Supervision of employees—Handbooks, manuals, etc.
   2. Behavior modification—Handbooks, manuals, etc.
   I. Roessler, Richard, 1944- . II. Title.
   HF5549.12
   658.3'02—dc20   93-36797
                                                        CIP

To our wives, Jo and Janet,
and to our children,
Brian, Amy, Jennifer,
and Kristin

Contents

SECTION I

Using the ABC Model to Improve Work Behavior

SECTION 2

Managing Behaviors to Affect Outcomes

SECTION 3

Improving Individual Employee Performance

SECTION 4

ABC From Top to Bottom

List of Applications, Figures, and Tables

Preface

For the past 25 years we have promoted and taught the use of behavior-centered management in industry, retail and service businesses, educational institutions, rehabilitation facilities, and prisons. During that time we have been pleased not only to see increased use of behavior-centered approaches in institutions where we have been consultants, but also to see the increasing number of research articles demonstrating the successful use of these procedures to solve the "bottom line" problems in areas such as productivity, quality control, net sales, shrinkage, customer service, workers' compensation claims, and worker dissatisfaction.

When we began presenting seminars and workshops to managers in industrial and retail companies, we also began receiving requests from the participants for written information about applications of the behavior-centered management procedures. Although there were many books on behavior modification, we found none that extended the principles of applied behavior analysis to the area of managing work behaviors. There were a few textbooks written for the college classroom, and there was a small percentage of books that applied a few of the principles of reinforcement to management. Although there were many applications of behavior analysis in organizations that had been published in journals, few of them had been collected or described in a book on behavior-centered management. Thus, it was Miller Williams, director of the University of Arkansas Press, who prompted and encouraged us to begin the first draft. He had invited us to present the behavior-centered approach to the department heads of university presses when they met in Fayetteville in 1987. Williams did not attend the session (Tom T. Hall, country music star and member of the Country Music Writers Hall of Fame, had just published his new book and was speaking at the same time in the next auditorium), but he did send some representatives of the U of A Press (either they didn't like country music or they were afraid of the boss). Anyway, somebody said something nice about the behavior-centered management approach, and so, here's the book.

We must thank all of those managers who through the years contributed their experiences and agreed to test the principles of applied behavior analysis within their organizations. Special thanks to Gene Harwood, past director of the Hot Springs Rehabilitation Center; Joe Sharrer and Joe DeDimonico, past directors of the Tennessee Rehabilitation Center in Smyrna; Bob Sarver, former Commissioner of Corrections of Arkansas; Mark Simmons, CEO of Simmons Industries; Ishmi Kazmi, vice-president of Superior Industries; and Suzanne Alford, senior vice-president of Wal-Mart.

We also wish to thank Kristin Henry for her assistance in typing and Eunice Millett for her many trips to the library to copy just one more article or to look up one more reference. But it was the dedication of Eileen Worthen to all the behaviors required in producing a book—typing, editing, copying, coping with the computer, and doing 90% of it on weekends—that resulted in a book. Her positive reinforcement of our efforts and usually subtle criticisms increased our quantity of work and improved the quality of the product. However, the polish to the product was added by our editor, Debbie Bowen. Not only did she edit and correct the text, but she also demonstrated the practices described in the book as she managed our behaviors.

Although neither of us was fortunate enough to directly study under B. F. Skinner, we knew him and studied his work. His influence is present in every application of behavior-centered management as described herein.

Managing Another Person

One person manages another in the sense in which he manages himself. He does not do so by changing feelings or states of mind. The Greek gods were said to change behavior by giving men and women mental states, such as pride, mental confusion, or courage, but no one has been successful in doing so since. One person changes the behavior of another by changing the world in which he lives. In doing so, he no doubt changes what the other person feels or introspectively observes (Skinner, 1974, p. 181).

Introduction

Richard Roessler and I occasionally are asked to speak on topics in psychology to a variety of audiences. On one occasion, I had been asked to speak in Little Rock, Arkansas, on the topic "How to Motivate the Unemployed to Return to Work." The audience appeared startled when I began my speech by saying that *we don't care* if the unemployed are *motivated* to return to work. What we do care about is whether they *return* to work. I then described the use of behavioral procedures to get people to return to work. One individual came up afterward saying he was in a big hurry to go to another meeting but that he had a lot of questions to ask me about those behavioral methods. He handed me a piece of paper with his name and telephone number, saying he would buy me lunch if I would give him a call whenever I was in Pine Bluff, a town in southern Arkansas. Not being a person who lets the opportunity for a free lunch escape, I tucked the piece of paper into my wallet. About a month later, after finishing my meeting in Pine Bluff, I dialed the number he had given me. I knew I was in trouble when the voice at the other end of the line said: "Tucker Prison Farm."

When the Period at the End of the Sentence Is Death[1]

I get nervous even when I'm driving within the speed limit and I pass those flashing blue lights where a police officer is giving somebody else a ticket. For my free lunch, I had to be escorted between two prison towers manned by trustees with shotguns. I stood petrified while trying to appear cool when they searched me and confiscated my keys and lighter. It turned out that my host, a full-time instructor with the prison system, had the unusual task of trying to teach eighth- to eleventh-grade English to the prisoners.

"You said forget motivation and center in on the behavior. I haven't been able to get them to do anything. I tell them the importance of good writing, the need to spell properly, to punctuate their sentences. I can't even get them to use the dictionaries." He went on to say that they had all these new dictionaries that had been donated to the prison and not one had been opened as far as he knew.

Still casting my eyes around the lunch tables where at least a hundred prisoners were eating and talking and, I was sure, watching me, I stuck my foot further into my mouth, "That should be easy, just shape them into—"

That was all he needed to hear. "Okay, come on into my class and show me. My class meets in just a few minutes."

With thoughts about there being no such thing as a free lunch, I stuck close to him as we passed through more metal gates and guards on the way to his classroom, a huge room with the library on one side and about 20 chairs facing the teacher's desk and blackboard on the other. As the "students" came slouching in, smoking and talking, I noticed a guard with a shotgun following them in and closing the door. At first I thought the guard might be taking the course, but he positioned himself against the door, holding the gun like a hunter at a deer stand.

"Aren't we in the middle of the prison, with all those gates and guards between us and the outside?" I asked.

"Just about dead center," the instructor replied.

"Then why the guard?"

"State law. Whenever prisoners from maximum security, where they're waiting for the electric chair, come to class or whatever, we have to have an armed escort present."

Many thoughts about motivation passed through my head about then: (a) I was motivated to get out of there, and there was only one door, blocked by an armed guard; (b) I was motivated not to get shot, and it occurred to me that amongst the prisoners there were some with nothing to lose who were sitting between the guard and me; and (c) How do you motivate men to learn the difference between a noun and a verb or where to put a comma in a sentence when they are waiting for the electric chair? Do you tell them the devil may check their punctuation before he will let them in the less-than-pearly gates?

The specific procedure used with the prisoners is presented in detail in a later chapter. But the challenge to the prison instructor and to those who attended my speech in Little Rock is the central theme of this book: We can ignore motivation if we attend to behaviors.

—Jack Marr

In *Supervision and Management: A Guide to Modifying Work Behavior*, Marr and I will prove that there are rules of management that can change the way people work. We will demonstrate specific manager behaviors that will enhance profitability; increase productivity; improve quality; reduce inventory shrinkage; increase work safety; improve customer service; diminish employee health costs and workers' compensation claims; reduce absenteeism, tardiness, and theft; and improve communication. Our approach is called behavior-centered management. It teaches managers the "what," "where," "when," and "to whom" rules critical for organizational success. In fact, we will show that when behavior-centered rules are followed, good attitudes, employee satisfaction, high morale, and motivation occur as natural byproducts of effective management behaviors.

—Rick Roessler

The Focus on Behavior

The behavior-centered perspective on management stresses that the behaviors of people at work are a function of the environment in which the work occurs. Because the managers' behaviors are part of that work environment, they influence the performance of the workers. Two important types of manager behaviors exist: management antecedent behaviors and management consequence behaviors. Management antecedent behaviors are those actions a manager can take before the employee begins the targeted work behavior. Management consequence behaviors are those actions the manager takes after the targeted behavior.

Although the behavior-centered approach does not reject attitudes, motivation, feelings, or personality, it defines them as covert or hidden states that we cannot directly observe. Behaviors, on the other hand, are directly observable, overt events. According to the behavior-centered approach, manager antecedents and consequences are far more efficient and effective techniques for changing behavior than approaches based on concepts such as attitudes, motivation, or personality. By their own actions, managers can alter conditions of the work environment which will, in turn, change unsatisfactory employee behaviors.

The Bottom Line: Is It Successful?

Behavior-centered management strategies focus on the work behaviors of employees and on the supervisory techniques that can be used to encourage employees to adopt and maintain such behaviors. The behavior-centered approach originated in the field of applied behavior analysis that is often called behavior modification. Most of the principles and procedures were developed from research in operant conditioning and, to a lesser extent, respondent conditioning, social learning, and cognitive psychology.[2] Since the 1960s, the behavior-centered approach has been successfully applied to individual and social problems in many "helping" professions such as clinical and community psychology, psychiatry, psychiatric nursing, nursing, medicine, rehabilitation, social work, preventive dentistry, and public health.[3] When used to treat individual problems of patients, the procedures are more often called behavior therapy. More recently, business and industry, sports, physical education, and recreation have been using behavioral procedures. The merger of the principles of applied behavior analysis with the field of management is referred to as organizational behavior modification or O. B. Mod.[4] The behavior-centered approach has been proven to be successful in all of these fields.

What Is the Alternative?

Managers do need help, but sometimes they are confused by competing management theories. In a recent survey of studies conducted across different organizations, occupations, geographical locations, and time periods, over 60% of the workers studied said that their immediate supervisors created the most stressful aspect of their jobs.[5] Most employed adults reported that they are working for or had worked for "intolerable" bosses. The survey suggested that between 60 to 75% of managers are incompetent. Even if that startling statistic might be an exaggeration, it suggests that many people hold managerial positions for which they have had no significant prior training. As a result, many managers rely on their experience with other managers or their own personal ways of dealing with people.

Suggesting that managers need to learn to manage is not a new, earth-shaking revelation. Dozens of management and leadership training programs have been developed and used by military establishments, industrial and retail corporations, and human-service delivery organizations. A number of books have been written presenting a variety of theories of leadership and management. Some of these advocate another approach to management: the personality approach.

For example, one theory recommends that we screen managers using a personality inventory that identifies managers with traits on the "dark side" of personality, such as dependency, fear of failure, arrogance, attention-seeking, lack of common sense, interpersonal sensitivity, and untrustworthiness (see note 5). Presumably, use of that screening instrument would reduce management incompetence within organizations, which would, in turn, result in decreases in job stress, absenteeism, sabotage, and grievances and increases in productivity. Notice that the solution to management problems requires administration of a personality inventory to screen out managers with dark-side traits or to identify managers who need training in ways to overcome their dark sides.

Blaming dark-side traits of the supervisor leads to the circular reasoning commonly associated with the internal, personality approach to management. The supervisor is an A (she has dark-side traits). Therefore, she acts in certain ways. She acts in certain ways; therefore, she is an A. Certainly, traits, whether they be dark or light, predict behaviors across situations with some validity. A "dependent" manager would be more likely to call for help, ask his supervisor, or even do nothing when he had to make a decision than would an "independent" manager. But, before we turn to personality tests to screen managers, it is important to recognize that no personality test has perfect validity in predicting behaviors or even high predictive validity for every area of management responsibility.

Productivity

Consider production. Increased productivity is an essential goal of managers regardless of the industry in which they work, and managers and their *behaviors* are vital to the productivity equation. Because they have the greatest influence on the overall productivity of the labor force, managers must know how to perform their roles effectively and not shift the blame to anyone or anything else.

Finding Fault

When productivity is low, where shall we place the blame? Is it the fault of the workers, or is it the fault of the manager?

Blaming the employee. Consider where the blame is placed in this scenario:

"He's got a bad attitude!"

Two warehouse managers are discussing George's problem. George is always behind in his work.

"Everyone in the warehouse is waiting for George to move pallets of freight to locations where they are needed. I'm at a loss," his manager says. "I have warned him that he'd better speed up or else. He just doesn't care. He doesn't seem to have the right personality for work—no sense of responsibility. What do you do with people like George?"

The other manager thinks a minute and says that George's problem is clearly one of attitude. "George probably doesn't want to work in the first place. I've got one just like him. They just have a bad attitude about work. They really don't care. If personnel would just hire people who want to work, half of our problems would disappear."

Personality, sense of responsibility, attitude—which is it, and how do we know? If we ask the supervisors how they know that George doesn't care, doesn't have a work personality, or doesn't have the right attitude, we are liable to hear circular reasoning that doesn't explain anything:

Because he doesn't do B, he's an A.

Because he's an A, he doesn't do B.

Even though most managers readily recognize that circular logic is not helpful, some may lapse into personality-oriented explanations for poor productivity. Examples of manager explanations for poor performance that rely on personality attributions are provided in Table I-1. Each attributes the cause of the problematic situation to some internal (personality) construct of the person.[6] Personality explanations for poor performance lead nowhere other than to try to change the employee's attitude or to fire him and replace him with someone else, who, in all probability, will turn out to have an attitude problem as well. But suppose we focus on the attitudes and personalities of the managers instead. Does that help resolve productivity problems any better?

TABLE I-I
Personality Attributes for Unsatisfactory Performance

Internal	Non-Specific
Lacks purpose	Moody
Bad attitude	Bad actor
Unmotivated	Rebellious
Close-minded	Procrastinator
No work ethic	Negative
Self-centered	Trouble-maker
Strong-willed	Instigator
Know-it-all	Lazy
Immature	Sloppy
Burnt out	Obnoxious
Doesn't care	Careless
Spaced out	Whiner
No spirit	Non-attentive

Blaming the supervisor.   Listen as Bill's supervisor blames him for the productivity problem in the department.

> "We still have problems in Department 10. Bill just can't seem to motivate his people. Production has been down for weeks there. No matter how much pressure I put on him, freight doesn't move any faster. He doesn't seem to have the personality necessary for leadership."

Here we go again—another internal cause for problems in productivity. How was Bill chosen for a management position in the first place? Either he was promoted based on his supervisor's recommendation or the personnel department selected him. If the supervisor made the recommendation, was it based on demonstrated behaviors of leadership, on the "good old boy" career ladder, or on the belief that the best worker would automatically make a good manager?

If the personnel department selected him, what were the criteria for selection or promotion? Because personality characteristics are hard to assess via standard interviews of people applying for management positions, personnel departments too often select managers for aesthetic appearances rather than for competence. Or, they depend upon personality screening tests of questionable validity.

Instead of blaming productivity problems on worker traits or on manager personalities, we should focus on the behaviors of the employees and the supervisors. When we do that, we are taking a behavior-centered perspective on productivity problems.

In *Supervision and Management,* we show how to apply behavior-centered management in profit and nonprofit organizations, retail businesses, industrial plants, hospitals, universities, rehabilitation centers, and government offices. The specific applications address two types of employee behaviors—behaviors that cause problems for the employer because they are too infrequent (e.g., not waiting on customers) or because they are too frequent (e.g., personal telephone calls). Unsatisfactory outcomes of behaviors, such as shrinkage, cash shortages, workers' compensation claims, and accident rates, are also discussed. In almost all cases, the applications demonstrate effective use of the behavior-centered procedures in changing behaviors of employees and, therefore, management outcomes.

The more similar the setting of a particular application in the book is to the setting in which the reader wants to apply the intervention, the more likely the same effects will be found. The applications throughout the book occur in small grocery stores, restaurants, administrative sections of hospitals, real-estate offices, large industrial plants, large retail stores, and even the territory of the self-employed beaver trapper. In every case, we have selected interventions that demonstrate the principles of behavior-centered management implemented in carefully controlled studies that include behavioral measures of success. Although data on worker satisfaction and attitudes toward the behavior-centered approach are often included, no study was selected if it solely relied on questionnaires or surveys, no matter how controlled or rigorous the research.

The Organization of the Book

In the early chapters of *Supervision and Management,* we discuss the basics of behavior-centered management. First, a distinction is made between identification of outcomes and management of outcomes. Outcomes such as superior production rates, higher product quality, increased net profits, and lower numbers of customer complaints are the goals of management and must be identified, but not managed. Once identified as goals, the outcomes enable the manager to define the behaviors that will produce those goals.

The need to pinpoint the employee behaviors that produce unsatisfactory or superior outcomes is essential. Unless the specific behaviors are identified, the manager cannot apply the strategies of behavior-centered management. The procedures described in the early chapters of this book are management antecedent and consequent behaviors that successfully modify behavior. Cases in industrial, retail, educational, and human-service delivery settings are used to illustrate the successful application of behavior-centered principles. Managers will understand the variety of approaches available for changing the behaviors of employees by reading chapters 1 through 5 in that order.

Chapters 6 through 10 describe methods for influencing behaviors that affect organizational productivity and net profits, quality and error rates, tardiness and absenteeism, safety, employee health, and customer service. These chapters may be read in any order. Some of the techniques address behaviors that enhance or disrupt rate, quantity, or quality of production, and some address those behaviors that cause high accident rates or high workers' compensation claims. Chapters 11 and 12 are focused on individual problem behaviors related to the effective operation of an organization, whether it is an industrial plant, a retail store, a hospital, or a school. These behaviors include arriving on time, dressing appropriately, responding to supervision, initiating actions to prevent or correct errors, working successfully with co-workers, bizarre behaviors that disturb others, and sexual harassment.

Chapter 13, the final chapter, is directed at implementing the behavior-centered procedures throughout an organization. How do upper- and middle-level management get first-line managers or supervisors to use the procedures, or vice versa, we might add?

At any point in this book, you may be convinced that a particular behavior-centered procedure will work in your business or organization. But how can you prove it to yourself, your boss, your employees, or even your stockholders? To do so, you will need the information in the appendix, "Proving It With Hard Data the Easy Way."

Summary

Managers need a clear set of guidelines on what to do to solve problems related to profitability, attendance, safety, etc. Too often it has been a matter of trial and error as managers attempt to change those work outcomes. Sometimes, blame for the lack of success is placed on the inner characteristics of the employee; for example, bad attitudes or lack of motivation. Sometimes, blame is placed on managers and the dark side of their personalities.

We believe that a more successful approach to management exists. Referred to as *organizational behavior modification,* it has its roots in the field of applied behavior analysis. O. B. Mod. avoids the frustration of trying to change or select for the inner characteristics of attitude or personality and, instead, concentrates on management behaviors that effectively and efficiently change the work behaviors of employees.

To demonstrate the effectiveness of this behavior-centered approach, a variety of applications in profit and nonprofit organizations are presented throughout this book. Each of the applications uses a well-controlled research design. In the first half of the book, the basic principles of the behavior-centered approach are described. In the last half of the book, the principles are implemented in solving problems with production, safety, tardiness, absenteeism, and employee health. The last chapter describes the procedures by which upper-level management can increase utilization of behavior-centered management throughout the organization. Finally, the appendix is available to help readers when they are convinced of the value of behavior-centered management and are ready to prove its effectiveness in their own setting.

Notes

1. This incident precipitated the introduction of applied behavioral analysis into Arkansas prisons, which was later described in part by Marr, Lilliston, & Zelhardt (1974).

2. The father of behavior modification, B. F. Skinner, predicted the extensive application of operant conditioning procedures in business, industry, and other economic endeavors in his book *Science and Human Behavior* (1953).

3. Skinner and his students were largely responsible for the growth and expansion of the applications to all of these fields or in influencing those professionals who first introduced the procedures in their respective professions.

4. Luthans & Lyman (1973); Luthans & Kreitner (1985). Those who are most active in basic and applied research and applications of O. B. Mod. are usually members of the Division of Experimental Analysis of Behavior of the American Psychological Association; the special-interest group, Organizational Behavior Network, of the Association for Behavior Analysis; or the special-interest group, Organizational Behavior Management Network, of the Association for the Advancement of Behavior Therapy.

5. Hogan & Morrison (1990).

6. Because those terms put the blame on something inside the person, such as mental state or cognitive process, this viewpoint has often been called the internal explanation for what people do. Luthans & Kreitner (1985), p. 3.

Using the ABC Model to Improve Work Behavior

CHAPTER I

Affecting Outcomes by Using the Behavior-Centered Approach

Outcomes

Managers are judged by the outcomes of their stores, industrial plants, or businesses, and outcomes are the results of management or mismanagement. They are the tracks in the sand; they are what is left after the action is over. They can be examined 1 minute, 1 hour, 1 day, and often 1 year later. Because managers are judged by these outcomes, they sometimes try to manage outcomes. But that is like trying to manage history. Accountants who doctor the books are managing history by changing the data that produced the profit-and-loss statements. A president was threatened with impeachment for supposedly attempting to modify recorded conversations. Managing history can be an impeachable offense.

Cautioning one about managing history does not mean that we oppose changing outcomes. Sometimes we want to change outcomes. For example, film editors are paid to modify the actual events recorded by the camera. We pay millions to the movie theaters to see these works of art. But net profit or safety records aren't works of art; they are the outcomes of events in business and industry. Although we cannot manage outcomes, we can manage the causes of outcomes. Therefore, it is important to discriminate between causes and outcomes. Table 1-1 shows a number of different types of unsatisfactory outcomes.

Causes of Outcomes

What causes unsatisfactory outcomes? "The activities of people," we reply. But what causes people to act that way? The answer to that question is critical.

3

TABLE I-I

Unsatisfactory Outcomes

Trash on a public beach	Customer complaints
A child's failing grade report	Half-empty shelves in a store
A dirty shirt	An empty truck waiting to be loaded
Being 30 pounds overweight	Shrinkage in inventory
A wrecked automobile	Flaws in a manufactured product
A decrease in productivity from 60 to 40 units/hr.	Workers' compensation claims

The procedures used by management to remedy problems and achieve desirable outcomes in the organization depend upon what is perceived to be the cause of the problem. Shakespeare put it well: "Find out the cause of this effect, or rather say, the cause of this defect, for effect defective comes by cause." Taking Shakespeare to heart in their studies, psychologists have found that although people frequently ask why something happens, the answers they give to the "why" often depend upon whether the outcome is defective. Many times, superior outcomes are judged to be internally caused; for example, we may say, "We won the game because of our superior ability." But external causes are often blamed when we fail; for example, we say, "The referees gave them the game."

Similarly, poor outcomes are attributed to internal or external causes, depending upon who was involved, we or they. "I flunked because the professor gives impossible tests." But, "My roommate flunked his test because he has no self-discipline." The fundamental attribution error is one in which the observer overestimates the importance of traits and underestimates the importance of situations when seeking explanations for another's behavior.[1]

We see this attribution error too often as managers identify outcomes and the attributed causes. Managers may attribute an excellent outcome to their superior management style, but a poor outcome may be attributed to the economy, poor luck, or the kind of people working for them. Since the solution depends upon the cause that we identify, it is important that we look at the different types of attributions of causes. In this section, we examine different types of attributions, then present the reasons for choosing a behavior-centered approach.

The s-O-r Model

Sometimes, people and organizations use a medical or illness model to find their solutions. When our children stop eating or run a fever, we say that they are sick and that we need the doctor to determine why. The physician examines the child and identifies the cause of the illness. When management adopts the medical model, unsatisfactory profit-and-loss statements are attributed to some underlying illness. The company is sick, so a doctor must be called. Typically, the doctor is a consultant or a team of consultants from within or outside the organization. The unsatisfactory outcomes are symptoms of an underlying disease that must be identified.

Similarly, causes are sometimes attributed to inner states of the individual. This s-O-r model is adopted from the traditional mental health model of the psychologist. The first symbol, "s," stands for any and all stimuli that affect "O," the organism or person, and "r" stands for the person's response to that "s." Stimulus (s) and response (r) are easily understood, but it is the big "O" that causes us problems. Psychologists have put all kinds of mysterious entities which they call hypothetical constructs or intervening variables inside the big "O"; for example, motivation, personality traits, attitudes, morale, self-esteem, feelings of self-regard, need-achievement, drive, and spirit. They select one or more to explain an unsatisfactory outcome. Poor grades reflect a lack of motivation. The activities that caused the divorce reflect a bad attitude toward marriage. Low production indicates poor morale. An empty truck waiting to be loaded shows the laziness of the workers.

Consider the parent who comes home from work and sees empty garbage cans at the curb in front of his neighbor's house. And sure enough, there are his own garbage cans filled to capacity in the carport. His son was supposed to take the cans down to the curb before he left for school. The father walks into the house, infuriated. "Wait until that kid gets home," he tells his wife. "He didn't take the garbage cans down again. He's *lazy*. He has no *sense of responsibility. All he cares about* is playing and watching TV."

Note the s-O-r inferences in these comments. When the boy does come home, he will receive the usual lecture, a consequence that is at least 7 hours too late. From the boy's perspective, the lecture is a consequence of coming home. It will probably do little to stimulate him to take the garbage cans to the curb on pickup days.

Companies that take the s-O-r approach believe that unsatisfactory outcomes are due to workers with the wrong attitudes, poor motivation, and little pride. These companies treat problems by trying to fix the workers and by being more selective when hiring new employees. Or the company may try to get its managers to change the poor attitudes that their subordinates have toward work, which may serve only to frustrate the manager and annoy the employees.

Psychology has generally found that it is nearly impossible to change an attitude without changing the behavior of the person first. A number of psychologists have found that changes in roles, circumstances, or context will first change employee behaviors and then later their attitudes.[2] Sometimes the change in attitude required by the change in behavior is in conflict with the original attitudes.[3] *cognitive dissonance → change of attitude*

Behavior-centered management stresses that outcomes are caused by the behaviors of people. Therefore, behaviors that lead to unsatisfactory outcomes can and should be changed.

Behavior Problems

Because unsatisfactory behaviors are the source of an unsatisfactory outcome, it is necessary to identify the specific behaviors that cause a particular outcome. They can be of two types—behaviors that occur too seldom or those that occur too often. Those that occur too seldom are *behavior deficits*, and those that occur too often are *behavior surpluses* or *excesses*.

When behavior deficits occur, jobs that need to be done are not getting done. What is the person *not* doing that should be done? If management increases those desirable behaviors, the outcomes will take care of themselves. Note the following examples of outcomes and behavior deficits:

Outcome: Blemishes in the paint.
Behavior Deficit: The painter is *not* inspecting the spray gun or cleaning the nozzle periodically. As a result, many toys, wheels, or fenders are poorly painted.

Outcome: Too few repeat customers.
Behavior Deficit: The employees do *not* greet the customers when they come into the store. As a result, many customers leave the store reporting that the employees are unfriendly.

Outcome: Empty shelves.
Behavior Deficit: The employee does *not* walk the aisles looking for shelves that need to be restocked, and he does *not* re-order early enough in the week. As a result, many customers can't find merchandise, and sales plummet.

Behavior excesses may also cause unsatisfactory outcomes. Employees who are busy playing practical jokes, making personal phone calls, or taking extra long breaks are not doing their jobs. The behavior excesses can cause mistakes on the job; or, they may cause behavior deficits. For example, when making personal phone calls, employees may miss flaws in the products they are supposed to be inspecting; they are not waiting on customers; or they are not stocking the shelves when they should be.

Behavior Specificity

Too often, managers do not describe the specific behavior problems to the employees, but instead they speak in generalities. If they operate out of the s-O-r model of management, they make inferences about the inner states of the person. To tell the employee that he is careless, irresponsible, not motivated, or lazy has a wide range of negative effects. It may anger the person, produce resentment, or create a feeling of helplessness. The manager may be referring to the shelves not being stocked when she tells the employee that he needs to show more concern for the stock or that he is not keeping an eye on the merchandise. Since the manager wasn't specific, the employee may think the customers are stealing.

Parents who take their children out to restaurants may fall into the same trap by warning them to "act like ladies and gentlemen." Each child has a different interpretation of that directive. When asked what their parents mean, they reply, "I can only go to the bathroom three times while inside"; "I should talk quietly"; "I have to say *please*"; or "I shouldn't pick my nose."

If we want the clerk to keep the greeting cards sorted at Christmas, we should not simply tell her to be alert. Instead, we need to be specific and tell her to inspect the card rack every 15 minutes or every hour and to separate the "Get Well, Grandma" cards from the "Happy Anniversary, Lover" cards, and to separate other misplaced cards from the different categories of Christmas cards.

There's an easy way to determine whether we have been specific enough in identifying the behavior deficits or excesses that cause the unsatisfactory outcome. All we need to do is to conduct the following test: If three people were asked to count how many times the targeted employee acted in the unacceptable manner, would they all come back with the same answer? "Go observe Sally and count how many times she displays a bad attitude toward the merchandise." The reports from the observers would have little reliability; that is, the observers would often disagree about examples of "bad attitudes." When the behavior problems causing the unacceptable outcome are described in such a manner that observers would have high reliability, we have taken the first step in using the behavior-centered approach. "Go observe Sally and count the number of times that she rearranges the card rack."

The Behavior-Centered Approach

The behavior-centered approach directs management efforts at changing the behaviors of employees. Instead of trying to alter attitudes or personality characteristics, the behavior-centered manager focuses on the behaviors that cause the outcome. Because behavior is controlled by antecedents and consequences, it can be changed by antecedents and consequences.

The Distinction Between Antecedents and Consequences

Both antecedents and consequences influence behavior. The difference between them, however, is that antecedents precede the behavior and consequences follow the behavior. They are like two guides who have been hired to take us to our destination. Antecedent (A) is in front, and Consequence (C) is behind. Without A, we would not know which path to follow. Without C, we would fall further and further behind. Anything that is done before which activates the correct behavior—prevents the behavior deficit—is an antecedent. Anything that is done before which suppresses inappropriate behaviors of employees—prevents the behavior excesses—is also an antecedent. When the manager has identified the behavior problems that cause the unsatisfactory outcomes, anything that she does to prevent those behavior problems from occurring is an antecedent.

Some would refer to antecedents as activators. Although *activator* is an easier term to remember, it does not accurately describe the role of an antecedent. Some management antecedents do not activate behavior but instead suppress behavior. For example, two salesclerks may meet in the aisle between their departments every Monday morning to talk about their weekend activities. If the assistant manager appears, his presence suppresses this socialization but may not activate work behavior. Similarly, other antecedents suppress behavior excesses (such as horseplay, gossip, and theft) that interfere with work.

Consequences are those actions that a manager applies after the correct or incorrect behavior occurs *and* that increase the employee's correct behavior in the future. Consequences are also those actions that are applied after the incorrect behavior *and* that decrease the behavior excesses.

Notice in Application 1-1 that many traditional coaching methods were used. Motivating speeches, lectures on the need to win, and prompts to "pay attention," "stay alert," and "keep your eye on the ball" were common locker room occasions. More than likely, they had little effect on a team worn out from traveling by bus from one game to the next. But when the specific behaviors needed to produce a better outcome were identified, incentives posted, and payoffs made, the outcomes of the games improved; thus antecedent—behaviors—consequence.

Did the players' attitudes change? Who knows. Did they develop a will to win? The team's owner or the fans may have thought so. You can almost hear them saying, "When the going gets tough, the tough get going! Yeah, team."

The Basic ABC Model

Table 1-2 depicts the behavior-centered management model that is the foundation for this book and the basis for the intervention with the tired ball players. Behavior is influenced by that which precedes it and that which follows it. Conditions preceding behavior are referred to as *antecedents* (A),

---

APPLICATION 1-1

How to Win a Pennant

The behavior-centered method was used to improve offensive production of a professional touring baseball team.[4] This minor-league team attracted many young, talented players who saw their performance with the team as an opportunity to be selected by scouts for major-league tryouts at spring training camps. The efficiency average (EA) of the players was selected as the measure best reflecting the offensive behaviors contributing to the team's run production. EA was calculated by summing the hits, RBIs (runners batted in), walks, sacrifices, and HBPs (hits by pitch), all divided by the number of trips to the plate.

For the first 28 games (baseline), traditional coaching was used. For the next 2 weeks, a behavior-centered approach was used. A sign (antecedent) was posted announcing that after every seven games, prizes of $5,

$3, and $2 would be awarded (consequence [It was 1973]) for the 1st, 2nd, and 3rd best EAs, respectively. The team EA increased from 0.681 during baseline to 0.831 during the ABC intervention, and runs scored per game increased from 5.2 to 7.4 after the sign was posted.

After 2 weeks of the intervention when the payments for top EAs stopped, the coach was surprised to see that the team EA and runs scored continued high, 0.824 and 7.9, respectively. Observation of the players' behavior on the bus, however, revealed that the highs were due to the competition among team members since they were calculating their own EAs and betting amongst themselves. Although HBPs had doubled after the ABC procedure was initiated, they returned to near the baseline level after it was stopped. No gain, no pain?

---

while conditions following behavior are referred to as *consequences* (C). Another way to state this principle of behavior management is to stress that behavior is influenced by manager actions *before* it occurs and manager actions *after* it occurs.

Applied Behavior Analysis in Business and Industry

Assessment is the first step in behavior-centered management. During the assessment phase, it's important to identify not only the specific behavior deficits and excesses but also to identify existing antecedents that may be triggering the incorrect behaviors or that may be suppressing the correct work behaviors. Similarly, it's important to identify the consequences of inappropriate behaviors or the lack of consequences for appropriate work behaviors. Identification of these influences helps to identify solutions to the problems.

Parents are trying to remove one type of antecedent and replace it with another when they try to control the friends that their children invite over to the house. Teachers control antecedents to trouble when they rearrange the seating chart after they have spotted the troublemakers. Psychologists are trying to control the consequences of oppositional behaviors when they ask parents to stop responding to their children's arguments.

In a business setting, if the target behavior is the speed of the cashier (rings per minute) when there are many customers waiting to check out, the manager notes that the antecedent to pausing or slowing down is the cashier commenting on the customers' purchases, appearance, or children.

TABLE 1-2
The Behavior-Centered Management Model

1. The first task of the behavior-centered manager is to identify the specific behavior deficits and excesses that cause a particular outcome.
2. Management antecedents (A) and consequences (C) change behavior (B).
3. Antecedents are used before the excess or deficit behaviors can occur.

4. Consequences are used after the correct or incorrect behaviors occur.
5. The second task of the behavior-centered manager is to select which antecedents and consequences she will use.

Changing an unsatisfactory outcome is as easy as ABC.

Identification of that antecedent allows the supervisor to advise the clerk that when there are other customers waiting in line to not make such comments until she has totaled the sale and packaged the purchases. Identification of the antecedent to pausing or slowing check-out behaviors is likely to be more effective than just telling the cashier that she is too slow.

Similarly, assessment should include identification of the consequences that regularly occur immediately following the inappropriate behavior. If, whenever the employee delays stocking the empty shelves, the department supervisor assigns another employee to help stock, who wouldn't wait if delay results in assistance!

Behavior-centered management requires a behavioral-analysis approach. The problem of an unsatisfactory outcome is assessed with an ABC analysis. (1) What behaviors must be changed to produce a satisfactory or superior outcome? (2) What antecedents must be put in place or replaced to change or create those behaviors? (3) What consequences must be put in place or replaced to change the behaviors? Application 1-2 illustrates the use of the ABC method in an industrial setting.

The changes in output reflected in Application 1-2 did not just happen. This manager used a variety of behavioral techniques that enabled her and the crew to reach the goal.

What antecedents (A) and consequences (C) did she apply? The manager

1. Operationalized the unsatisfactory outcome by identifying a quantifiable production outcome. (A)
2. Determined the level of current production related to that outcome. (A)
3. Through discussions with the team, selected behaviors and procedures that would make the production process more efficient. (A)
4. Provided the work group with information on current performance and involved them in setting goals for new levels of production. (A)
5. Helped to implement the new procedures and provided feedback on their impact on performance. (A and C)
6. Reinforced behavior consistent with the new procedures immediately after the behavior occurred. (C).

The behavior-centered approach is also being used extensively in retail businesses. In fact, recent research in the area of retail sales suggests that the "people factor," that is, customer-service behavior, may be one of the primary elements distinguishing successful from unsuccessful retailers during times of narrow profit margins and increased price competition.[5] Retail managers who teach and reinforce behaviors consistent with superior customer service are more likely to achieve the best outcomes. The use of the ABC approach in a retail business is illustrated in Application 1-3.

APPLICATION 1-2

ABC in Industry

As an illustration of the behavior-centered approach, consider the manager who wanted to increase the average number of electronic components assembled per hour by a team of workers (the outcome). She first gathered some baseline data (worker production levels before intervention) for 2 weeks and determined that each worker, on the average, assembled 40 components per hour. Having charted her baseline data, she met with the work crew to determine whether they had suggestions as to more efficient or new techniques that would increase the production rate. She learned some very important facts about (a) the way materials were brought to the workstations, (b) the sequence of steps in the assembly process, and (c) the repetitive quality checks that slowed production. Together the work team and the supervisor drafted changes in methods of procuring materials, organizing assembly steps, and conducting adequate, but abbreviated, quality-control procedures. These new steps were written on a flip chart and modified until they clearly stated new behaviors or performances that would result in improved output. She reviewed these procedures with the work crew and answered all questions.

She next applied a procedure called participatory goal setting to initiate the new program. She reviewed the baseline performance with the team (average production of 40 units per hour) and involved everyone in a discussion of new goals. To what extent could production improve with the new procedures? Some workers stated that they could improve their output by 8 units an hour, others by 2 units an hour, and still others by 4 or 5. Based on that information, she asked for a team vote on a new production goal somewhere between 41 and 45 units per hour. The team settled on 43 units per hour as the production average to strive for during the next 2-month period. The manager mentioned how pleased she was with their suggestions and said she would post their progress.

To help the workers know how well they were doing, the manager posted daily graphs on average hourly production based on data gathered at random times during the workday. The graph included a red line at the 43-unit mark. As she saw the employees perform the targeted behaviors, she praised them, and when the graph reached the 43 mark, she placed a large star on the graph. The program was successful, and both the manager and the employees were pleased with the team effort.

APPLICATION 1-3
ABC in a Retail Business

Komaki, Waddell, and Pearce (1971) have reported an interesting study of the effects of antecedents and consequences on the behaviors of two employees in a small grocery store. The store manager had identified three behaviors that he believed were influencing customer satisfaction and sales. The employees were spending at least 50% of their work hours in the back room instead of being in the store near the merchandise. They were offering help to entering customers within 5 seconds only about 35% of the time. And they were maintaining the shelves filled to at least 50% of their capacity only 57% of the time.

Next, the manager informed the employees that if he found that they were in the store and not in the back room 90% of the time when he observed them, he would give them an hour off with pay per week. That targeted behavior increased to an average of 87% across the next few weeks. Accordingly, he next targeted the customer and shelf behaviors. Again he informed them that they could earn another hour off with pay per week if they met the 90% goal for each. Offering help to customers within 5 seconds jumped to an average of 87%, and shelves stocked to at least 50% of capacity jumped to an average of 86% over the following weeks. The authors reported that not only were the customers heard to comment on the improvement in service, but the employees also voiced their pleasure.

What antecedents and consequences did the manager use in that small store?

1. He first identified the unsatisfactory outcomes—unhappy customers and low sales. (A)
2. He identified specific employee behaviors that contributed to those outcomes. (A)
3. He analyzed the situation and identified the lack of consequences for those employee behaviors. (A)
4. He identified a consequence that the store could afford. (A)
5. He informed the employees about the targeted behaviors in specific terms. (A)
6. He gave an incentive for meeting a specific goal. (A)
7. He gave time off with pay for meeting each of the goals. (C)

In the material to follow, ABC strategies are explained in more detail via discussions of principles and examples. In later chapters, examples are provided of ways to apply these techniques to behaviors that occur in the workplace. Sometimes the strategies are used to increase the frequency of a behavior; other times the strategies are used to decrease the frequency of a behavior. In all cases, the behaviors targeted for change are those identified as causes of unsatisfactory outcomes.

Summary

Outcomes leave tracks in the sand. They are the historical records of the activities of employees and managers. Because managers are judged by those outcomes, they are tempted to try to manage them. Such efforts are as fruitless as are those of the parent who tries to change an unsatisfactory grade report by screaming at the child that his grades are unacceptable.

It is necessary to determine the causes of unsatisfactory outcomes whether they be high shrinkage or low production rates. When we search for possible causes, we must avoid making the fundamental attribution error of overestimating the traits of employees and underestimating the situations that cause people to do or not do the things that produce unsatisfactory outcomes.

Reliance on the illness models of medicine or s-O-r models of psychology contributes to the problem. We then too often rely on the variables inside "O," such as attitudes or low morale. Even if managers are practicing psychologists, they have been notably unsuccessful in changing attitudes without changing behaviors first.

The behavior-centered approach requires that we first identify the specific behaviors that cause the outcomes. Then we can use antecedents (A) and consequences (C) to change those behaviors (B). Changing unsatisfactory outcomes in business and industry is as simple as ABC.

Notes

1. Ross (1977).
2. Beer & Walton (1990).
3. Bem (1968); Festinger (1957).
4. Heward (1978).
5. Weitzel, Schwarzkopf, & Peach (1989).

CHAPTER 2

Antecedents: From Directives to Stimulus Control

Preparing the Employee to Work and Getting Work Started

In this chapter we describe a variety of management antecedent behaviors that influence performance in the workplace. Each behavioral technique may be applied to one of two common work situations: (a) situations in which workers have never learned what to do, and (b) situations in which workers may know what to do, but they do not do it.

When workers have never learned what to do, it is usually because managers have not provided adequate direction or instruction for them to understand how to complete a task. In the second instance, managers have not arranged conditions so that desirable behaviors are elicited and maintained. Fortunately, behavior-centered techniques can be applied successfully to both of these situations—eliciting and maintaining employee behavior consistent with an organization's mission and goals.

Manager Antecedent Behaviors

An antecedent is an event that precedes a behavior and affects the occurrence of the behavior. The telephone rings, and we pick up the receiver and say "hello." When a customer walks into the store, the employee is supposed to smile and ask if any help is needed. We don't answer telephones unless they ring, and employees don't ask if they may help if there is no customer.

In the study described in Application 2-1, the outcome was an ugly path across a beautiful lawn, but the behaviors of walking across the grass were the targets (behavior surpluses in this case). Note that the ugly path was not blamed on the attitudes of the staff or students. Nor was the blame placed on their lack of motivation to improve the appearance of the campus. Instead, two different antecedents were used to decrease the surplus behaviors: a request and a directive.

Directives. A manager uses many directives to control the behaviors of employees. More are used or should be used with new employees than with experienced ones. Some common directions include "Start work at 8 A.M."; "Take a 15-minute break"; and "Wear a hard hat." Some directives are company policies, and employees are asked to read and follow directives in the policy manual. Many written rules are ignored unless there are also follow-up and verbal directives to follow the procedures. Once employees learn that

---

APPLICATION 2-1
Antecedents and Consequences on a Campus

A few years ago, I sent some of my students to count the number of students, faculty, and staff who were cutting across the lawn on their way to the Student Union between 12 and 1 P.M. As can be seen in Figure 2-1, the path worn in the grass was an ugly outcome of their attempts to save time on their way to the building. Over 300 people were observed going to the union between 12 and 1 P.M., saving 6 seconds out of their lives by not following the sidewalks. (There was no shortcut path blazed to the library.) The students decided to try an easy antecedent first. They placed a sign, "Please do not walk on the grass," at the beginning of the path (point 1), waited a week, and then planted an identical sign at the beginning of the other path (point 2). The first sign only reduced the number taking the shortcut at point 1 to 275 and, of course, had no effect at point 2. When the sign was in place at point 2, the number dropped to 270. Thus, those antecedents had little effect on the target behavior.

Next, the students placed a second sign, "Prepare yourself not to walk on the grass," at point 3, 50 yards in front of the first sign. The average number taking the shortcut daily dropped to 30. When the students repeated the procedure at point 4, the number dropped to 25. Most of those who continued the shortcut hadn't passed the signs at points 3 and 4, but had passed between buildings to the north and south.

One student suggested a more drastic solution based on consequences, a sprinkler that automatically turned on whenever a person took the shortcut, but his suggestion was vetoed since some students might choose to get wet or race the sprinkler.

FIGURE 2-1

Antecedents on a Campus

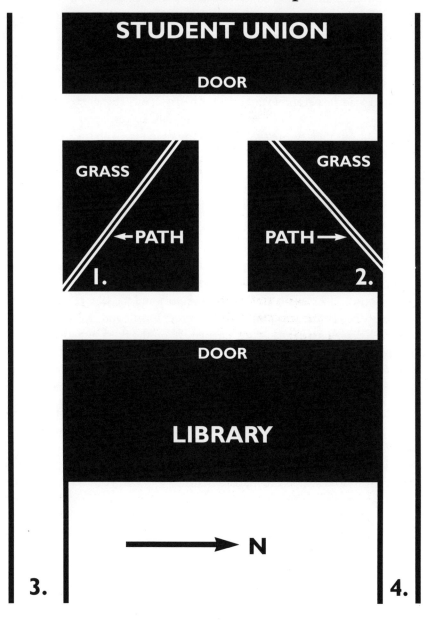

management does not require them to conform to a policy, employees begin to test the other policies. If a written policy is not enforced, it should be omitted from the manual or changed to describe when and where it is to be followed. Otherwise, we are teaching employees that store or company policy is irrelevant.

Similarly, if a command is given but the manager seldom checks on whether the employees do as they are told, they come to ignore his directives. Some of the senior employees will even tell the new person, "Don't worry about it, Mac; he never remembers what he says"; or, "He never checks on it."

How many times do we see parents in public places saying, "No, no, no, Johnny, no" as their 3- or 4-year-old continues to play with the merchandise or bother the other customers? To the child, his mother's "no" has as much relevance to his actions as does the color of her hair, because she never does anything after she says "no." The directives we say to children or adults only become antecedents that control behavior if there are follow-ups and consequences for obeying or disobeying.

Expectations.   When the manager includes when, where, or what standards of performance or outcome in the directive, an expectation is being used as an antecedent. Such statements as "I expect you to put the tools away before going home"; "I want you to check the inventory and the sales rate of all items on the shelves before you complete the reorder form"; and "I do not want to see any ladders or pallet jacks left unattended on the floor" are expectations. Each expectation implies follow-up on the part of management. Each will become an antecedent for appropriate work behavior only if employees have reason to believe that there will be follow-up and appropriate consequences.

Information.   Although we don't always know why, information alone will change the behavior of people. An illustration is the application of an antecedent in the form of public information to reduce theft as shown in Application 2-2. The reduction in theft rates may be due to the employees being more attentive to the marked items or may be because many people who take items don't consider themselves to be shoplifters. If they take those items, they are labeling themselves. Care must be taken in using this procedure because other research has shown that when items such as cigarettes and candy are so marked, those items become an attractive target for teenagers who like the greater risk, and, as a result, theft rates increase.

By the way, that antecedent method of reducing shoplifting produces a greater reduction than do warning signs which say shoplifters will be prosecuted[1] or the practice of publishing the names of shoplifters in the local newspaper.[2]

APPLICATION 2-2
Antecedents to Reduce Theft

In this study, an antecedent consisting of the public identification of specific items was used to reduce theft in retail stores.[3] Signs were placed on clothing racks and walls near the targeted items.

> **Attention Shoppers and Shoplifters**
> The items you see marked
> with a red star are items
> that shoplifters frequently take.

The results showed that young ladies' tops were stolen at a daily rate of 6.6% before the signs and 6% after the signs were in place and after the items had been identified with stars. Pants stolen dropped from 5% before the signs to 3% after the signs. There were no changes in the rates of sales.

The same procedure was used in a large grocery store in Sweden.[4] Sales of the nine target items increased slightly, while thefts were almost eliminated. These improvements can be seen in Figure 2-2.

The procedure was also found to be effective in small drugstores, one located in Memphis, Tennessee, and the other in Fayetteville, Arkansas.[5] Both stores showed significant decreases in thefts when the high-theft items were publicly identified. In the Memphis store, prophylactics showed the highest theft rate before and the greatest decrease after!

Certainly, management directives and expectations are types of information that affect employee behaviors. How many times has a manager (or a parent) heard the phrase "Nobody ever told me" or "How was I to know"? These questions reflect the need to repeat directions and to ask new employees to repeat directions to make sure the directions are understood.

Information, however, should be a two-way street. Managers gain information that can be valuable in correcting problems when they encourage employees to suggest ideas for improving production, quality, safety, or sales. Some supervisors routinely ask individual employees for suggestions. When employees see their supervisors act on their suggestions, they are more likely to supply helpful information and suggestions in the future. Suggestions may be solicited through suggestion boxes or at team meetings. One illustration of how not to solicit suggestions is provided in the following scenario which was reported by an employee of a government agency.

The manager had either heard at a management training seminar he attended or read in a management self-help book that asking employees for suggestions was good for morale.

FIGURE 2-2

Theft Reduction in a Grocery Store

Public Identification of High Theft Items

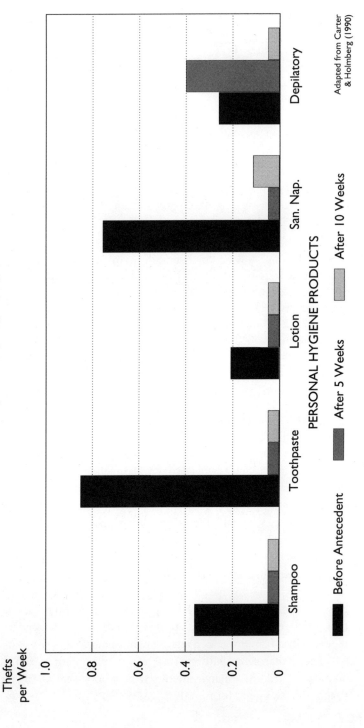

Adapted from Carter
& Holmberg (1990)

On Friday morning, Mr. "O," the supervisor, called a meeting of all the staff.

Mr. O: I believe that as humans we have the brain power to solve our own problems. Now, we have long lines of people waiting, and that shouldn't be. I want you people to use your brain power to solve this problem.

All employees present raise their hands.

Mr. O: Please don't think I don't have some ideas of my own.

All hands except one are lowered. Mr. O calls upon Employee No. 1.

Employee No. 1: Why don't you tell us your plans, and then we can make suggestions that will fit in with them?

Mr. O: No, I don't want to do that; I want to welcome your suggestions.

Employee No. 2: How about moving the telephone so that the receptionist can . . .

Mr. O: No, no. I've already decided to leave the telephone where it is, and that's nonnegotiable.

Training. The behavior-centered approach to training focuses on the behaviors needed by the employees to perform the jobs they have been assigned. The manager must assess the skills the person presently has and teach him to do those that are new or that must be performed in a different manner than he has done before. Some individuals must unlearn habits from previous jobs that are unacceptable in the new position, and some must learn completely new skills.

If the job requires a highly skilled person, much, but not all, of the training is reduced by careful hiring procedures. The job is advertised so that the necessary skills are specified. Similarly, the interviewer can screen out those who have too little experience or training. Even when the person has met the qualifications, some training is usually necessary because each position has unique requirements. Questioning the person who has been hired will allow the supervisor to determine how much additional training is necessary. However, some new employees will claim more experience or skills than they actually have. In such cases, observation or an initial demonstration of their skills is required.

Thorough training of new employees will avoid many problems that interfere with satisfactory performance. Time spent initially implementing well-designed training will save time later and prevent unsatisfactory outcomes. Although developed for training or retraining the older worker, these rules are helpful in training employees of any age.[6]

1. The training material should be clearly seen as relevant to the job.
2. The training procedures should provide positive feedback so that the person can clearly see that he or she can do the work.

3. The training should be organized so that the new knowledge and skills are clearly related to existing knowledge and skills of the trainee.

4. The training should be structured so that the trainee gains complete mastery of previous components before being moved on to the next step of a training module.

5. Training material and procedures should be presented so that memory requirements are limited.

6. Training procedures should not include paced or time-limited situations.

The behavioral approach to training starts with a clear description of the behaviors to be learned. If the trainer cannot describe what it is that must be done and when, where, or whom it must be done by, the new employee is not going to learn the task. When a task analysis has been conducted so the separate behaviors necessary to complete the task have been identified, a number of behavior-centered procedures are available to train the person. These include training by modeling, by chaining, and by training to criteria.

Training by modeling. Modeling involves learning by watching experienced workers do a task. Practicing the new behavior under supervision is referred to as role playing. To use modeling as a training technique, the supervisor must first clarify what the learner is to learn; that is, spell out the steps of the task. It is wise to label these steps with an easily remembered term and review these terms with the worker. In the actual teaching process, the model should exaggerate the steps involved and proceed slowly through them. Albert Bandura, a well-known psychologist who has studied modeling and its effects, has described four factors that are critical to structuring a successful modeling program.[7] Here, they are described as applied to work situations:

1. *Attention.* The worker should be told what to look at and listen to in order to learn what is being modeled. If this is not done, the observer may watch wood chips fly out of the lathe instead of notice how to use the tool effectively and safely.

2. *Retention.* Individuals will learn and remember more of what they are to observe if the steps are labeled using familiar words and described in proper sequence before they are modeled. The observer should also repeat step names before he sees the demonstration. Then, before starting each step, the model must state the step's name and sequence number; for example, "this is the first step in which I secure the material." Finally, the instructor should ask the observer to repeat the name (secure material) and sequence number (first step) of each step to complete.

3. *Practice.* Overt practice of what the trainee has seen and remembered is necessary if the person is to learn that he can do the steps that were modeled. The trainee should practice the steps in sequence, naming them if necessary, until he masters the task.

4. *Motivation.* Although they may know how to do something, people often will not act unless they expect some payoff for their efforts. Therefore, during the modeling procedure, the trainee should see the model receive praise for work performed. Reinforcement of the model creates an expectation for similar outcomes in the observer. The supervisor must also emphasize the relevance of what is being modeled to the employee's job so that the learner clearly understands the connection between the steps modeled and the outcome of those behaviors. By the way, proper use of training by modeling also helps the employee better understand the importance of his job.

If no direction is provided, new employees will choose their own model. Unfortunately, they may select the worst worker to imitate if that individual happens to be accessible and friendly. Employees who are effective workers may appear to be poor models to the new employee because they are not outgoing or friendly. They may also be poor teachers because they complete the steps of the task without allowing the trainee to participate. Hence, experienced workers should be carefully selected for modeling. They must demonstrate the skills in question, such as proper tool care, stocking, freight handling, tool clean-up, and appropriate work-break behavior consistent with the previous guidelines. They must encourage the worker to learn the steps and reinforce the learner for improvements.

Supervisors should also remember the importance of reinforcing the model for the training assistance. Often, time spent introducing another worker to the job comes at the expense of other activities that the experienced employee needs to do. Recognition for the help in training makes the experienced worker feel that her efforts are valued. Such supervisory recognition also sends a message to the trainee that experience is valued and that the behaviors being demonstrated are directly related to reinforcement by the supervisor. One final caution is in order about modeling—do not overwork any one employee as the model. Distribute the modeling (training) responsibilities among the senior workers so that everyone receives some praise for the activity and so that one worker does not assume an unfair share of the teaching.

Many interesting examples of the use of modeling in production and retail settings exist. In one use of modeling, the supervisor of construction crews on a large apartment building project noted that his carpenters were not returning to work promptly from breaks. A little lost time by several crews over several weeks quickly added up to a significant loss. To confront this situation from a behavior-centered perspective, the supervisor first determined the behavior that needed to change, that is, not returning to work promptly. He then selected modeling as the change or intervention strategy; he asked the senior carpenters on each work crew to make a special effort to return to work from breaks on a timely basis. The supervisor provided a rationale for the change that was needed and even shared a brief log of the total amount of time lost per day by all crews multiplied by 22 workdays and the dollars per month lost on the project. Understanding the rationale for the requested change, the senior carpenters committed to the program and agreed to model several behaviors; for example, standing up at the appropriate time following breaks and lunch and saying, "It's time to get back at it." This simple no-cost strategy, the modeling of appropriate behaviors by high-status persons, resulted in increased work time, which decreased project costs.

Modeling is usually linked with the term "role playing." Role playing refers to the learner's efforts to demonstrate correctly the actions modeled. Chances are excellent that the trainee will repeat the steps correctly if the modeling procedures have been carefully followed. However, the chances are also good that some aspect of the trainee's performance will need to be modified. This modification of performance is actually a consequence strategy referred to as corrective feedback.

When giving corrective feedback, be sure first to identify and mention at least one acceptable aspect of the person's performance.[8] The positive feedback gets the trainee's attention and reinforces her for listening. Once she is listening and has not "tuned out" the supervisor, he can provide the corrective (negative) feedback about an aspect of the performance that needs to change.

In giving performance feedback, it is very important to specify not only the behavior that is acceptable but also the one or ones that need to change and how they need to change. For example, a supervisor of bank tellers might tell a new teller that she really likes the way the teller mentions the customer's name and makes eye contact, but that the teller also needs to remember to smile at the customer and to thank the customer for the business at the end of the transaction. The manager should then demonstrate the target behaviors to the employee. Used properly, modeling, role playing, and corrective feedback are inexpensive and efficient ways to enable people to perform more effectively.

Training by chaining. Chaining is an important instructional technique in which the task is broken down into a series of small steps. It is especially useful in training an employee to accomplish a complex task that has many steps that must be carried out in a specific order. Three types of chaining strategies may be tried: (a) total task presentation, (b) forward chaining, and (c) backward chaining. In all three methods, the first step involves dividing the work task into separate and sequential behavioral steps. The steps are then taught one at a time.

In the total task presentation method, the trainee is required to do all the steps from the beginning to the end of the chain over and over again until all can be performed in order without error.[9] Thus, the new cashier must first greet the customer; scan the merchandise; bag the items; total and ring the tax into the computer or register; state the total cost to the customer; take the money, placing it on the drawer, not in it; ring the amount received; count the change once to himself and again, aloud, to the customer; and finish with the appropriate thank-you statement—all done *in order without an error*. If an error occurs, the trainee must start over at the beginning. The total task presentation method requires less time for the trainer than do the other chaining procedures. In general, the more intelligent the trainee, and the simpler the task (few steps), the more the total task presentation method is preferred in training.

In forward chaining, the worker is taught the first behavioral step and all subsequent steps in order until the task is completed. The person is taught and reinforced for carrying out the first two steps, then steps 1, 2, and 3, and then steps 1, 2, 3, and 4, etc. Instruction (an antecedent strategy) and reinforcement (a consequence strategy) continue until the person can do all of the steps without error.

In backward chaining, the individual watches the instructor complete the steps in the task, and then she is taught to do the last step. Next, after observing the instructor do all but the last two steps, the worker completes these two steps herself. Backward chaining continues; that is, the individual is taught the last three steps, then the last four, etc., until she follows the behavioral steps without error.

For example, a "Rapid Car Care" outlet might teach a new employee to change oil using either the forward or backward chaining method. To use the forward chaining procedure, the trainer would first place the oil collector can underneath the car, select the proper wrench, demonstrate how to remove the oil plug with the wrench, etc. For individuals having difficulty learning and remembering steps, the first three steps would be repeated before further ones were taught.

In backward chaining, the same job would be taught by reversing the procedure. The instructor would first demonstrate where to throw the empty cans after the oil has been poured into the motor. Next, the trainee would watch the instructor insert and tighten the oil plug into the engine before pouring the new oil into the engine. She would then be prompted to pour the last can of oil into the filler tube. The trainee would then be taught how to pour all the cans of oil into an empty engine and then dispose of the empty cans properly. Next, she would learn how to insert the oil plug into the engine before filling the engine with oil and throwing the cans away. Backward chaining would continue until the learner demonstrates mastery of the steps involved.

Backward chaining to teach the Olympic style power snatch is illustrated in Application 2-3.

Training to criteria. Too seldom do supervisors require that new employees train to some standard or criterion. To perform the task from beginning to end while being observed is one criterion, but too often it is insufficient. To perform the task without error five times in a row while being observed is more likely to produce the behavior that will result in successful

---

APPLICATION 2-3
Chaining the Power Snatch

As a project in the behavior modification course taught by Marr in 1992, Kevin Norman, a weight-lifting instructor, decided to try backward chaining as a method to train a coed to perform the power snatch, a weight-lifting event used in the Olympics. First, he did a task analysis of the lift.

1. Proper starting position: feet at shoulder width, knees bent, back straight, bar on mat close to shins, and wide hand grip on the bar.
2. By slightly straightening legs, bring bar to level just below knees while keeping the back straight.
3. By shifting weight to the toes and simultaneously shrugging shoulders, bring bar to level above knees.
4. By shrugging shoulders while straightening legs, bring bar to waist level.
5. By again shrugging shoulders and raising elbows high, raise bar to chest level.
6. Finally, drop under bar and catch it with arms extended.

The instructor then started the training by assisting the trainee in lifting the bar to the chest level with elbows out. The first training step was to teach her to perform step 6. Next she was taught how to move the bar from her waist to her chest level, step 5 followed by step 6. Then came steps 4, 5, and 6. Continuing the backward chaining, and repeating a step only when necessary, she quickly learned how to move from step 1 to step 6. Norman reported that this rather complex athletic movement was very easily learned by the coed, who had no previous experience with this lift. The whole procedure took about 37 minutes, about half the time that it normally takes an athlete to learn to perform the lift.

---

outcomes. To illustrate the importance of training to criterion, we often ask workshop participants who arrived on the airlines how many error-free departures they would like their pilots to have had before the participants boarded their flights.

Once the person meets the criterion, continuous observation is discontinued, but occasional checks should be made. Thinning out the observation can then take place as satisfactory performance continues.

Stimulus control of employee behavior. The alarm clock ringing in the morning serves as a stimulus to initiate the day's activities. Similarly, the telephone ringing serves as a stimulus to the behavior of picking up the receiver to answer a call. Anything in the work environment that triggers the appropriate work behavior is a stimulus that controls behavior. Thus, the red line painted on the floor around a dangerous machine serves as a signal to the workers that they are to walk around the line and should not approach the machine.

Some stimuli do control the behaviors of most employees and customers. Examples are "Please Use Other Door" and "Exit Only" signs, the factory whistle to start work, and written instructions. Even supervisory behavior can be controlled as is seen in Application 2-4.

APPLICATION 2-4
Stimulus Control of Supervisory Behavior

At one of the behavior-centered management seminars, a manager asked what to do if a person knows what to do on the job, but just forgets. When asked to be more specific, he said that zoning in his store, that is, maintaining a clean and well-stocked area, was the responsibility of the department supervisors, but they often forget to do it on any regular basis. He explained that zoning included such behaviors as filling the empty or partially empty shelves; facing the merchandise to the front, dusting, and picking up debris; and cleaning countertops in the area of responsibility.

When it was suggested to the manager that the public announcement system be used as an antecedent to remind all supervisors that it was time to initiate zoning directives to the employees, the problem was easily solved. He used a timer to cue the designated person to play the reminder song four times a day, which in turn prompted the departmental supervisors to initiate zoning checks. The actual reminder song used was "Hi-ho. Hi-ho. It's off to work we go . . ."

When the behavior of the employees is not being controlled by the stimulus, the signal may be too weak or imperceptible. The solution may be as simple as increasing the intensity of the stimulus or repositioning the sign. Notice the need to change the location and message on the sign as in the "Antecedents on a Campus" example, Application 2-1, given earlier.

Also, a stimulus may not control the behavior of the employee if the employee doesn't know the meaning of the stimulus, as when the red light flashes on the intercom in front of the new secretary or when the computer monitor prints "type pathname." The problem is then a lack of adequate training. The new employee may have been informed as to the actions necessary when that stimulus occurs, but was never trained to criterion—required to perform the task three to five times while being observed.

"Gotcha" management is the practice of not training employees to recognize the signals to perform certain behaviors or to correct errors independently. Then, when detecting a mistake, the supervisor berates the employee. The worker believes the manager intentionally hides his knowledge so that mistakes will be made. Workers need to know the meaning of key stimuli. What are the signs, early on in the report, that predict that the statement won't balance? What is it about the consistency of the paint that signals too much variation in its thickness before it is sprayed on the product? What additional information is available to the employee to make sure that too much or too little stock will not be reordered? Repeated errors in a department are signals to higher-level management that training is inadequate or follow-up is incomplete or possibly too negative. Errors may be caught before higher-level management occurs, but low morale may be a sign that the supervisor of the department is not adequately transferring his or her knowledge to the employees or is too critical of their attempts to gain the information.

A feeling of helplessness on the part of employees frequently accompanies "gotcha" management. Whenever employees ask for help, they are ignored, criticized, greeted with "Look who needs help again," called "stupid," or otherwise embarrassed. But if they do not get help or instruction, they will make mistakes that bring about even worse consequences. Thus, they are in a state of helplessness, being caught between a rock and a hard place. Besides producing very unhappy employees, "gotcha" supervision may produce more serious misbehavior that can range from doing no work, lying, and hiding of mistakes to sabotage of production.

Summary

The "A" in the behavior-centered management approach, ABC, stands for *antecedent,* any event that occurs before and that affects the behavior of employees and the outcomes of those behaviors. A variety of such events is under the control of the manager. The behaviors of the manager in such cases are referred to as *management antecedent behaviors.*

The simplest antecedent is a directive which tells the person what to do. Expectations are statements by the supervisor that spell out rules about when, where, what, how, and by whom the manager wants the work accomplished. Neither directives nor expectations, however, are effective if there is no follow-up. Follow-up behaviors by supervisors allow employees to learn whether expectations, policies, and directives have any predictive power, that is, real meaning relative to the consequences of doing or not doing work.

Information alone can serve as activators or suppressors of behaviors. As was seen in the studies in retail stores, public information can significantly reduce such behaviors as theft of merchandise. Why these antecedents are so effective is not always known.

Training is a management antecedent behavior that has probably been used as long as some people have supervised the behaviors of others. Training by chaining behaviors is comparatively new since it is a much more complex teaching procedure. Whether forward or backward chaining is used, this type of training reliably teaches employees to perform complex tasks that require a number of different behaviors to be performed in a set order, such as those required of a pilot, a cashier, or a mechanic. Training to criterion is also effective because it requires the new employee to perform a task without error a number of times. The repetition, although time-consuming, decreases errors and costly mistakes later.

When the more informal type of training is used by letting the new employee learn on the job, the person is often likely to gravitate to the friendliest employee in the department. Being friendly does not mean that the person is the best role model of the behaviors needed to complete the task. It is important that management choose the model. Clear demonstrations combined with patient observation of the attempts to imitate are important characteristics of the person selected to model appropriate work behaviors. When the model or the manager does not follow the rules of attention, retention, practice, and motivation, modeling work tasks can be a waste of time for everybody involved in the training.

Stimulus control of employee behaviors is a very cost-effective way to produce the right behavior at the right place at the right time. Whether it be a sign that has messages, questions, or directives that change daily or weekly, or music that signifies a time for certain tasks, employees and first-line supervisors can use the stimulus as a cue to change tasks, perform certain jobs, or even return from breaks.

Notes

1. Thurber & Snow (1980).
2. Ross & White (1987).
3. McNees, Egli, Marshall, Schnelle, & Risley (1976).
4. Carter & Holmberg (1992).
5. Mullen & Marr (1993).
6. Sterns & Doverspike (1989).
7. Bandura (1986).
8. Marr & Roessler (1986).
9. Martin & Pear (1992).

CHAPTER 3

Antecedents: From Preparation to Follow-through

Learning Theory and Cognitive Psychology

The psychology of learning is one of the areas in psychology that has produced the largest number of behavior-centered management applications. In this chapter, management procedures based on learning theory and cognitive psychology are presented that influence how and whether people learn to work appropriately. Learning to discriminate among different things, places, people, times, and events is especially important.

Discrimination learning. Most people don't say "Good morning" when they approach the front door to the building unless there is someone (stimulus) standing there. Similarly, most people do not pick up the phone and say "hello" unless it rings (stimulus). If they did, we would worry about them. In each case, they have made the easy discrimination between the presence of a stimulus (a person or a ringing telephone) or its absence. Many of the discriminations made at work, however, are much more difficult. The automobile mechanic listens to the same sound that we do but often is able to instantly tell that all the car needs is a tune-up.

Some difficult discriminations require years of experience or lengthy training. Without proper training, many line assembly workers, chicken sexers, and quality-control employees could not be accurate in the many repetitive discriminations they make per hour. Based on their training and experience, pilots, physicians, and pharmacists make life and death discriminations as a regular part of their job. We can tolerate no errors in their discriminations.

The goal and outcome of discrimination learning in work settings is to decrease errors. When a person makes an error,

1. He is not making a response to a stimulus that should be made; for example, he's not placing the item on the shelf so that its label can be read by the customer. *Outcomes:* Low sales of the item or customer complaints; or

2. He is making a response to a stimulus that he shouldn't make; for example, he's trying to lift a box that is too large or too heavy to lift by oneself. *Outcomes:* Too much workers' compensation being paid out for back injuries or too much breakage when boxes are dropped.

When either error is made, we sometimes hear the supervisor make the fundamental attribution error, by accusing the worker of laziness, carelessness, irresponsibility, or a lack of concern for the job. The behavior-centered leader does not make that attribution but instead considers the method of changing the behavior in order to change the outcome.

When the same type of error is repeated, or committed by many people, the problem may be one of inadequate discrimination training. What if we could improve quality of the product (outcomes) by using birds that have been given discrimination training? In Application 3-1, note how one pharmaceutical company trained pigeons to discriminate between good and bad pills.

Discrimination training. The manager who takes the time to teach staff to recognize the stimuli that signal the need for corrective behavior will be rewarded by increased productivity, fewer errors, and higher morale. Instead of telling the employee to do the task, readjust the machine, or return to the truck dock for stock, the manager teaches the employee which stimuli alerted the manager to the need. Knowing the signs (stimuli) of impending trouble, the employee will not need to be prompted in the future. Asking the employee to describe the conditions of an unsatisfactory merchandise aisle alerts that employee to (a) the half-empty shelves that need restocking, (b) the cans that need to be faced to the front, (c) the boxes that need to be priced, and (d) the debris on the floor that needs to be picked up. As the employee describes each sign or stimulus, the manager asks the trainee to describe what needs to be done to correct the problem.

Removing control by fading. Sometimes stimuli that control behavior need to be put in place to signal when, where, or what to do. Once employees are performing tasks correctly, in the proper sequence, or at the right time, the stimuli may be removed. The step-by-step partial removal of these stimuli is referred to as "fading." The working parent, tired of coming home and finding none of the household chores done and the 12-year-old watching television despite numerous confrontations about the condition of the house,

Pill-Pecking Pigeons

Not really. The pigeons never actually touched the pills, but they did prove to be pretty good quality-control workers in their discrimination between correct pills and skags.[1] Skags are pill capsules that are discarded because they are off-color, have gelatin sticking out, a dent, or a double cap. In this large pharmaceutical plant, up to 2 million capsules might be inspected daily by a quality-control team of 70 women. The employees were paid on a group bonus schedule employing "error cost." For example, if the supervisor found more than three or four minor imperfections in a batch of capsules that had been inspected, the inspector had to reinspect the whole batch which reduced her output and, therefore, her bonus.

The director of research at the plant gave his permission for pigeons to be trained to do the inspections. Each pigeon was trained in a box that allowed it to see each capsule as it passed on a conveyor belt. First, they were trained to peck a key that illuminated the capsule. They then either pecked at a different key if the capsule was a skag or at the same key if not. Either of those pecks would turn off the illumination, move the next capsule forward, and turn on the food hopper, if correct. If wrong, the chamber was blacked out for 30 seconds. Capsules could be brought into view one at a time at the rate of two per second. During training, skags made up 10% of a batch. By the end of the week, the birds were 99% correct in their choices. At that rate, two birds inspecting each capsule simultaneously would make an error 1 out of 10,000 times. Although the directors of research and pharmacology were delighted at the pigeons' discrimination ability, the board members had misgivings, "Who would trust medicine inspected by pigeons?"

his laziness, and his poor attitude, finally resorts to a fading and follow-up behavioral method. A list is posted on the refrigerator door:

Hang up coat
Let dog out
Empty dishwasher
Start homework

When the youngster complains that it is embarrassing to have the card where his friends might see it, the parent informs him that it will be removed when he has completed the tasks on time 3 days in a row. When the boy has met that criterion, the fading procedure begins. The parent cuts off the right side of the card (one-fourth) so that it reads:

Hang up
Let dog
Empty dish
Start homew

Two days later, presuming everything goes well, another slice is cut off. Fading of the instructions is continued until there is no stimulus, but the behavior is maintained. If the child does not follow the instructions on any day, the parent replaces the card or uses the overcorrection positive-practice procedure described in the "Consequence" section of the next chapter.

A manager is fading out a stimulus that has behavioral control when at first she gives directions every day to the new employee and then gives fewer and fewer as the demands of the job take control of the behavior. Soon the sight of the half-empty shelves controls the behavior of restocking or reordering. The bell over the front door of the store begins to control the new salesperson's behavior of approaching the customer. Or the time elapsed since the blade was last sharpened or the machine was last oiled takes control of the employee's behavior of replacing a blade or oiling, instead of his depending upon a flawed product or directions from the manager to perform those work behaviors. Although these examples illustrate the value of experience on a job, they also demonstrate how controlled fading speeds up the discrimination learning that comes with experience.

Sometimes a stimulus has an effect on behavior even though we do not know whether or not the person can detect it, as in Application 3-2. What would happen if the different odors in the industrial plant were faded in and out?

Errorless discrimination training. When a person is first taught to discriminate shapes, colors, sounds, or objects, she may experience considerable tension because of the difficulty of the task. As she learns, she makes errors which cause frustration. Sometimes new employees become discouraged and want to quit, or they ask for a transfer to a new job or department. One way to prevent the frustration and to simplify the task is through errorless discrimination training.

Through errorless discrimination training, the employee is taught to make difficult discriminations without ever making an error. Consider the case where a trainee for a quality-control position must be able to discriminate among three types of shapes: O, D, and Q. The shapes move by the inspector on a conveyor belt:

O O D Q O Q D D Q O Q D O Q Q D O O D Q D O Q O Q Q O D D, etc.

The inspector must reject Os and Ds by placing an O in the left basket and a D in the right basket and not touching the Qs, which are transmitted to packing by the conveyor belt. In errorless discrimination training, we arrange the training situation so that there is little chance for error. In the first few minutes of training, it appears that there are only Os on the belt because the Qs are so small that they look like periods.

O O . O . . O . O O O . . O . O . O O . . . O . . O . . O . . .

and the right basket is covered so that he can only place the Os in the left basket. Next, we enlarge the Qs but make them easy to discriminate from the Os, O q O q O q q q O O q O q O q q, while leaving the right basket three-fourths covered. Then, the format is O O q O q q O q q q O O, until finally we present O Q O Q O Q O Q Q O O. If there is an error, we have faded in the Qs too fast. When discrimination is perfect, we can start the presentation of the Qs again as periods with only Ds present on the belt, D . . D . D D . , etc., with the left basket covered, so there are no placement errors.

Errorless discrimination training has had a number of uses in teaching people to make difficult discriminations. For example, the procedure has been successful in teaching children to remember and apply math facts,[6] and in teaching adolescents and adults with mental retardation to assemble 15- and 24-piece bicycle brakes[7] and to correctly match and attach lock nuts and bicycle to axle posts.[8] There has been little application to training in other industrial settings, possibly due to the lack of dissemination of knowledge about the procedure.

Generalization. When the newly trained behavior of the employee happens in a variety of situations, we say that generalization has occurred. For example, if we train the new salesclerk to smile and greet the customer in the stationery department, will she remember to smile at customers when she works in other departments? If she does, the behavior is said to have generalized to those other assignments. Similarly, if the new waiter is trained to take an order and deliver the food appropriately to a table of two people, will he deliver the correct orders to a table of six people who have consumed at least two drinks each by the time they ordered?

Managers have programmed generalization when employees perform the correct behaviors in other situations. Programming for generalization includes the following steps:

1. Train the person in a situation as close to the performance area as possible. Although the employee may be trained to operate the spray-gun equipment in an isolated part of the plant, training isn't complete until he is shown how to do it when the product swings by him on line, when he is wearing a mask, and when the shape of the products change. Similarly, the cashier must make the correct chain of responses when the customer hands her a 10-dollar bill to pay for a purchase; that is, put the 10-dollar bill in the cash register, leave the clamp of the 10-dollar-bill tray up, withdraw the correct change, and count the change out loud when returning it to the customer.

2. Vary the situation in which the training is conducted. After he has learned to perform the task without distraction, add sights and sounds that normally occur in the work location. If he is to work in different locations, have him drive the forklift in those locations while adhering to safety regulations.

3. Program common stimuli. Use the same cues (stimuli) for similar behavior in all of the places where employees work. Programming common stimuli is done routinely in some manufacturing plants; safety zones around machines are all painted in yellow or a fluorescent orange. All company trucks have the same color paint on the windshield wiper control and a different color paint on the light switch. The code for merchandise type is located in the same place on boxes no matter what their shape. (Employees are more likely to restock shelves if they know they can find the merchandise without a long search.)

Behavioral contracts.   If the previous antecedent strategies prove ineffective or are not feasible, a behavioral contract may solve the problem. A contract is a formal written and signed agreement specifying performance goal, deadline, specific steps, and consequences (what will happen) if the goal is reached or not reached. Terms of the contract are worked out jointly between the supervisor and the worker, with the first step involving clarification of the target behavior. Agreed upon changes in that behavior, either decreases or increases, are spelled out in writing, with several days or weeks dedicated to gradual approximation of the performance goal.

An agreement to decrease tardiness is an example of a behavioral contract. Usually, if an employee has a bad habit of reporting for work late, returning from lunch late, or taking too much time for breaks, his supervisor might give him one warning and then fire him when he is late again. But if the employee's skills are difficult or expensive to replace, that is, when extensive training has occurred, the consequences described in a behavioral contract may change the employee's bad habits.

For example, the supervisor might baseline the amount of time lost by an employee who neither arrives at work in the morning on time nor returns from breaks and lunch promptly. Total minutes lost per day could be charted for review by the worker and the supervisor. She then shows him or describes the less desirable job he has been assigned until he has reached a more acceptable goal in minutes lost per day. The employee should agree to chart timelines during the contract period and discuss progress periodically with the supervisor. Interim goals, say for 3-day periods, should be established when the employee can return to his regular job or assignment as a result of his *achieving* those subgoals, not for just coming close. Stipulations of the contract should be followed when the employee achieves or fails to achieve the final goal.

Managers often make informal contracts with their employees. An informal contract is usually for a short period of time and is not put in writing. "Hurry and clean up the area, and we all can go home early." The case described in Application 3-3 was an informal contract but could have been printed on a large sign and placed where everybody on the team could see it. When the incentive for the employees is listed where they can see it, it acts as an antecedent to greater effort.

Feedback allows the employee to redirect his efforts, and it propels him to make the effort. When feedback is not given or is infrequent, the employees not only continue making errors but appear to not want to work. Work does not get done, production is down, and employees are uncertain about their

APPLICATION 3-3

Twenty Boxes for Breakfast

At one of the behavior-centered management institutes, a manager reported that she had used an oral contract with the evening shift in order to get greater productivity. The employees had been unloading the trucks at the rate of 12 boxes an hour, which sometimes required them to just stack the boxes on the dock until the next night when they could then relocate the boxes to their proper storage areas. When the number of truckloads arriving began to increase, the store began to have a serious problem in merchandise disburse-

ment. The manager informed the dock workers that if they could increase their unloading rate to 16 boxes an hour, she would supply coffee and doughnuts; if they were able to average an unloading rate of 20 boxes an hour, she would buy them all breakfast. Imagine her surprise when her assistant manager reported that they had reached 20 per hour by the third day. The savings in overtime as well as the improvement in the organization of the storage area more than made up for the breakfast costs.

jobs. Similarly, delayed feedback is deadly to morale. Immediate feedback produces task-oriented workers who follow directives and remain on tasks until the job is done.

Note that the manager in Application 3-3 set the goals of 16 and 20 boxes unloaded per hour but never told the team how to do it. She let them decide. In the antecedent strategies that follow, management turns much of the control over to the group or individual worker.

Work teams. The reorganization of employees into work teams gives the semi-autonomous teams the responsibility and information they need to manage their own work. When self-managing work teams are organized, their success seems in part due to their receiving responsibility for whole tasks rather than each individual being responsible for only part of a task and to the flexibility allowed by the shared responsibility among group members.[9] Work teams can be very large or very small and can be used in departments within a factory or a human-service delivery organization. The manager should be highly familiar with the training, development, and supervisory requirements of such teams before attempting this type of intervention. As we will see in later chapters, the success of the procedure of organizing employees into work teams has been mixed.[10]

Quality circles.   The management antecedent strategy of establishing quality circles (QCs) can solve many work-related problems. Although QCs first became popular in Japan, their use in the United States has produced some significant effects on production quantity and quality, absenteeism, and communication.[11] However, the reader should be cautious in initiating QCs because reviews of the literature reveal very few well-controlled studies that would support the many testimonials and claims.

Typically, experts in implementation of quality circles are brought in to initiate the program. Participant employees are first trained to analyze work problems through such activities as brainstorming, cause-effect analysis, and the use of problem-analysis flow charts. They practice these skills in QCs that are organized much as work teams, described in the previous section. The QCs meet weekly for about an hour.

Such training and placing of employees in QCs is said to enhance the decision-making abilities of employees, give them more knowledge about production problems, improve communications among employees and with management, and make the workers feel a greater sense of responsibility for the outcomes of their work.[12] Evidence of their success in improving productivity and reducing absenteeism will be given in chapters 6 and 8, respectively.

Self-instructional training.   Self-instructional training is a self-control strategy in which people change their own behavior through covert instructions that they say to themselves.[13] To use self-instructional training, the instructor first specifies the situation in which the behavior is to occur, followed by a series of questions designed to make the person think about what she should do in that situation. The instructor asks, "What is the first thing you should ask yourself when in this situation?" Without waiting for the employee's response, the instructor answers the question. Then she says, "What should you do next?" Again the instructor answers the questions immediately. Next, the instructor asks, "Is that an effective thing to do?" and answers, "Yes, that is effective because . . ." The instructor states how the action or actions resolve the problem and result in positive outcomes for the employee.

In the second phase of the training, the instructor asks the questions and waits for the employee to repeat the answer. The last question is followed both with an answer and the self-reinforcing statement about why the action would be effective. When the worker can make all of the correct responses in the proper order, the instructor reinforces the learner and urges him to continue to practice the responses learned through self-instructional training. Use of self-instructional skills is encouraged if the employee works through the technique in a variety of related situations in several self-instructional lessons.

A supervisor of a packaging team in a plant producing large recycling bags for home use might adopt this technique with new packers who have demonstrated some difficulty in reaching expected quality and production rates. For example, the supervisor might first review the steps of the task with the new packer:

1. Count out five bags.
2. Visually scan the bags for defects, for example, rips, ragged edges, loose trimmings, etc.
3. Repair or eliminate defective bags.
4. Fold each bag twice and place it in a stack of five bags.
5. Place the bags in the carton with the bag openings facing the front of the carton.
6. Tape five twist ties to the carton lid.
7. Repeat quality-control scanning.
8. Replace carton on line, product label toward operator.

Using self-instructional training, the supervisor would review the steps and then ask the operator what the first step is. Before the operator can answer, the supervisor gives the answer and so on until all steps are reviewed and answered. The final step leads to the self-reinforcing statement as to the effectiveness of the entire operation. Then the supervisor asks the employee to repeat the steps in order, followed by the self-reinforcing statement. As in any other learning situation, "practice makes perfect," and the employee should be encouraged to repeat these steps until they are committed to memory. In the movie *The Dirty Dozen*, we saw James Coburn teach his 12 paroled prisoners how, and in what order, to carry out their assignments behind enemy lines by having them repeat over and over again the numbered assignments, naming the assigned person, the task, when, where, etc.

Follow-up.   When antecedents are used to initiate behaviors that will produce the desired outcomes, follow-up behaviors by management are necessary to determine whether employees have initiated the behaviors and have continued them until the task was completed. Follow-up is used to apply the consequences that ensure performance of the behaviors in the future.

Learning about one's rate of production, safety record, or attendance record has no real meaning until it becomes clear how that rate is interpreted by the employee and the supervisor. At that point, the feedback takes on new meaning and becomes either positive or negative. People will work to maintain or change their behavior based on feedback, depending upon the way that they have been taught to interpret the feedback.

Because many directives are company policies, employees are asked to read and follow those required procedures. Many of these directives are ignored unless there is managerial follow-up. Managerial follow-up is a consequence. Without follow-up, employees will conclude that management is not really serious about the policy and, as a result, begin to test other policies.

Similarly, if a directive is given but the manager seldom checks on whether the employees do as they are told, they come to ignore his directives. Some of the older employees will even tell the new person, "Don't worry about it; he never remembers what he says." Each directive will become an antecedent for appropriate work behavior only if employees have reason to believe that there will be follow-up.

Consider the study described in Application 3-4. Feedback to employees, to supervisors, and even to the psychiatric residents produced a reduction in errors.

Management follow-up is one of the most necessary steps in preventing and correcting unsatisfactory outcomes and in maintaining worker behaviors that produce satisfactory or superior outcomes. Most managers will claim that they do follow-up to see that the work is being done. However, more detailed questioning indicates that their inspections are only cursory; their follow-up is too late; the feedback they give is too general; or the workers don't know that there was any follow-up inspection. In some cases, when the employees are questioned, there was no follow-up, as is illustrated in Application 3-5.

Follow-up activity by managers should be directed at behaviors of employees, should be visible, and should be unpredictable with respect to time. It saves management time in the long run if follow-up occurs as a natural part of the manager's daily schedule. Reinforcement of productivity, correction of communication errors, inspection, and modification and adjustment of directives can occur in the informal daily walk-around.

Feedback about the behavior of stocking shelves has greater impact on future stocking behaviors than does feedback about an outcome such as a stocked shelf. Research on delay of reinforcement and delay of punishment has shown over and over again that more immediate feedback has the greater impact.

Positive feedback indicates that behavior is producing the desired results; that is, the previously set goal is being achieved or exceeded. For example, charting the cartons processed per hour in a freight area results in production data that can easily be compared with previous performance or with a goal

APPLICATION 3-4
I'm Gonna Tell!

This study illustrates the importance of feedback to employees. A high rate of staff errors in stamping residents' cards was the outcome targeted for change in a psychiatric institution in Ohio.[14] Residents were required to participate in an employment preparation program in which they received training and experience in reporting for work on time, dressing appropriately for work, staying on task, etc. Although such programs can be beneficial in the rehabilitation of psychiatric residents, many of these residents were not completing their employment contracts due to the high number of errors made by staff; that is, staff members were marking cards with unearned stamps.

The first step was to replace the stamps with notations that would more clearly identify time, place, person, etc. When staff received written feedback on their errors, errors dropped from 62% to 45%. When immediate supervisors began receiving feedback on employee errors, errors dropped to 37%. However, when feedback was given to the highest level of supervisors, errors increased to 40.5%! When all feedback stopped, errors returned to 57.5%.

Note that feedback to employees or supervisors up to this point had not included any systematic set of consequences for employees who made errors. Since it was believed that residents had been nagging staff for stamps they didn't deserve, a negative consequence was placed on residents for unearned stamps; that is, residents were required to file a report (explaining how they received the stamps) that could result in loss of privileges. Errors decreased to 35.5%. And finally, when top-level supervisors were instructed to take action (unspecified) regarding errors by subordinate staff, errors dropped to 16%.

set prior to data collection. Comparisons between current and past or desired performance creates the conditions for the feedback to take on meaning— positive or negative. The feedback becomes positive if the expectations are reached and negative if they are not.

However, feedback can be beneficial to performance only if the new employee can actually use it. For example, one study found that when workers scheduled their own work rate, feedback improved performance.[15] But in situations where there was considerable constraint placed upon work rate (e.g., machine paced), feedback had little effect.

Positive feedback is used in another way as well. Complimenting a worker

APPLICATION 3-5

Who Follows Up on the Main Boss?

Employees in a large human-service delivery institution were asked to describe what problems they had doing their jobs.[16] Of the over 1,000 problems described, one-third were attributed to the fact that their supervisors did not follow up on their directives. Their complaints were of this type:

He tells us what is supposed to be done but never checks to see that we do it. My co-workers know that he doesn't check back so they don't even try or don't help if I do start the job. Then a week later, he yells at all of us if he gets complaints.

As consultants in that project, we not only recommended that the first-line supervisors be directed to do more immediate follow-up, but that their supervisors follow up to see that it was happening. Before you ask if we followed up to see if the follow-up on the follow-ups was taking place, we are pleased to say that we did not have to, because the top-level supervisor put a committee system in place to follow up on each of the consultant recommendations.

on aspects of a task completed properly is a form of positive feedback which, of course, has reinforcing qualities. And when corrective feedback must be given, it is more effective if positive feedback is given first (to keep the person listening), followed by the corrective or negative feedback.

Summary

When a person makes an error, a response is either not being made when it should be or is being made when it shouldn't be. The error may be due to a problem of discrimination. The failure to discriminate can be corrected using a number of the training and follow-up procedures described in this chapter.

One method is by accentuating the differences among target objects through color, size, sound, etc., and then fading out those characteristics of the stimuli that are not natural to the task. We can fade out differences in words, shapes, or even people in order to produce the discriminations necessary on the job. In errorless discrimination training, we prevent the person from making a mistake from the very beginning. Once the new employee is able to make a fast and correct response to one object, we fade in another part of the task at a rate where he continues to make only correct choices.

Making a behavioral contract with employees is an antecedent procedure that can produce desirable changes in deficit behaviors such as reporting for work on time or excess behaviors such as taking too many breaks. Contracts require exact descriptions of behaviors, goals, times, places, consequences, and persons. As employees reach the contracted subgoals, they gradually satisfy increased demands until they are performing at the level required by the job.

Self-instructional training, an antecedent procedure, teaches employees to talk themselves through a complex task. The supervisor first models the correct description of the steps of the task and then requires the worker to answer the self-imposed questions about the job one step at a time. When the employee is able to ask and answer the questions in the proper sequence, he is able to talk himself through a complex task.

The next two chapters describe the powerful effects of management consequence behaviors.

Notes

1. Verhave (1966).
2. Dember (1991).
3. Parasuraman (1991).
4. Adler (1991).
5. Yagi (1991).
6. Haupt, Van Kirk, & Terraciano (1975).
7. Gold & Barclay (1973).
8. Irvin (1976).
9. Watson (1976).
10. For an excellent review of the successes and failures resulting from reorganizing employees into work teams, see Sundstrom, De Meuse, & Futrell (1990).
11. Marks, Hackett, Mirvis, & Grady (1986); Rosenberg & Rosenstein (1980).
12. Barra (1983); Mirvis & Lawler (1984).
13. Meichenbaum (1983).
14. Andrasik & McNamara (1977).
15. Knight & Salvendy (1981).
16. Marr, Roessler, & Greenwood (1976).

CHAPTER 4

Consequences to Increase Behavior

Behavior-centered strategies classified as consequences are management behaviors that follow employee behavior and that affect those behaviors. A simple description of the role of the consequence in the ABC model can be taken from everyday practice in business. When the manager demonstrates what the worker needs to do, an antecedent strategy is being used. But when the worker is praised for the correct performance of the task, a consequence strategy is being applied.

Consequences may have two different effects on behavior. Some consequences may *increase* the tendency of the person to do the correct behavior in the future and some may *decrease* the behavior excesses that occur in the workplace. In either case, the consequence is occurring after the behavior. In this chapter, methods of increasing behavior with consequences are presented, and in the next chapter methods of decreasing behavior excesses are discussed.

Management Consequence Strategies to Increase Behaviors

Positive Reinforcement

The consequence that most easily changes behavior of employees and the most powerful consequence that can be used by management on a day-to-day basis is positive reinforcement. It is defined as any event that is presented after the target behavior that results in an increase in the occurrence of that behavior. The chain of events is as follows:

First Event	Second Event	Third Event
Target Behavior Occurs	Manager Reinforces	Behavior Increases

Note that both the second and third event must occur for the process to be called positive reinforcement. The manager says something positive or presents a pat on the back when he observes the employee performing the target behavior, and the employee performs that behavior more frequently in the future.

When given orally, positive reinforcement is inexpensive, quick, and effective. But it is typically the management activity that is most often neglected. Employees, supervisors, and managers report that they do not receive enough positive reinforcement. Too often, managers act as if the pay and benefits they provide are sufficient. Yet numerous studies have shown that money for work is not even among the top five reasons as to why people seek and maintain a job. Appreciation and recognition, on the other hand, are usually among the top two reasons.

Oral reinforcement should be given sincerely, positively, and immediately. If we are not sincere, then we seem manipulative, and employees resent it. If we present only negative consequences, we create a morale problem, and our employees direct their actions at avoiding the punishment by doing only the minimum. And if we delay reinforcement by limiting our positive words to outcomes, we will have little effect on behavior.

The rules of reinforcement and the effects of reinforcement have been studied for almost 100 years, but the practice of giving reinforcement is still both a skill and an art. Some managers do it easily; others act as if it is a difficult, unnatural act. Psychologists know that some children never receive positive reinforcement from their parents but only receive attention when they have done something wrong. Yet the most popular and well-adjusted children receive frequent positive statements at home. Unfortunately, some parents don't care; some don't know any better; and some simply don't know how to reinforce their children because they were never reinforced themselves as children. Similarly, there are managers who need training and encouragement to develop this skill. Like anything else, the more they practice it, the better they get.

Management by walking around (MBWA) is one kind of management behavior that allows managers to deliver reinforcement in a positive manner when the correct behaviors are occurring. When the manager is out on the floor, moving from one department to another, she can not only get to know her people but can deliver a word of praise when she sees the shelves being stocked. She can see the smile and customer assistance when it happens and deliver a positive statement of regard for the behavior. Employees who receive positive consequences at the time they are working appropriately are employees who not only are happier because of the feedback, but who initiate the correct behaviors without constant supervision.

Several important principles must be kept in mind when using positive reinforcement. Never provide the reinforcer unless the behavior is demonstrated. Reinforcement is a manager action *after* the behavior (consequence). When the behavior occurs, reinforce the worker immediately. The more immediate the reinforcement, the clearer the connection between the desired behavior and reinforcement.

Remember that workers differ in their reinforcer preferences. Although most managers appreciate the workers' need for reinforcement, some managers are better than others at recognizing differences among their workers in terms of reinforcer preferences. Some individuals prefer a pat on the back accompanied by the words, "Good job. I appreciate having your inventory in on time." Others may be embarrassed by such open praise and prefer a brief note or less conspicuous recognition given privately.

To understand more clearly differences in reinforcer preferences, supervisors might think of individual employees as they answer the following questions:

1. What topics of conversation does the person enjoy?
2. What does the worker do in his or her spare time?
3. Who are the worker's friends on the job?
4. What does the worker like to do during breaks?
5. What would the worker like to receive as a small present?
6. What would the worker purchase with an extra $5 or $10?
7. What would the worker hate to lose?
8. What would the worker like to have, to do, or to hear?

The answer to each of those questions reveals a potential reinforcer for that employee. Since the answer would be different depending upon which worker we are referring to, the reinforcements must be tailored to the individual. And that's an art and a skill.

Positive reinforcement is a powerful behavioral technique that helps an organization achieve its goals. But many people confuse reinforcement with rewards. Rewards are not always reinforcing because they are not given immediately after the behavior but are given a week or more later—the gold watch for 30 years of work. Rewards may also not be reinforcing because they don't always increase the likelihood of the person performing the targeted behavior—a certificate for 100% attendance during the year. Also, so-called rewards are sometimes not reinforcing to the employee because they are given more from the manager's perspective than the employee's—enrolling an employee in a second training program because she completed the first one so quickly.

Some people call positive reinforcement bribery. But that's not correct because a bribe is something given to a person to perform an illegal act or promised to a person to do a job that he is not required to do. Positive reinforcement, on the other hand, is anything that occurs *immediately* after the *correct* behavior and that *increases* the likelihood of the person repeating that behavior. Brief words of praise or other forms of recognition represent immediate reinforcers that can be used effectively. When paired with other long-term strategies such as stock-option programs, quarterly performance and end-of-year bonuses, and safety and loss-prevention incentives, praise and recognition contribute significantly to organizational success.

Discipline is a management activity that is also too often practiced without the positive. Consider the effect on the associate of being reprimanded by a manager who limits his comments to the faults of the person. Although he may temporarily improve the employee's behavior, the employee is also likely to criticize the supervisor frequently to other employees. He may even decrease other appropriate behaviors and increase inappropriate behaviors such as tardiness, absenteeism, and theft.

Compare that approach to the effect attained by the manager when he includes a description of all the things that the associate does right, a statement about the seriousness of the problem behavior, a request for a plan about what the person will do to correct the problem, and a request for a plan about what the person wants management to do to help him correct the problem. He will probably return to work believing that his manager appreciates his work and intending to correct the problem.

Incentives.   An incentive may act as both an antecedent and a consequence. When the manager informs the employee about the reward, the incentive is being used as an antecedent. When the employee learns that he has earned the incentive, he is being positively reinforced, which is a consequence. Table 4-1 shows a number of different incentives. Notice the variety and the different costs to the organization of the different activities. More than one incentive might be offered because different people prefer different reinforcers. We have all heard the phrases "What's sauce for the goose is not sauce for the gander" or "Different strokes for different folks."

TABLE 4-1
Examples of Incentives

Preferred parking space
Preferred workstation
Preferred work hours
Extra breaks
Paid vacation trip
Extra vacation time, paid
Extra vacation time, half paid
Swimming pool or movie passes
Opportunity to win a drawing
Paid lunch
Half day off with pay

Longer lunch
Reduced price at day-care center
Patches or T-shirts with insignia
Bonus based upon behaviors (sometimes outcome)
Coupons that are redeemable for prizes
Coupons that will purchase extra days off
Coupons that will purchase family activities

Sometimes employees may choose their own rewards from an existing menu. Application 4-1 describes the use of a reinforcer menu. Where else but in a restaurant? Notice how the sales of fresh fish increased when the manager first directed the hostesses to promote the purchase of fresh fish but then decreased until the incentive was added.

The problem with the procedure used in Application 4-1 is that the consequence was placed on outcome and not behavior. Two or three of the hostesses may have been responsible for the increase in fresh fish sales, while all received the reward for the increase. If the manager had tied the incentives to the number of fresh fish orders placed at the tables served by each hostess, the reward would have been more closely associated with the target behaviors. Reinforcing behaviors instead of outcomes might have resulted in the restaurant placing first in the district instead of third and fourth during the treatment phases of the study. Managing behaviors instead of outcomes might also have maintained the suggestive selling behaviors after the rewards were withdrawn.

Although there are a number of incentives that are effective as behavior-change consequences, some are more costly than others; for example, prizes may be more expensive than issuing a preferred parking space. The general rule is to use incentives that are just large enough to get the behavior to happen. The larger incentive is not always the best, though, as can be seen in Application 4-2. Not only did the greater amount of money not prove to be more attractive, but also there was some evidence that the greater amount was a disincentive.

How About a Snapper Today?

In this study, the manager began by prompting the hostesses in a popular seafood restaurant to point to the fresh fish list posted on chalkboards at the same time they gave menus to the customers.[1] Notice in Figure 4-1 how the prompting at the beginning of the baseline period produced a spurt in sales of fresh fish, followed by the characteristic decline that takes place when a manager gives a directive but does not include a consequence.

To start the treatment phase, the manager called another meeting and asked the hostesses to suggest fresh fish on 100% of the orders. The manager said that he would post charts showing the daily number and percentage of orders of fresh fish sold.

Posted in an "alley" where all food received final preparation before serving, the charts also showed the percentage of fresh fish orders for the previous week.

At the end of each week, if the restaurant was ranked in the top five in the region for orders of fresh fish sold, the manager rewarded the hostesses with a free lunch and, if ranked number one in the region, with a free dinner. Figure 4-1 shows the increase in sales of fresh fish sold in each of the incentive phases as the restaurant ranked third in the region during the first intervention period and fourth in the second.

No, we do not know whether the hostesses ordered fresh fish for their free lunches.

Although producing significant savings, the lottery approach to incentives should be used carefully.[2] Note the following:

1. When only one name is drawn, many are not being rewarded. The lottery system can backfire by producing resentment for not winning when the person has improved the targeted behavior in order to earn lottery tickets. For example, when mothers were given lottery tickets for engaging in a variety of steps that enhanced the health of their children, many of the mothers were upset over their failure to win prizes in the lottery.[3] But when a trading-stamp approach replaced the lottery, there was increased participation in the program and more enthusiasm for the steps necessary for rearing healthy children. Improvement in a work behavior is more likely to be maintained if more names are drawn and rewarded.

2. In a lottery incentive program for attendance, if a person is late by 2 minutes in the first week of the month, there is no incentive to not be late or to not miss a day of work for the rest of the month. Greater gains in punctuality and attendance are likely if:

FIGURE 4-1

Incentives for Suggestive Selling of Fresh Fish

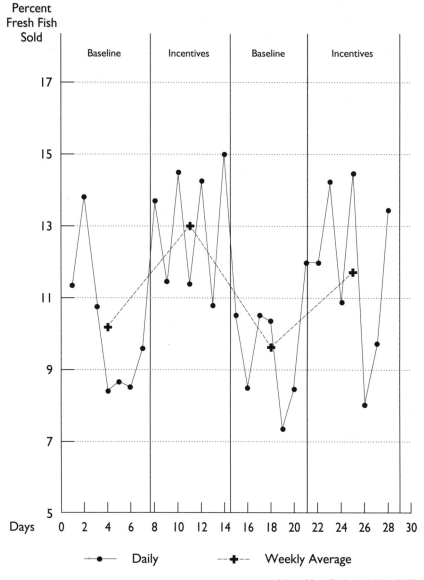

Adapted from Beckman & Marr (1987)

When More Is Not Better

To test the assumption that more is better, incentives that might be used to attract young males to enlist in the navy were studied.[4] In the first study, 860 males between 16 and 22 years of age were interviewed, and in the second, 854 were interviewed. Among the incentives compared were such items as receiving a bonus of $1,000 for enlisting versus a bonus of $3,000, and 2 years of college versus 4 years of college for enlisting. The men were asked to indicate what effect the incentives would have on their interest in the navy by choosing from 1 to 5, where 1 = "I would think less favorably of the navy" and 5 = "I would think more favorably of the navy." Counts made of the most favorable response to each incentive revealed that 8% chose the $3,000 bonus while 27% chose the $1,000 bonus. Furthermore, the mean attractiveness of the lesser bonus was greater. There were no significant differences in response to the years of college incentive. In the second study there was no difference in attractiveness between a one-time $1,000 enlistment bonus and a bonus of $1,000 a year for 3 years. A bonus of 10% of base pay for good performance was found to be more attractive than a bonus of 25%! Although the authors of the study admittedly did not know why more was not better, they reasoned that too large an incentive may lead to distrust, anger, or such feelings as "I can't be bought."

a. There is a second drawing for half of the monetary award for persons late only once.

b. The winner of the reduced reward must be there for the drawing which is held on a randomly selected day.

c. All employees whose names are in the basket get a playing card. They can keep it or give it away. The best poker hand at the end of every five drawings wins another reward.

Negative Reinforcement

Negative reinforcement is another procedure that causes confusion. People often think of it as punishment. When a person is punished, something aversive is applied following a behavior in order to decrease that behavior. But negative reinforcement is defined as the *removal* of something aversive or undesirable following a correct behavior in order to *increase* the probability of that behavior. The person escapes something unpleasant by performing the behavior.

Once while riding in a friend's car, we were suddenly blasted with loud static from his radio. He reached over and hit the dashboard with his fist! We know that behavior was not described in the radio manual. How did he learn to do that? He probably tried the dials first, turning them in different directions and maybe even turning the radio off and on. When those behaviors didn't work, he may have been so frustrated that he hit the dashboard with his fist. "Aha, it worked!" From then on, whenever he heard the loud static, he hit the dashboard to escape the static.

Unlike punishment which is designed to decrease a behavior, negative reinforcement is used to increase a behavior. The person tends to repeat those behaviors that have been found effective in escaping unpleasant situations. Releasing a probationary employee from participating in weekly monitoring sessions and from maintaining a detailed activity log when 2 consecutive months of acceptable sales are achieved is an example of negative reinforcement. In other words, the employee is encouraged to maintain the effective sales behaviors by the removal of the monitoring requirements.

Parents use nagging as a form of negative reinforcement. They stop nagging (usually) when the adolescent does his chores, hangs up her clothes, or comes to the dinner table. The teenager does what she is being nagged to do because her actions make the nagging go away. Parents continue to use nagging to try to control the teenager's behavior because it works sometimes.

Employees may complain about the work environment, and thus prompt management to take steps to reduce the heat, the noise, or other adverse working conditions. Now workers are more likely to say, "If all of us would complain, maybe something would be done about it." It is better to take care of such conditions before the complaints rather than after, because the latter reinforces the behavior of complaining.

What Should Be Reinforced?

In our workshops on behavior-centered approaches to management, we often present cases to the managers to help summarize the principles of feedback and reinforcement. Too often we find that these seemingly simple procedures are still misapplied.

> An employee has completed a number of hubcaps that have blemishes in the paint. Antecedent to change the outcome: He is told to clean the spray-gun filter.

> A driver leaves his truck in the dispatch yard with chicken debris clinging to the bottoms of the cages. Antecedent: He is informed that all drivers are expected to hose out the cages before leaving work or leaving for another pickup.

The price changes given to the clerk at 8 A.M. have not been marked on the merchandise at 1 P.M. She says she has been busy stocking shelves and facing merchandise. Antecedent: Her supervisor informs her that price markdowns are to be done first because customers enter the store looking for those items priced as advertised.

We then ask the workshop managers what the supervisors of these employees should do next. Most of the managers will say follow up by checking the hubcaps, the truck, and the markdowns, and by reinforcing the persons if the jobs are done right. We reinforce the managers for saying they will follow up, but then point out that if they wait for the jobs to be completed when they follow up, they are managing outcomes. If we want to change the behaviors of those employees, we must be prepared to reinforce behaviors not outcomes. Reinforcing the behaviors of cleaning the filters, hosing out the cages, and marking prices will change the outcomes. Thus:

Directives (A)

Behavior (B)

Follow-up and Reinforcement (C) of Behavior

What Steps Are Reinforced During Chaining?

If a job consists of a sequence of behaviors, which behaviors in the chain should we reinforce? When training a new employee, all steps should be reinforced at first. Later, we can thin the reinforcement as she becomes more proficient at completing the chain (Rules on thinning reinforcement are presented later in this chapter under Schedules of Reinforcement). Skilled, experienced workers need little if any reinforcement as they chain the steps of production, reordering merchandise, or construction. Reinforcing their outcomes is sufficient, and sometimes little, if any, supervisory praise is necessary.

Why is so little reinforcement necessary in those cases? We often say it is because the employees take pride in their work. Maybe, but we do know that getting something done can be reinforcing in itself. Completing the job of changing the oil in your car, finishing a report, or ringing up the sale feels good. Each of these outcomes resulted from a sequence of behaviors. And in each case, the last behavior performed was more closely followed by the reinforcement, completion of the job, than were the behaviors it took to get the job started. The steps necessary to clean the painting gun include the last step, screwing the filter cap back on. The steps necessary to clean the chicken truck are nearing completion when the driver turns the water off. It is the steps early on that are most distant from the reinforcement, and it is those "getting-started" steps that need supervisory reinforcement when we want to change "careless," "irresponsible," or "lazy" workers.

Sometimes, getting-started steps seem unrelated to getting the job done. It is not obvious to the beginner why behaviors which are distant from the reinforcements are necessary, even though the manager says the steps are very important. Is it really necessary to call prospective clients on the telephone in order to sell cars or houses? The experienced manager says it is, but trying to get the new salesperson to do it is difficult. Application 4-3 illustrates how management attacked the early part of a chain of sales behaviors in order to improve the outcome.

It is not unusual for managers of real-estate brokerages or of car dealerships to use incentives to increase sales. However, those programs are usually directed at outcomes and not behaviors. The salesperson who sold the most units during the quarter gets an all-expense-paid trip for two to Hawaii. At the end of the quarter, one salesperson gets sunburned; the rest just get burned.

APPLICATION 4-3
Face-to-Face Selling Behaviors in Real Estate

The annual goal of most real-estate companies is to increase market percentage, the percentage of total property sales made in a region by a company. The particular company described in this study had already tried a number of the usual steps to increase sales and dollar volume.[5] It had hired more sales agents, invested heavily in various training programs for agents, remodeled the offices, enlarged office spaces, purchased more desks and telephones, and added secretarial help. Despite being the largest brokerage in the area, the company ranked only seventh in sales and dollar volume out of 15 active firms.

The task of management was to identify, increase, and maintain those behaviors that might lead to increased listings and sales. Ironically, adding more agents had resulted in an actual decrease in profitability for the company. Low-productive persons were occupying positions that were draining resources from the firm.

Following his training in behavior-centered management procedures, the sales manager announced a new behavior-centered program. Nine of the 27 full-time sales agents resigned. The remainder had from 1 to 5 years of selling experience with this brokerage and were representative in age and sex of agents with other companies. The two behaviors targeted for increase were those face-to-face contacts related to sales volume: (a) initial contacts with clients concerning property or sales, and (b) follow-up contacts with clients.

continued on next page

continued from previous page
Following the dinner to introduce the program, and during the 2-week baseline period, all agents were required to fill in a "smile sheet" that requested information on the who, what, where, when, and how of client contacts. To verify contacts, a "courtesy" card or telephone call by the manager to over 100 of the clients included questions on the nature of the contact. No inaccurate smile sheets were turned in by agents. Individual charts, coded so only the agent could identify his or hers, were posted where all could see them. Charts showing weekly contacts, listings, and sales were also posted.

At another dinner period, a token economy intervention was introduced that lasted another 15 weeks. For each week, after 15 follow-ups and 6 initial personal contacts, each of the next 16 contacts earned a token, and each after that earned 2 tokens. Contacts were reset to zero at the end of each week. Tokens could purchase any of 60 items, for example, 11 tokens for 10 gallons of gas or 1,000 for a slate pool table.

After the 15 weeks of intervention, the token intervention was withdrawn, amongst grumbling, and then reinstated a month later. Figure 4-2 shows the effect of the token reinforcements on the face-to-face selling behaviors. Before the program was begun, the average real-estate agent income per year in the district was $7,570, while agents in this company averaged $6,927. During the program the average in the district was $6,400, but in this company the average was $14,000. Only 4% of their sales force were million-dollar salespersons before the program, but during the program year 31% of the salespersons reached that level. How about those tokens?

The Token Economy

Application 4-3 not only illustrates the effect of reinforcing sales-related behaviors rather than outcomes, but shows also the value of reinforcing behaviors that usually have no immediate reinforcement. A token economy is a method of reinforcement that has the advantage of delivering the reinforcement immediately after the targeted behavior while giving each person a choice from a list of available reinforcements. It has three components—the target behavior, the token, and the menu of back-up reinforcers. In Application 4-3 the behaviors targeted for change were personal contacts with prospective buyers. Generally, it is best not to target more than five different behaviors because of the difficulty of trying to observe and reinforce more than five during the same time period.

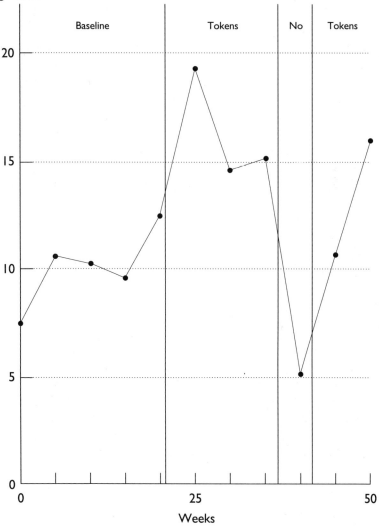

FIGURE 4-2

Follow-up Contacts in Real Estate

Mean Contacts
During Week

Adapted from Anderson et al. (1983)

The tokens can be any type of unit that is easy to deliver, such as poker chips, check marks, points, stamps, or coupons. In Application 4-3, tokens were awarded for each personal contact over 6 and each follow-up over 15.

The menu of back-up reinforcers is a list of activities or items that the employees might buy with their tokens. The cost of each item in tokens is also listed. The general rule for pricing these items is based upon the principle of supply and demand. The more expensive or desirable the item, or the more difficult it is to deliver, the higher the cost in tokens. In Application 4-3, 10 gallons of gas cost 11 tokens, while the pool table cost 1,000 tokens. In the women's prison, the most desirable activity and the most difficult to provide to the prisoners was that of going fishing at one of the ponds at the Cummins Prison Farm. Since two guards and a truck were needed for about 4 hours to provide security and transportation, the fishing activity cost 1,000 tokens to be divided across 8 or 10 women prisoners. They earned points by sewing prison uniforms. Many of the women had refused to work when paid real money on a piece-rate basis, but they worked very hard for tokens to purchase the right to go fishing.

In the introduction, we described how Marr found himself in the predicament of trying to modify the classroom behaviors of "unmotivated" prisoners, some of whom were waiting for death in the electric chair. Application 4-4 describes how he used a token economy to shape the behaviors of using a dictionary.[6]

When and How Often Should We Reinforce?

Positive reinforcement cannot practically be given every time an employee performs the correct behavior. If it could be, it would be called a continuous reinforcement (CRF) schedule. When parents are trying to teach a child to say "please," they try to use a CRF, but usually can't because the child is liable to say the word at times when the parent isn't present or when the parent is too busy to notice and give praise. By the same token, a manager cannot be there at the time clock to praise each employee who arrives on time.

Schedules of Reinforcement

The alternative to CRF schedules are intermittent schedules where reinforcement is delivered after some, but not every, occurrence of the behavior. Instead of trying to reinforce the worker every time he does a job right, we reinforce him only occasionally. The two ways to do this are to reinforce him only after a certain number of correct responses (a ratio schedule), or by reinforcing him only once in a while (an interval schedule) if he is still doing it

APPLICATION 4-4

A Token Economy for Prisoners

I had put myself in this situation by suggesting that the prison instructor should be able to get his "students" to use dictionaries by shaping their behaviors. He said, "Show me," and there I was, in the middle of Tucker Prison, with 15 tough-looking prisoners looking at me like I was the busted flush in last night's poker game, with a shotgun-toting guard leaning against the only door.

After threatening them with being put on report, my host-teacher got them to put their cigarettes out and sit down. Having established that classroom atmosphere, he introduced me and then sat down. His introduction caught me off "guard" as I had been waffling between trying to figure out where the safest place to stand was and who were the targets of the guard's concern. So I chose a behavior familiar to most college professors when in doubt, and walked to the blackboard and asked the students a question. I then proceeded to ask one of the most naive (stupid) questions I have ever asked. "All right, men, what do you want to do in here that you presently can't?" With little hesitation and a lot of laughs, they proceeded to tell me in somewhat graphic but definitely pornographic terms what they would like to be doing.

I said, with what was meant to be a laugh but that was more like an anxiety-type giggle, "No, I mean what would you like to do in this class-room that's possible, that you presently are not permitted to do?"

Hesitation, and then one said, "Yeah, when we come in here at night and use the library, we get to smoke cigarettes. But he don't let us smoke no how." I wrote "Smoke a cigarette" on the board.

Another said, "I'd rather go over to the library and read comic books than sit here and study this English ———." I wrote "Go to library for 15 minutes."

Another, "I want to go to the window and watch the baseball team practice." I wrote "Go to the window for 15 minutes."

After a few more items were added, I went to my briefcase and pulled out a pack of 3 x 5 cards that I usually carry in case I want to make notes. Holding the cards up, I returned to the board and wrote numbers such as 5, 10, 15 next to each of their preferred activities and said, "When you have that many of these cards, you can purchase those activities."

Silence, and then one said, "What do you mean?" The con sitting next to him looked at him. I walked over to the looker and said, "You have just earned a card for looking in the direction of the dictionaries."

They all looked, and I gave them cards. One moved his foot, and I gave him a card, saying, "You just earned

continued on next page

continued from previous page
a card for moving your foot in the direction of the dictionaries."

One got up, with a grin, and walked over toward the dictionaries, and when I gave him a card for being near the dictionaries, the others followed and received cards, as if they were playing a silly game with the visitor.

One reached over and placed his hand on a dictionary and received his card. Some of the others reached over and grabbed dictionaries and as one "student" was jostled out of the crowd, I gave him a card for having a dictionary in his hands and moving toward his desk.

The others, kidding, pushing, and some carrying dictionaries on their heads, returned to their seats and got cards. As I stood at the front of the room, feeling relieved that I had survived so far, I saw one of the men "accidently" put his hand on his pencil.

But before I could reward him for having a dictionary on his desk and a pencil in his hand, my feelings of relief were terminated by the shout, "Wait!" One of the prisoners had gotten back up and started toward me with a slow shuffle. As I was looking to make sure the guard was still there, the man reached the desk, slapping his cards down one by one,

"One, two, three, four, and FIVE."

Pointing at the blackboard where their preferred activities were listed, he reached into his pocket and pulled out a pack of cigarettes —taking one, lighting it, all the time looking at me, then the teacher, and then sauntering back to his seat, in a cloud of smoke. This released a hoard of buyers, and as they settled back into their seats, smoking cigarettes, I realized we had taken an important first step in establishing a token economy in the classroom. I gave half of the cards to the teacher, and we started reinforcing the students for opening the dictionaries, writing down words, copying their meanings, and using the words in sentences.

About a month later, I received a call from the Commissioner of Corrections of the State of Arkansas, who said, "Aren't you the guy who started the 'motivational' system down at Tucker?

"Well, we've got two eighth- to eleventh-grade English classes in our prisons. They're still having trouble with the one at Cummins Prison, just getting them to sit down in their seats in class, but I think those guys at Tucker know more words out of a dictionary than most of you college professors. I want to talk about putting that system in some other places in the prisons."[7]

right. Table 4-2 shows these two basic types. Notice that each is subdivided into fixed and variable schedules.

There are many advantages to using these intermittent schedules of reinforcement:

TABLE 4-2
Intermittent Reinforcement Schedules

Type	Effect on Behavior	Example
Fixed Ratio (FR)		
Reinforcement after x number of responses	High rate of behavior with pauses after reinforcement[8]	Piece rates—$2/per bushel of apples picked
Variable Ratio (VR)		
Reinforcement after *average* of x number of responses	Very steady rate of work behavior	Tips to waiters, commissions for sales
Fixed Interval (FI)		
Reinforcement after x minutes, hours, days	Behavior occurs immediately before reinforcement is due	Showing up for work only on payday
Variable Interval (VI)		
Reinforcement for the behavior only if it is occurring after an average of x units of time	A low, steady rate of behavior	Checking the display for neatness when time for visit by supervisor is uncertain

Name of Schedule	Definition
FR 5	Reinforcement after every 5th response
FR 8	Reinforcement after every 8th response
VR 5	Reinforcement on the average of every 5th response
FI 5	Reinforcement on the 5th day if behavior occurs
FI 8	Reinforcement on the 8th day if behavior occurs
VI 5	Reinforcement on the average of every 5th day if behavior occurs on the day reinforcement is due

1. The employee doesn't get tired, bored, or turned off with the supervisor's reinforcing statements. For example, concerning safety the manager might say, "That's great that you put on the goggles before you start up that machine."

2. Employees work more steadily when reinforcing statements are unpredictable and occur only occasionally.

3. Appropriate work behaviors will continue for long periods of time when there are delays in reinforcement if the employee can't tell which of the on-time, retail customer, or production behaviors are going to be reinforced.

The effects of intermittent schedules explain some of the patterns of behavior we see in the workplace. Notice how the waiter shows up more and more frequently as the time to give a tip approaches. "More coffee, sir?" "How was your dinner?" "May I bring you dessert?" "More water?" Where was he when I needed ketchup? He was on a *fixed interval schedule* (FI). We would receive much better service if we told him that we would give him a tip on the average of every 10 minutes if he came to the table—a variable interval schedule.

Another example of schedules at work is seen in the effect of consumers' buying habits on the turnover of salespeople. When a VR schedule (see Table 4-2) changes slowly, people will continue their work behaviors. But when it changes quickly, work stops. The salesclerk may use the same sales speech with each customer that he approaches. He is reinforced with a commission on the sale only when he sells a car. When many customers are in the market, he sells a car on the average of every third sales presentation. But, during a recession, he may sell a car only on the average of every 15 presentations. If the economy declines slowly, the switch from a VR3 to a VR15 is slow, VR3—VR5—VR9, etc., and he will probably be trapped by the schedules into continuing as a car salesman. But if the market changes quickly his attempts to sell will end quickly, and he will look for another job.

Although variable ratio schedules produce a much steadier rate of behavior, fixed ratio schedules usually produce a higher rate. This can be seen in Application 4-5 where both schedules produced significantly greater gains than did hourly pay, but the fixed ratio schedule produced greater effort.

Usually a manager is better off with a VR schedule than an FR schedule. You only have to estimate the number of responses instead of counting the exact number to determine which of the responses to reinforce. When you begin to thin the reinforcement, you put an anchor on the work rate by changing the variable ratio slowly as in the salesman example above.

Interval Schedules

Interval schedules explain and also suggest management practices to change workers' behavior. Ordinarily, managers would not find fixed interval schedules useful because they tend to produce patterns of work behavior

Schedules of Reinforcement in Training

One demonstration of the superiority of consequences tied to actual behavior is shown in a study of the trainees in an electronics program.[9] Using self-paced programmed texts dealing with basic electricity and electronics, trainees were compared on straight hourly pay, variable ratio (VR), and fixed ratio (FR) schedules of reinforcement. Behaviors measured and targeted for improvement were the number of text units studied or passed, products completed, etc.

Trainee effort and performance on both FR and VR were superior to that on the noncontingent hourly pay procedure, and performance did not differ between the two types of ratio schedule trainees. However, trainee effort was greater on the FR schedule than on the VR schedule.

where the employee does almost no work until it is almost time for the reinforcement to occur. What behavior is being reinforced when the employee shows up at the pay window on Friday to receive her check? The answer—going to the pay window on Fridays. However, fixed interval schedules are operating in the world of work. Consider the second shift worker who wants a parking space near the building where he works. If he arrives before 3:30 P.M., the first shift has not ended, and he will receive no reinforcement; that is, he will not get a desirable parking spot. If, however, he arrives after 3:45 P.M., all the desirable parking spaces have been taken because his second shift co-workers got the empty spaces during the short period that they were open. Such a schedule is called *fixed interval with limited hold* because there is only a limited amount of time to make the response and get reinforcement.

Buyers who travel to New York, London, or Paris prior to the fashion shows will be able to select the latest fashions; but if they wait too long, they are liable to find that the competition has bought all the best items. Similarly, sending a truck driver to Warren, Arkansas, for special tomatoes too early results in lost time because the tomatoes aren't ripe. Sending him too late results in spoiled tomatoes.

Variable interval schedules of reinforcement are useful because they produce very steady work behavior. When the manufacturing vice-president of Standard Steel Corporation walks through the melting shop every day, he varies the daily visit so that he arrives at different times. He then reinforces the first appropriate work behavior he observes.[10] If he does that only once a day, and if he reinforced the same type of behavior, we could say that he has the employees on a VI 24-hour schedule.

Another use of variable interval schedules is illustrated in a study where the supervisors in a large rehabilitation center were directed to visit with each assistant supervisor once a week on randomly selected days.[11] Each time, a supervisor would ask the assistants which of the new behavior principles of management they had used the previous week. Whenever they were able to describe a specific instance (who, what, where, when) of use, he reinforced them. Figure 4-3 shows the increase in use of the procedures as the VI 7-day schedule of monitoring continued. Note that the assistants could not predict when they would be questioned, and possibly reinforced, each week.

Many industrial, retail, and trucking firms are concerned about the problem of gasoline costs for their trucking fleet. Some have used incentives for gasoline conservation, while others have used variable interval schedules of reinforcement. In one firm, drivers were given cash after 1 month (the interval) for limiting their driving to essential trips, thereby reducing mileage and conserving gasoline.[12] Although that procedure produced a 20% decrease in miles driven, the researchers were not satisfied. As illustrated in Application 4-6, a simple FI 7-day schedule that earned small reinforcements was used, but a large reinforcement for meeting the criteria for 4 weeks in a row was added.[13]

When Reinforcement Is Thinned Too Fast: Ratio Strain

Did you ever wonder what ever happened to those nice, polite kids of ages 7 through 9? At ages 11 through 13, the kids act like savages—as if they were raised in a barn or a pig pen. The answer is probably ratio strain. Kids at ages 5 through 9 who were praised for covering their mouth when they coughed, for saying "please" when they asked for something, or "excuse me" if they interrupted a conversation, are expected to do those things at age 10. However, the parents stop reinforcing them for being polite. Behaviors that are learned under continuous reinforcement schedules where every instance of the behavior is reinforced will disappear very quickly when reinforcement is no longer given. This is called *ratio strain*. The change in the ratio of reinforcement occurs so fast that a strain is put on the behavior and it decreases. Remember the car salesmen who quit during the recession? Ratio strain.

Behaviors that are reinforced only occasionally will continue for a much longer time when reinforcement is removed.[14] We can see that rule in operation when we try to eliminate some types of inappropriate work behaviors. An example is the practical joker on the assembly line. On the average of every fourth time he plays a practical joke, he gets a big laugh from the other workers, a VR4 schedule. Practical jokes are very difficult behaviors to eliminate

FIGURE 4-3
Modeling Versus Supervision

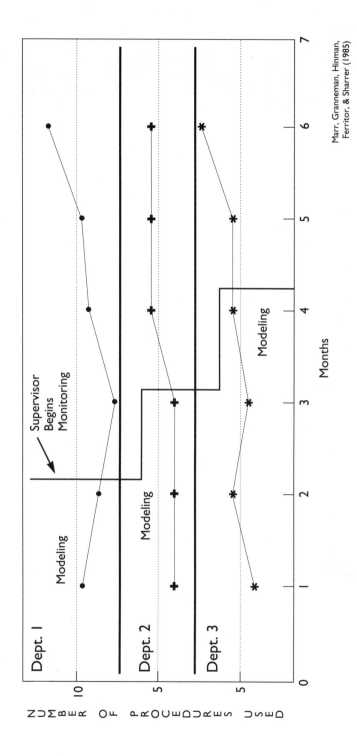

Marr, Granneman, Hinman,
Ferritor, & Sharrer (1985)

Decreasing Driving by Chaining the Schedules

In this study the success of the ABC method of scheduling reinforcement on both an FI 7-day and an FI 4-week in promoting gasoline conservation was demonstrated. During the 3 months of the study, odometers were checked five times across 33 days before the behavioral interventions were initiated. One group (reinforcement) was then given a personalized fuel conservation guide (the antecedent) that explained how each person could earn a weekly prize of $1, $1.50, and $2 for reducing their driving by 10%, 20%, and 30%, respectively. Additionally, averaging 10% for the month earned $5, and another $2.50 for each additional 10% reduction up to 30%. To be eligible for grand prizes of $10, a person had to have at least a 10% reduc-tion in each of the previous 4 weeks.

Another group (self-recording) was taught to calculate average miles driven per day and given weekly and monthly prizes for turning in their mileage records (no reduction in mileage required). Eight odometer checks were made of each person in the groups during the 28 days of the interventions. The reinforcement group showed a 22.5% reduction in mileage during the intervention, and the self-recording group had a 12.5% reduction even though their prizes were given for only turning in their mileage records. It was interesting to note than when the reinforcements stopped abruptly, almost all individuals increased their driving to near the pre-intervention levels.

unless the supervisor can eliminate all reinforcement by convincing the other workers not to laugh. Even if that is possible, the jokester will continue his pranks for quite a while because he was only getting laughs occasionally before the reinforcement was totally eliminated. Positive discipline is usually called for in these situations; for instance, state at least one positive aspect of the person's work, confront the problem behavior, describe the rationale for why the behavior is a problem, and issue directives regarding future performance. If that doesn't eliminate the problem, we must move to a different type of consequence.

Another part of the art of reinforcement in the workplace is to maintain the optimum quantity and quality of work behaviors with a minimum of reinforcement. To attain that result, the manager needs to reinforce the new worker frequently and then thin the schedule by *slowly* giving less-frequent reinforcement across time. If the schedule of reinforcement is shifted too quickly, the behavior that is being reinforced will begin to decline. Did you ever see people try to stack beer or cola cans? When one tried to put the next can on top of the stack too quickly, the whole stack came tumbling down. Behavior, too, can come tumbling down if we forget to thin reinforcement slowly. The rule is to continue the reinforcement even when the worker is doing everything correctly, but to reduce the amount to a practical level that will still maintain the performance.

Summary

Consequences are the second type of tool in the behavior-centered management approach. One of the most effective and least expensive consequences that a manager can give is positive reinforcement. Any event that occurs after the behavior and that increases the likelihood that the employee will repeat the behavior is a reinforcement. Words of praise are positive reinforcers that are highly effective in changing behavior. Frequent positive reinforcement strengthens both the positive feelings employees have toward their jobs and the effects of negative feedback when it must be given.

Incentives act as antecedents and consequences. Knowledge that a positive consequence will occur (antecedent) propels employees to correct errors and to increase productivity. Receiving incentive such as bonuses or time off (consequence) strengthens and maintains desirable performance. Whereas verbal reinforcements are tailored to the individual, incentives are usually objects or events that all workers want. Incentives do not have to be large to produce changes in behavior.

Negative reinforcement is another effective means of increasing desirable work behaviors. Often confused with punishment, negative reinforcement is sought by employees because it means the removal of something unpleasant or aversive. Waiting to improve the working environment until the employees complain does, however, reinforce the behavior of complaining.

Schedules of reinforcement refer to the act of reinforcing the behaviors occasionally. Ratio schedules reinforce the person after every few responses, while interval schedules reinforce the person for a response that occurs after a specified period of time. Schedules, if thinned slowly, allow us to maintain the target behaviors at the desired rate while reducing the reinforcement to a level that is easier to deliver. If the reinforcement is reduced too fast, ratio strain occurs as the behaviors decrease to a pre-reinforcement level.

Notes

1. Beckman & Marr (1988).
2. Wallin & Johnson (1976).
3. Guthrie, Guthrie, Fernandez, & Estrada (1982).
4. Korman, Glickman, & Frey (1981).
5. Anderson, Crowell, Sucec, Gilligan, & Wikoff (1983).
6. This incident was the precipitation of the introduction of the behavioral system in Arkansas prisons, which was later described in part by Marr, Lilliston, & Zelhardt (1974).
7. C. Robert Sarver was commissioner of corrections during Gov. Winthrop Rockefeller's administration and led the prison system through the changes that replaced the armed trustees in the towers with guards, introduced strong rehabilitation and education programs in the prisons, and moved the correction system out of the situation characterized in the movie about Arkansas prisons, *Brubaker,* produced by Mann & Silverman (1980).
8. The fixed ratio schedule produces pauses after each reinforcement, and the pause is proportional to the size of the ratio. For example, a piece rate of being paid for sewing buttons on 5 shirts produces a shorter pause after the fixed ratio of 5 shirts than does a fixed ratio of 20 shirts.
9. Pritchard, Hollenback, & De Leo (1980).
10. Hellriegel & Slocum (1979).
11. Marr, Granneman, Hinman, Ferritor, & Sharrer (1985).
12. Foxx & Hake (1977).
13. Hake & Foxx (1978).
14. When reinforcement no longer follows a behavior, that behavior will disappear. We call that *extinction*. However, when reinforcement is removed following intermittent reinforcement of that behavior, extinction takes much longer. This is called the *partial reinforcement effect* (PRE). It can be used to the advantage of management when we want to delay or thin out the frequency of reinforcement for appropriate work behaviors. But it is to our disadvantage if we try to eliminate surplus behaviors such as practical jokes, complaining behaviors, etc., that have received intermittent reinforcement.

Consequences to Decrease Behavior

Each of the strategies described in Chapter 5 is applied immediately following the target behavior as was the case in Chapter 4. However, these consequences are methods designed to decrease the frequency, duration, or intensity of the target behavior. When using any strategy to decrease a problem behavior, a balanced approach should be used. When using techniques to decrease undesirable behaviors, be sure to add positive reinforcement for desirable behaviors. People leave or, even worse, sabotage situations characterized by inattention and too much punishment. A little reinforcement for appropriate actions goes a long way.

Management Consequence Strategies to Decrease Behaviors

Extinction

Because it requires the least effort, "extinction" is the first method that should be considered for decreasing the frequency of a behavior. The manager must remove the attention or any other type of reinforcement that is maintaining the targeted excessive behavior. The effectiveness of extinction depends completely on the ability of the supervisor and others working with the person to eliminate the consequences that are maintaining the behavior.

Having removed all reinforcement for the behavior, the manager must be prepared for the behavior to get worse before it gets better. Look what happens in the morning when the child says, "Mom, where're my shoes?" and there is no answer. Louder, "MOM, where're my SHOES?" No answer. "MOM!" No answer. "MOMMMM. MOM, MOM, MOM."

At first there may be little observable effect when the manager uses extinction on the employee who hangs around waiting for attention. But if she continues to ignore the person when he is "hanging around" and gives him attention when he is working, then his hanging around will decrease.

One of our university students once asked whether extinction would work on the behavior of a person complaining about her physical problems. The student explained that she worked as a part-time clerk in a retail store and was beginning to dread going to work because of the physical complaints made "all the time" by one of the other clerks. Although sympathetic, the student was tired of hearing about the pain the woman suffered after an operation, her arthritic aches and pains, her backaches, and her headaches.

The student was informed that extinction was a common part of the treatment package used in pain clinics. Relatives of pain patients are instructed, in the presence of the patient, that they are often unknowingly conditioning their loved ones to show pain behaviors. Patients are not even aware that they are being conditioned. Their pain-elicited facial expressions, gestures, and complaints increase as family members increase their attention whenever they see signs of pain. The family is instructed to increase its attention to the patient when the person is not showing symptoms of pain and is reminded not to respond to any of the pain behaviors. They are further instructed to respond to their loved one whenever the person asks for help, "please, get me my pills," "help me down the hallway," "get me the heating pad," etc., but to do nothing else at that time. Patients and family are amazed at the improvement over time.

Thus, our student was instructed to increase her attention to her co-worker when she talked about anything else except her pains, and to turn away, look away, and never respond when she complained about her physical ailments. A month later, the student happily reported that the woman rarely mentioned her pain but did talk about the customers, the merchandise, and even showed an interest in the student's university courses. Although feeling guilty and insensitive at first, the student soon realized that she couldn't help the woman with her pain and couldn't stand the job if the complaining continued. Interestingly, the student also reported that the extinction procedure hadn't stopped the woman from complaining to others who continued their attention! In a later chapter, we will examine how delaying attention when an employee is a frequent complainer can extinguish the complaining while still giving the manager an opportunity to respond to the person's real problems.

Differential Reinforcement of Incompatible Behavior (DRI). Differential reinforcement of incompatible behavior (DRI) is another powerful method for decreasing excessive behaviors that can have the added benefit of increasing desirable behaviors. The DRI procedure consists of reinforcing the behaviors that are appropriate in order to decrease those that are not. It could be called the "teeter-totter" principle. If you want one end of the teeter-totter to come down, do something at the other end to make it go up.

When the problem behaviors are such things as too much visiting with co-workers or too much horseplay, increased reinforcement of specific work behaviors results in an increase in those behaviors and a proportionate decrease in the behavioral excesses. The successful use of the DRI procedure can be seen in the study described in Application 5-1.[1] Managers in this large retail store had been trying to stop the inappropriate employee behaviors of visiting, standing around, or leaving workstations by tersely reminding or scolding the salespeople if they were absent, were slow in helping customers, or had not stocked shelves. When appropriate behaviors occurred, supervisors said nothing but were often overheard complaining about employees lacking motivation.

The incentives of time off with pay or the equivalent in cash were very effective. Notice that when the incentive was removed, the appropriate retailing behaviors continued.

Punishment. Punishment involves adding aversive consequences following a behavior with the express purpose of decreasing the frequency of the behavior. Over-reliance on punishment in an organization can lead to resentment, turnover, and absenteeism. Resentment is expressed in many costly forms—decreased attention to equipment maintenance, higher accident rates, and decreased production. In fact, the title of a famous book might be changed slightly to characterize the situation, for example, *The Crime of Punishment* or even *The Cost of Punishment.*

When a verbal reprimand is used where the manager believes that the employee just did not know better, it should be immediate and instructive in nature, "No, that's not correct. Watch me and do it this way." When the individual does it the correct way, she should be verbally reinforced immediately, "Right. That's the way. Good work."

When it is used to stop a behavior that the manager believes the worker knows should not be done, it is important to follow the rules that psychology has developed out of 80 years of research.

1. The verbal reprimand should be immediate.
2. It should occur after each and every occurrence of the behavior.

Enough to Get Started

This well-designed and controlled study examined the effect of positive reinforcement on increasing the retailing behaviors of the salespeople, while at the same time decreasing such inappropriate behaviors as standing around, visiting with each other, etc. Employees in 8 departments in this 100-department retail store were given a positive consequence for their appropriate merchandising behaviors and were compared to employees in 8 other departments who were not.

Before the intervention, all employees in the study had worked at least 6 months and had been instructed in the appropriate merchandising behaviors, such as selling, stocking, handling returns, talking with supervisors, etc. Each merchandising behavior was very specifically defined; for instance, selling: conversing with, assisting, or showing merchandise to customers as well as ringing up sales and filling out charge slips.

Trained observers visited each of the 16 departments twice per hour per day to record the behaviors across the 12 weeks of the study. After the baseline, all employees were told that the observers were gathering data on their performance. The employees in the 8 experimental departments were told that they would receive time off with pay or the equivalent in cash in proportion to their attainment of performance standards. In addition, for each week that an employee met the standards, his or her name was entered for a drawing for a 1-week paid vacation for two, the drawing to be held after the 4-week intervention period. When the reinforcement ended, observers continued their measurement for 4 more weeks. Figure 5-1 shows that the appropriate behavior increased during intervention and remained high after the reinforcement was withdrawn while inappropriate behaviors decreased and remained down.

3. It should be given at its most severe level and not increase in severity as the behavior reoccurs.

4. There should be no reinforcement for the behavior.

5. The employee should be given training or suggestions for an alternative or acceptable behavior that will earn the reinforcement that she has been receiving for the unacceptable behavior. Punishment does not always have to come in the form of degrading or disparaging comments or loss of privilege, pay, or employment. Instead, some punishment strategies such as "response cost" can be very effective in changing behavior.

FIGURE 5-1

Effects of Reinforcement on Idle Time and Retail Behaviors

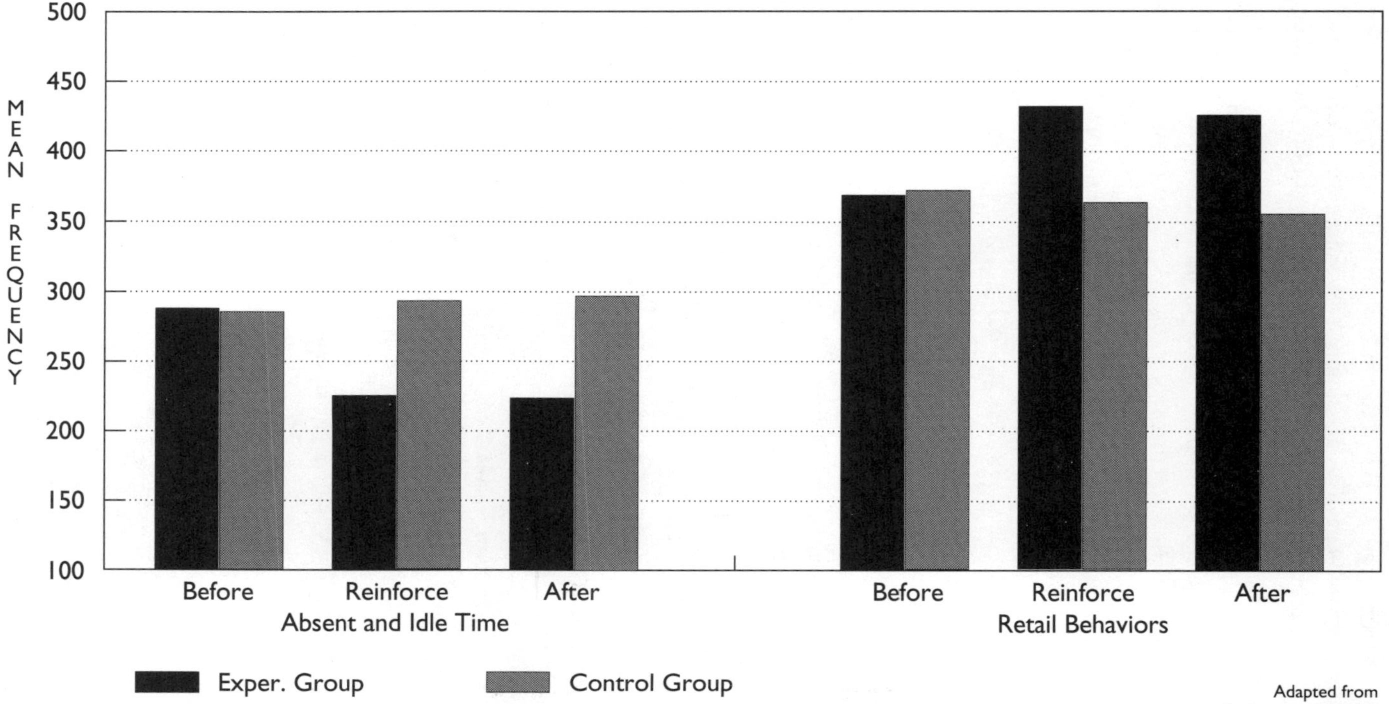

Adapted from
Luthans et al. (1981)

Exper. Group   Control Group

Response cost.   When reinforcers are withdrawn as a consequence for inappropriate behaviors, a response-cost procedure is being used. This procedure has been used extensively in behavior-modification programs as a method of reducing undesirable behaviors.[2]

An excellent example of how a response cost was used to reduce business costs by a telephone company is seen in Application 5-2. The author of that study suggests that the procedure might be used anywhere that a business finds a costly or precious service or commodity being consumed unnecessarily.[3] He cites the request for water in restaurants and hotels located in drought-ridden areas of the country. Generally, response-cost procedures are very effective in suppressing behaviors while not generating any serious emotional reaction. In fact, sometimes the introduction of response-cost procedures produces happier employees as will be seen later in Application 11-4.

The successful use of a response-cost procedure to reduce cash shortages in a business setting has also been reported.[4] When cash shortages were subtracted from employees' salaries, the size of the shortage was sharply reduced. Since the overcorrection behavioral-analysis method described later in this section has been shown to be effective for cash register shortages and is a

---

APPLICATION 5-2
Using the Book Saves Money

Although the telephone company in Cincinnati had been urging customers to use published directories for information instead of using directory assistance, subscribers had continued the use of the information service even though the typical request was for numbers that had been listed in directories for several years.

Since all subscribers were subsidizing the cost of providing the service, company officials believed that a response-cost procedure for local calls would benefit the over one million subscribers by decreasing the use of costly directory assistance by those who were abusing the service. The first 3 calls per month were free, and a 20-cent charge for each week was initiated for each additional call. Whereas there had been approximately 65,000 to 80,000 calls per month in the years 1971 thru 1973, after the response-cost procedure was begun, local directory assistance calls dropped to approximately 20,000 from 1974 through 1976. Meanwhile, long distance directory assistance requests for the same periods were not charged and continued their slow increase in frequency.

less-severe consequence than loss of salary, response cost is not recommended as the first choice of procedures to use in decreasing cash shortages.

It is interesting to note that children and adolescents, if given a choice, prefer a response-cost disciplinary procedure to a severe verbal reprimand. Do speeders send in their checks for speeding tickets because they don't want the inconvenience of going to court or because they don't want to hear the lecture from the judge? Some do go to court and take the risk of the fine and the lecture. Regardless, whether they be charges for personal phone calls, fines for parking in customer or reserved parking places, or decreases in pay proportionate to work not accomplished, these response costs are effective means of decreasing behaviors that are costly in time, money, or customer service.

Overcorrection

A set of procedures that has only recently been applied to behavior problems in business and industry is overcorrection. There are three different types: (a) overcorrection positive practice, (b) overcorrection restitution, and (c) overcorrection behavior analysis. All are directed at decreasing excessive behaviors or increasing deficit behaviors. Each procedure is discussed in terms of its actual or potential application to business or industrial problems.

Overcorrection Positive Practice

Although used extensively and successfully to increase deficit behaviors and to decrease excessive behaviors of children, overcorrection positive practice is rarely reported in research in business or industrial settings. Basically, it consists of telling the person the following, "Because you did the inappropriate behavior, you must now practice doing the appropriate behavior." Here are some examples. Parent: "Because you didn't hang up your coat when you came in, you are to put it back on, go outside, and then come back in and hang up your coat." Then when she does it, the parent says, "Good, but since you forgot to do it before, you need to do it two more times to get practice so you won't forget in the future." Another example, "Because you didn't put your bicycle away, I want you to practice putting it away three times. And the next time you leave it out on the lawn all night, you will get to practice five times." Or, "Because you didn't carry your plate and glass back to the kitchen when you finished your lunch, you need to practice . . . ," etc. Parents are delighted with the method because it is so effective when it is combined with praise for remembering to do the appropriate behaviors.

Although it could be used to decrease repetitive errors during training, most managers would be reluctant to use the positive-practice procedure on experienced employees because it might be seen as demeaning to an adult. However, we have suggested to managers that it might be used as a consequence for certain repetitive errors that seem to be due to carelessness, provided that it be put into effect as a retraining consequence for costly errors such as shortages at the cash register, incorrectly filled out reorder forms, or incorrectly mixed substances in an industrial setting. Thus, when the error has been made for the third time, the supervisor informs the person that he will need retraining. This would consist of having the individual repeat the correct set of procedures three or more times without error. He would then be told that the next time an error is made, he will again be given a chance to practice doing it the right way. When there has been improvement, the supervisor must be just as prompt with her praise as she is with her retraining procedure.

Overcorrection Restitution

This is similar to overcorrection positive practice in that the consequence is related to the behavior that was inappropriate. Overcorrection restitution requires the employee to take extra time or make extra effort as a result of his negligence. Instead of practicing the correct behavior, he must make restitution by repairing the damage or restoring the work environment to a state that is superior to its prior condition. Thus, failing to sweep the aisle has a consequence of sweeping, mopping, and waxing the floor in that aisle. Some readers may recall their first sergeant's restitution methods during basic training if he found so much as a match littering the barrack's floor.

Restitution in the form of money taken out of one's paycheck for cash register shortages, broken tools, or damaged merchandise is generally not recommended because of the negative feelings and behavior generated in the employee. A percentage of the cost of the damage is more likely to be seen as fair by the employee.

Overcorrection restitution in the form of money repays the employer for the cost of the error or carelessness and makes the employee more careful in the future. The teenager who has to pay a percentage of the increase in car insurance that resulted from her accident is a lot more careful than one who does not. Overcorrection restitution and positive-practice procedures are most effective if they are accompanied by positive reinforcement in the form of praise for improvement.

Overcorrection Behavior Analysis

This procedure has been used in business settings as well as in human-service delivery organizations.[5] The consequence for an inappropriate behavior is a written analysis of the antecedents, behavior, and consequences of the misbehavior with a plan for improvement. Application 5-3 describes the first use of the procedure in a large rehabilitation center to solve the problem of lost keys and meal cards of residents. Figure 5-2 shows the overcorrection behavior-analysis form that was used to handle the lost key problem.

The overcorrection behavior-analysis procedure has also been effective in reducing loss of keys in university dormitories,[6] and, according to one of the

---

APPLICATION 5-3

The Red Tape to Get a New One

Staff at a large rehabilitation center asked for help in decreasing the serious security problems created by residents who frequently lost their room keys and meal cards. The usual consequence for loss of a key or a card was a replacement of the item following a lecture that might include criticism or sympathy. A low-cost intervention that could be easily taught to the staff was needed.

Figure 5-2 shows the overcorrection behavior-analysis form. It took approximately 7 minutes to complete and required an analysis of the antecedents, behaviors, and consequences of the loss, and the development of a plan to prevent another loss in the future. Staff were instructed to give no more lectures but, instead, to have the clients complete the form in order to get a replacement.

In the 21 months before intervention, meal cards were being lost at a mean rate of 65 per month. In the next 12 months losses dropped to 45 per month, and a further reduction to 17 per month in the following year. Similarly, keys dropped from an average of 17 losses per month prior to intervention to 11 per month in the first year after intervention and 12 per month in the second year. These significant decreases took place despite the turnover of clients during the period of the study. Although each new resident was informed about the consequence of a key or card loss, some had to experience the consequence before a change in their methods of retaining such personal possessions took place. Of the clients who lost a card and had to fill in the form, 43% never lost another card. Some remarked that filling in the form in order to get a new key or card was a "pain in the neck."

FIGURE 5-2

Overcorrection Behavior Analysis: Keys

Name _____ Room # _____ Date _____ Time _____

Describe how you discovered you had lost your key:

When did you discover you had lost your key?

Where were you when you discovered you had lost your key?

What were you doing when you discovered you had lost your key?

When was the last time you remember seeing your key?

Where was your key when you saw it last?

Who had your key when you saw it last?

When was the last time you used your key to open your door?

Where did you put it afterward?

Where do you usually keep your key?

Have you lost your key before? How many times?

Do you carry other keys? If so, did you lose them too? If you didn't lose your

other keys, where do you keep them?

Has anyone else used your key?

Where else could it be?

Where did you look for your key?

Where else did you look?

What do you plan to do to avoid losing your key in the future?

Describe where you will keep your new key.

How will you remember to keep track of your new key?

Student Signature _____

managers attending the behavior-centered management institute, in reducing the weekly shortage of over $200 at cash registers. Its use to decrease excessive tardiness and unsafe practices will be described in chapters 8 and 9.

The overcorrection behavior-analysis procedure should be considered as a possible consequence when there is an unsatisfactory outcome, a variety of behaviors that may be causing the outcome, different employees performing the different types of inappropriate behaviors, and a variety of antecedent conditions associated with each of the behaviors. The form requires that the employee identify those antecedents and behaviors. The completed forms not only allow the manager to document reoccurring excesses and deficit behaviors of a particular employee, but also allow her to examine and compare the completed forms for common antecedents. For example, examination of forms completed for damaged merchandise in a grocery store may reveal that most of the damage was occurring because a forklift instead of a cart was being used to move cartons from the dock to the shelves. Possibly, the forklift operators need more extensive training or certain types of cartons should not be transported by forklift.

Prior to the introduction of an overcorrection behavior-analysis intervention, the supervisor should document the extent of the problems, explain the rationale for why the behaviors create problems, and describe desirable behavioral alternatives. Next, he should explain the rationale for the use of the form and how it would be used not to punish but to allow both the employee and management to better identify the causes of the problems and to develop plans to prevent the problem in the future.

Note that the overcorrection procedure can be used with some of the other behavioral interventions of modeling, participatory goal setting, charting and feedback, and positive reinforcement.

Reinforceability: A Word to the Wise

A manager who relies only upon negative consequences to correct deficit or excessive behaviors will very soon find himself with a morale problem. A manager who does not combine negative consequences with frequent praise and other positive reinforcements for the appropriate behaviors will also discover he is surrounded by an indifferent work crew or unhappy employees. It is important to be respected, but it is also important to be liked. Managers who are liked by their employees possess what we call "reinforceability."

Reinforceability. We discussed the need to match the reinforcement to the person in Chapter 4. What is reinforcing to one person is not reinforcing to the next person. We learn what is reinforcing to different employees by getting to know them. As noted previously, one person likes a pat on the back, another likes the phrase, "Good job," and a third likes to be teased.

But there is another consideration in reinforcing people. Does the person who says "Good job" have reinforceability for the person who receives the words of praise? The answer to that question depends upon the answer to these questions:

1. Does the behavior increase in frequency following the praise?
2. Does the person receiving the praise try to do other things that will earn praise from the manager?

If the answer is "no" to those questions, then the manager has little or no reinforceability. When the manager does have it, a wink, a nod, a smile, or praise directed at that employee will produce the behaviors that characterize an effective worker.

When Chicago was brought to a standstill by a crippling snowstorm that had not been forecast, very few people could get to work. The policy at the headquarters of a large merchandising corporation in that city was to not penalize any of the 3,000 managerial employees if they didn't show up for work under those types of weather conditions. Yet, despite the difficulties of travel, attendance in the various departments ranged from 39 to 97%! Who showed up? The answer was partially revealed by a survey of the employees' satisfaction with their job that had been done a few months before the storm. Attendance that day was strongly related to their satisfaction with supervision. Those who were most satisfied with their supervisors were more likely to make the extra effort to get to work when there was to be no penalty for not showing up.[7]

In the military, some officers are almost idolized by their men; and some, as in World War II, Korea, and Vietnam, were shot in the back or "fragged" by their own soldiers. The U.S. Army gives courses to their officers on discipline, praise, fairness, and concern under the title of "leadership." Yet it was only in recent years that psychology has begun to identify the variables that affect whether or not a leader is liked.

Social psychologists study the variable of attractiveness, and psychologists who specialize in the areas of learning and memory study the variable of conditioned reinforcement. In either case, the information is directly related to how a manager acquires reinforceability. The more reinforceability managers have, the more others want to please them. Some basic principles of reinforceability are:

1. The more the manager is associated with the satisfaction of the employee's basic needs, the more reinforceability he has.

2. The more the manager is seen as a source of need satisfaction of others, the more reinforceability he has. Thus, when some employees observe his management skills fulfilling the needs of just a couple of employees, his potential reinforceability for all increases.

3. The more reinforceability the manager has (a) the more the employee wants to please her, (b) the more aware the employees are as to what pleases her, (c) the more they will work to please her, and (d) the more they will work for her when she is not present.

When we discover that someone likes us, we like that person in return. This is the reciprocity principle—I like you because you like me.[8] But we also come to expect things from those we like. We decide that a person likes us when his or her behavior exemplifies three characteristics: behaviors of ego support, utility, and stimulation. Ego support involves telling a person things that make the person feel good. Getting to know the employee allows us to discover what is ego supporting for him.

An ego-supporting statement does not have to apply to work. Telling a worker who prides himself on his good taste in clothes, in front of the other employees, "I wish I had your good taste. When you wear a tie, it always goes with your shirt and trousers" is an example of an ego-supporting statement. Similarly, to compliment the person on the picture of her grandchild which she keeps in her wallet, or to compliment the person about his fishing ability or the way he can fix his own car, is as, or more, ego supporting as telling him that he is great with the customers. Note that ego-supporting statements are not necessarily positive reinforcements because the manager is not always being specific about what behaviors he is talking about, and his statement may occur when he is just visiting with the employees in the breakroom, in the lunchroom, or during a meeting. But the statements do make him more attractive as a person and give him greater reinforceability for everybody who responds positively to seeing a boss appreciate an employee as a person. Not only do managers need to be reminded to be a source of ego support to their employees, but we also need to be reminded to be a source of ego support to our spouses. "When was the last time you said something flattering to your wife *in front of others?*" the client with marital problems was asked. "I do it all the time," he replied. "Why just two years ago, I told her . . ."

Utility is another variable that is important in attraction. Utility is the extent to which one person does something that may or may not be needed by another. It is always a helpful action. Popular officers in the military were the ones who wouldn't hesitate to get out of their Jeep and help push when needed. Utility actions often keep a marriage going when ego support has disappeared over time.

Examples of utility behaviors include my secretary coming into my office and saying that she is going to get herself a cup of coffee and would I like one, too? Utility activities for management are helping the employee stock a shelf, answering a phone for a busy secretary, bringing in doughnuts once in a while, or working on the line alongside the employees to help them catch up. A busy manager cannot and should not do these things frequently, but she gains in her reinforceability when she is seen doing them occasionally.

Stimulation value is another variable related to attractiveness and reinforceability. Stimulation is innately needed by workers. To the extent that they are bored, they will seek stimulation by gossiping, making practical jokes, and taking breaks. We like people who will tell us an occasional joke or who say something unexpected. We are attracted to people who don't talk in monotones or who do put some expression on their faces. Do you always say and do the same things in front of employees? Do you always run the meetings in exactly the same way, announcements first, a little joke next, scheduling, and then a pep talk? Or, do you vary it just as an effective coach of the basketball or football team does at half-time?

There are other ways by which we know whether others like us. Sometimes these are unspoken cues such as eye contact, smiles, leaning toward the employee, or nodding one's head when the employee is talking. Let's see what happens when these cues are systematically manipulated in a situation that simulates the interactions between managers and their employees. In Application 5-4, we see the effect on production when the leader practices the behaviors of interest, openness, and friendliness toward production workers. Note that these behaviors had a positive effect on production only when the leader was directive and structured the job by telling subordinates specifically what the task was and how to do it.

Eye contact was used in that study to help communicate the impression of friendliness and interest. It is often claimed that the eyes are "the windows of the soul," and social psychologists have found that people use signals from the eyes to try to read other people's feelings. Most of us at one time or another have experienced talking to somebody who never looks at us during the conversation. He is looking around, at the papers on his desk, or at the picture on the wall when we talk. When he talks to us, he's looking over our shoulders or at one of our ears. One study actually tested the effect on others of looking at the person or elsewhere.[9] It found that experimental subjects judged other people to be cold and indifferent if those people during an interview only gazed at the subjects 15% of the time. But when gazed at 80% of the time, subjects judged the other person to be friendly and sincere. Of

Are You Getting Warmer?

In a study of leadership, male and female students in a Canadian university took the roles of workers in the "Fix It Company" that specializes in problems of other organizations.[10] For the first task, "workers" solved problems dealing with survivors of a plane crash in the subarctic. The manager supervised them as they worked. In the second task, the manager assigned them the job of completing arithmetic number problems and word problems taken from a business mathematics textbook. After instructing them, the manager left the room.

The question asked in this research was whether the manager's style of leadership during the first task would influence productivity in the second task when the manager was not there. In the directive approach, the manager told the workers how they should work to complete the task and gave feedback: "That's good work," or "That's wrong," or "That's poorly done." In the nondirective approach, he identified the problem and the need to solve it, but indicated that the workers should solve the problem themselves.

With half of the workers in both the directive and nondirective approach, the leader was "warm"; that is, he spoke softly, leaned toward them, looked them in the eye, and smiled frequently. With the other half of the workers, the same leader was "cold"; that is, he used a harsh, crisp voice and serious expression, leaned away, and avoided looking them in the eye.

Figure 5-3 shows the results. Not only were the workers more productive on the task when their leader was away if he was seen as a warm person, but they reported in the postexperiment questionnaire that they were more attracted to him, believed him to be more effective and helpful, and reported that they were more willing to work again for that leader. It is interesting that when leaders are warm but not directive, they were viewed as being effective, but productivity suffered when they were not there.

course, it is also possible to overdo a good thing. A constant gaze, such as a stare, not only makes others anxious but can communicate aggressiveness.[11]

We like people who provide ego support, utility, and stimulation. We like them if they are open, friendly, and interested in our opinions, preferences, and feelings. And we like them if they are direct and tell us specifically what it is we are supposed to be doing. Because we like them, we want to please them.

FIGURE 5-3

Leadership Style and Productivity

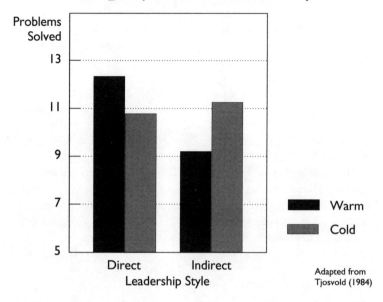

Adapted from
Tjosvold (1984)

And when the boss who is liked says, "you are doing a great job keeping those shelves stocked," the statement is reinforcing because he or she has reinforceability.

Summary

All of the consequences described in this chapter decrease behavioral excesses and require the use of positive reinforcement when the behaviors begin to change. The balanced approach of applying an immediate consequence after the inappropriate behavior and praising the person for demonstrating appropriate work behaviors decreases the negative reactions of employees when they must be reprimanded.

The least intrusive method of decreasing a behavior is extinction. Unfortunately, application is difficult because it requires the complete removal of the positive reinforcement or attention that the person has been receiving for the inappropriate work behavior. When the behavior is only directed at the supervisor's attention, it is easier to apply since the manager can ignore the person at those times and increase attention for appropriate behaviors.

Punishment in the form of immediate verbal reprimands is effective for stopping behaviors when the employee does not know better. It can be used to help teach the person that certain behaviors are unacceptable. When it is used, it is important to follow the general rules of punishment that have been established by psychological research during the last 10 years.

Response costs is the removal of reinforcers or the removal of opportunity to obtain reinforcers as a consequence for inappropriate behaviors. Response costs may be seen as a fine or as an added cost for service, but, when applied fairly and consistently, response costs not only eliminate problems, but may also produce happier employees.

Overcorrection procedures of positive practice, restitution, and behavior analysis are immediate consequences for deficits or excesses and include an aversive component. Positive practice requires repeated practice of the appropriate behaviors, while restitution requires the restoration of the environment to a vastly improved condition. Positive practice is not to be used as a demeaning procedure but can be used in business or industry as a method of retraining when inappropriate behaviors repeatedly occur. Overcorrection behavior analysis requires that the person analyze in writing the antecedents, behavior, and consequences when the inappropriate behavior occurs. It also requires a plan for correction in the future. Applications have been reported for losses of items such as keys and cash, but it could also be used for losses of tools, name tags, and even for tardiness or errors, as is described in later chapters.

An important determinant of how employees respond to all of these consequences is whether or not the manager is liked by the employees. If they like him, they will respond positively to the fair and consistent utilization of these procedures. Social psychologists have studied many of the factors that determine a person's likability. If the manager is seen as a frequent source of ego support, utility, and stimulation, she is liked and has reinforceability. Without reinforceability, her feedback has little effect. With reinforceability, not only are her consequences effective in producing the behavior changes necessary to produce superior outcomes, but the employees seek to perform the behaviors that are necessary even when she is not there.

Notes

1. Luthans, Paul, & Baker (1981).
2. Kazdin (1972); Martin & Pear (1992).
3. McSweeney (1978).

4. Marholin & Gray (1976).
5. Hinman & Marr (1989).
6. Marr & Granneman (1988).
7. Smith (1977).
8. Jones (1973); Shrauger (1975).
9. Exeline & Massick (1967).
10. Tjosvold (1984).
11. Forsyth (1987).

Managing Behaviors
to Affect Outcomes

CHAPTER 6

Increasing Production Quantity

Business and industry are always striving to improve productivity, whether it is described in terms of quantity of items produced, number of units processed, or total widgets assembled. Regardless of how it is described, managers are evaluated, in part, by the productivity of the workers they supervise. In this chapter, we address the behaviors that contribute to production; and the applications selected illustrate how the behavior-centered management approach, ABC, increases the quantity of work produced.

Many interventions have been found to be effective in changing productivity. These include methods used by management such as recruitment and selection, organizational restructuring, decision-making techniques, and work redesign.[1]

Although strategies for increasing worker productivity have been described as either "high- or low-tech" solutions, managers should not feel that low-tech strategies are any less important. Rather than involving capital investment in equipment and technology, low-tech approaches focus on learning techniques and organizational strategies that managers can use to enable employees to work more effectively and efficiently. We begin with a fundamental ABC step, pinpointing productive behavior.

Pinpointing Productive Behavior

What do employees do when they work? What behaviors do they perform when they produce a product? If supervisors have a taxonomy of the behaviors that occur during production, they can identify behaviors to modify that will increase the quantity of work. We must know what those behaviors are in order to (a) train new employees to perform the work,

(b) eliminate those behaviors that interfere with production, and (c) speed up production. Directing employees to "work harder" has as much impact as telling a student to "study harder." Similarly, pep talks and motivational speeches have very little lasting effects on effort.

Sometimes managers assume that the employees know what behaviors need to be changed, and the interventions focus on feedback about the outcome of their work; for example, the number of units assembled. But feedback about outcomes of their efforts is far less successful when employees are not clear as to which behaviors need to be changed in order to increase the number of units assembled.

During a training program, a rehabilitation supervisor asked for suggestions on how to respond to a worker who became very angry when he did not receive as much pay as the other clients. Because pay was on a piece-rate basis and because he didn't produce as much work, he often had one of the smallest paychecks.

After learning about the backward chaining procedure of training (Chapter 4), the supervisor was able to develop a training method that increased the productivity of that frustrated worker from 25% of the standard production rate to 75% in 2 weeks. She divided the work into three components, (a) production of a wooden bowl, (b) cutting the leather, and (c) attaching the leather cover to the bowl. Then she identified the seven behaviors that were necessary to attach the cover to the bowl. The worker was then retrained in this assembly phase by teaching him to do the last of the seven assembly behaviors, then the last two, then the last three, etc. His frustration disappeared as he learned the steps and saw the finished product. Pinpointing target behaviors, therefore, included specifying the three major tasks and the behaviors needed to complete each task, and, thus to produce the finished product.

Management Antecedent Behaviors

Rules and directives. Sometimes, behaviors that interfere with production can be controlled by clearly stating the rules about behaviors. For many people, talking to co-workers is more enjoyable than waiting on customers or working. It is important that management communicate the general and specific rules about socializing during work hours. In some departments, talking must be limited to communications about work-related events with other types of conversation limited to break periods. In other types of departments, socializing does not interfere with work and, in fact, may relieve boredom from repetitive work and be one of the reinforcements at certain workstations.

Some employees do not stop their socializing when work requires their attention or when the break or lunch periods end. Some managers even contribute to the problem by modeling inappropriate socializing on the job. If a manager moves from one workstation to another talking about athletic events, his car, fishing last weekend, or hunting, instead of supervising the work in his department, he may not only lose the employees' respect but also encourage them to imitate his nonproductive behavior. Some general rules, then, are:

1. Clarify the rules about socializing when employees are first assigned to a department.

2. Make sure that these rules are defensible. For example, to say that store clerks should never talk about anything other than work when there are lapses in work demands is both indefensible and demoralizing.

3. In some cases, calling a team meeting and asking for input on the rules on talk during work will result in a greater adherence to the rules than will imposing the rules from above.

4. The supervisor must make sure that she follows those rules. The fine line between talking about events outside work and the need to apply the principles of increasing the reinforceability of a manager (see Chapter 5) is often difficult to determine. In some cases, it is better to do slightly more than may be ideal to increase the feelings of approachability toward the supervisor rather than to promote feelings of fear and dislike of management. In other cases, supervisors have to suffer the consequences of leadership being a "lonely" position.

5. The rules must be explicit. For example, when a truck arrives, employees are expected to immediately unload it and move the cartons to their appropriate storage places. When a customer enters the store or department, employees are expected to greet the customer and offer assistance in finding or showing merchandise.

6. For those employees who regularly violate the rules, a performance coaching session, a response-cost procedure, or an overcorrection, positive-practice training procedure should be initiated. See chapters 11 and 12 for procedures to use to deal with work problems of an individual.

Training and instruction. Behavioral approaches to increase productivity have been very successful components of many different training programs. Frequently used techniques include task analysis, patient instruction with positive feedback, and practice with reinforcement. Videotapes may be used to demonstrate correct training methods. During training, the person should be required to verbalize aloud the steps in performing the job, including what to look at when approaching the workstation, what to do first, where to place hands, etc. Pilots and co-pilots read aloud items from their preflight check sheets before take-offs, which directs their attention to engines, flaps, etc. Similarly, describing out loud the steps in starting a machine, painting a part, or assembling a computer increases attention of the person to the training and allows the trainer to monitor the learning.

Many employees will nod their heads when asked after a demonstration whether they understand what they are supposed to do, even when they don't understand. Not only does the procedure of requiring them to describe the job allow for correction of misunderstanding, but it has been found to be a method that helps people to remember better. See Chapter 2 for ABC methods on better training.

Employee-Generated Plans

Employees are one of the best sources of information on how to increase production. Asking for suggestions in meetings and through the use of suggestion boxes are ways that employees can contribute to the development of a plan. Suggestions must be followed up by questions on who, what, where, when, and how. When suggestions are welcomed, praised, and, often, implemented, they are more likely to be made in the future.

One type of intervention that is clearly both a management antecedent behavior and a management consequent behavior is the establishment of financial compensation programs.[2] Financial compensation programs encourage employees to identify and suggest methods of improving productivity. The compensation may go to individual employees or to work teams. Setting up the compensation system is the management antecedent behavior; delivery of the incentives to the employees is the management consequence behavior.

Financial compensation programs by the navy, the army, and the air force have all demonstrated substantial productivity gains.[3] At eight sites where a gain-sharing (compensation for methods to decrease the time to complete a task) intervention was used, 853 army employees received $376,000 in compensation for methods that saved 74,000 person hours.[4] Similar productivity gains in such diverse federal programs as NASA, NSF, and DOD have also been reported.[5]

Quality circles. A program that first became popular in Japan and that has proven to be effective in increasing productivity is the establishment of quality circles. Everybody likes to participate in the decisions about their own work, and the quality circles allow the employees to get involved in the decisions of the where, when, who, and what of productivity. One example of the effect on work in one manufacturing division is shown in Figure 6-1. The authors of that study described the changes in the division, "Prior to the QC [quality control] program, for example, machine operators would wait for a set-up person to make a needed adjustment in a machine or other equipment.

From QC discussions, some employees learned how to make adjustments on their own, lowering the delay wait and increasing the percentage of time spent on actual production."[6] For a more complete description of quality circles, see Chapter 3.

Work Teams

Another way to enable employees to assume the task of identifying specific behaviors that affect productivity is to reorganize the work force into work teams. In one study, reorganizing production employees into semi-autonomous work teams produced dramatic improvements in output and

FIGURE 6-1

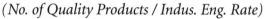

Production Efficiency and Quality Circles
(No. of Quality Products / Indus. Eng. Rate)

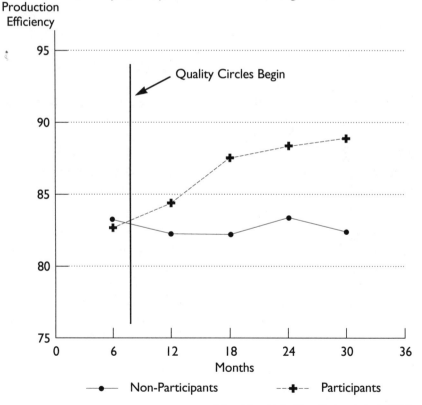

Adapted from Marks, Mirvis, Hackett, & Grady (1986)

decreases in costs.[7] Work in the Fisher Corporation had been done traditionally via an assembly line. Reorganization gave the semi-autonomous work teams the responsibility and information they needed to manage their own work. The gains in both production and savings were maintained over a 4-year follow-up period.

When self-managing work teams are organized, their success is due, in part, to their receiving responsibility for deciding who performs what tasks and to the flexibility inherent in the sharing of responsibility among group members.[8] However, the success of organizing employees into work teams has been mixed.[9] In one review of studies of work teams, performance improved in 4 out of 9 cases, including city maintenance crews,[10] air force cadet teams,[11] and engineering project groups.[12] But, such groups as cafeteria food-service groups, student project groups, army combat units, and moving crews showed no improvement in quantity or quality of performance.

Flextime.   Flextime for employees is another management antecedent implemented in order to increase productivity. Flextime or flexible working hours allows workers greater autonomy in setting their work schedules, yet does not detract from the technical, economic, or administrative requirements of production.[13] Employees determine their starting and ending times within periods of work which are set by the organization. They are also expected to smooth out individual variations by filling in for each other.[14]

Research results of the effects of flextime on productivity are also mixed. For example, in one study described in Chapter 9 of this book, there were no gains in productivity of work groups in a large corporation, but there were significant declines in absenteeism.[15] Other studies have shown productivity gains after the initiation of flextime,[16] but, overall, it would appear that other management practices must accompany the switch to flextime before it can significantly affect productivity.[17]

Goal setting.   When management specifies the level of performance that must be attained by employees, goal setting is being used to affect productivity levels. Goals that are set at high, but attainable, levels can improve quantity and quality of production. Note that "attainable" levels may, in part, be determined by worker input where the manager discusses the productivity problems with the employees and asks for their opinions. If production levels are set too high, workers become frustrated and angry or even depressed over their inability to do the job, and production suffers significantly.

It would seem that in this age of automation, there would be little room to affect those workers' behaviors that contribute to production. When speed is limited by conveyor belts, the time it takes a mold to heat, or a part to be spray painted by a machine, there would seem to be little room for variance in production rates. Improving production in such situations becomes a special challenge. It is easier to show an improvement when the present level is below a "fair" standard; that is, when production is clearly lower than what is possible. In the situation illustrated in Application 6-1, feedback and feedback with praise were used to change the number of pieces produced by workers in a furniture manufacturing company.[18]

A variety of tasks were included in that study. Activities in the fiberglass, punchpress, welding, plating, and upholstery units were all different in their requirements to produce various parts of office furniture. Additionally, the workers and supervisors were from different populations. For example, one department had all female employees with a female supervisor, while others had only male employees. Thus, we agree with Wikoff et al. that the procedures that they used in that study would probably be just as effective in a number of other industrial settings where the tasks are heavily automated and varied in their requirements in effort and time.

Management Consequence Behaviors

Appraisal and feedback. Goal setting by managers has been studied for its effects on task performance by a number of investigators.[19] Most of that work, however, has indicated that goal setting is most effective when combined with feedback. For example, in a study of five air force groups composed of approximately 80 individuals, productivity of electronic equipment repair and storage and distribution of materials and supplies were measured for 8 to 9 months.[20] For the next 5 months, the groups received monthly feedback on their productivity, which improved by over 50%. When formal goal setting (performance level set by management) was then added to the monthly feedback for the next 5 months, productivity increased another 25%. The authors of the study found that job satisfaction and morale improved but neither intervention had an effect on absenteeism.[21]

Appraisal and feedback include the assessment of the employee's performance of each part of the job with individualized feedback. When coaching assessments are provided more frequently than in the usual performance appraisal, productivity indicators increase significantly. In Application 6-2, we see this effect in a study of white-collar workers in a university.

Note that in the previous two applications reinforcement was given for improvement. But in the university admissions department, employees were praised while they were working at the rate designated by the goal set that morning. Praise was also given the next morning, but it may have been the

APPLICATION 6-1
Feedback for Furniture Makers

In this study, the number of furniture pieces per day for each worker was targeted for change in seven departments of this unionized, institutional furniture manufacturing company. First, baseline data were collected across at least 8 weeks in each department to determine production rates prior to intervention. Workers recorded their production data daily. Accuracy was verified by their supervisors.

Before the intervention, the principles of behavior modification which focused on ABC were presented to supervisors and department managers using slides, videos, and discussion. This included the presentation of case studies similar to those presented in this book. As the intervention was introduced in each department, supervisors began giving feedback daily in the form of a graph of each task of each worker showing the daily output. Graphs were coded to individuals (for anonymity) and placed behind a locked, glass-covered bulletin board. In addition, the supervisors explained the graphs to each person with no praise or criticism.

After anywhere from 8 to 35 weeks of this feedback-only treatment, supervisors were given another hour of training on the importance of praise as a consequence for improved performance, and the praise intervention was begun in four of the departments. Individual workers were praised whenever their daily production rates were 1% higher than the previous day's rate. Also they were praised by middle-level management for weekly improvements.

In Table 6-1 we can see that productivity increased after daily feedback was started and increased again after the supervisors began praising the workers for improvements. Although the improvement may appear to be small, when the percentage increase is calculated across the nearly 2 years of the project, the company had gained "approximately 800 additional labor hours per week or the equivalent of about 20 full-time employees"[22] at no increase in cost!

praise delivered during the working period that caused the dramatic improvement in production.

In the furniture factory, praise was also delivered the next morning based upon performance the previous day. Feedback with praise by the supervisor resulted in significant savings by the company, but the increase in parts produced might have been greater had the consequences been related more closely to the behaviors that produced the increase in productivity. This is not easy to do in a factory where a supervisor cannot always judge whether the

TABLE 6-1
Output After Feedback and
Output After Feedback With Praise*

Department	Baseline	Feedback Only	Feedback w/Praise
Fiberglass	96%	99	103
Upholstery	85	86	86
Punch Press	88	96	98
Welding	70	73	79

*Percentage of standard output for each task was defined by the industrial engineering department of the plant.

behavior of an employee that is being observed represents the behavior of that employee when he's not being observed. But as we have described in Chapter 4, the more immediate the reinforcement, the greater the impact on behavior.

Incentives. What happens when we use an incentive to modify production-related behavior? Incentives serve as both antecedents and consequences of behavior. We tell the employees what they will receive if they perform at a certain rate, and then we reinforce them with the money or other type of reward when they do perform at that rate. Ideally, the reinforcement is delivered as close in time to the actual improvement in performance as possible.

Based on one review of studies using ABC procedures to affect productivity, it was concluded that monetary incentives increased productivity more than goal setting, employee participation, and job enrichment techniques.[23] There is no doubt that monetary incentives have resulted in dramatic increases in productivity. For example, monetary incentives resulted in increases in productivity of 200–300% at Union National Bank in Arkansas,[24] 200% over a 10-year period at IBM, and 300% over workers in comparable industries at Lincoln Electric.[26] Application 6-3 illustrates the incentive plan used at Union National Bank.

The bank attributes its success to the five principles of behavioral psychology (see note 25). These are

1. The use of *positive reinforcement*
2. that is *immediate*

Goal Setting for Government Employees

This study directed interventions at three employees who were application processors in the admissions department of a midwestern university.[25] The tasks were (a) entering a student's application for admission into the computer, (b) recomputing the grade point average (GPA) of the student by calculating it from courses taken in high school, and (c) typing a label containing the name and social security number for the new file. Each employee made a check mark in the appropriate column of each task on a daily data sheet. Random checks of the data proved them to be accurate from 93 to 100% of the time.

The employees were first informed of the need and method of keeping the daily data sheets. After 1 month of collecting baseline data, the supervisor met with each employee in the morning to give an individual a specific goal so as to reduce stress from trying to catch up with the backlog of applications. Goals were set daily based on the highest number of tasks completed the day before: If the employee had completed between 40 to 70 different tasks, the new goal would be a number between 60 and 80. At the 5-minute morning meeting, if the employee was near or above the previous day's goal, she was praised. If she was below that goal, the supervisor redirected her efforts and gave encouragement. In addition, at least twice daily the supervisor examined the employee's data sheet and provided feedback with praise or correction. Table 6-2 shows the results of the goal-setting and feedback intervention across the next 35 weeks for each employee.

3. and *contingent on specific behaviors*

4. that *can be measured,* and

5. *individualized*—each person's reinforcement is tied to his or her own behavior.

Union National has been so successful with the proof and teller program that it now has 75 individualized incentive programs for 70% of its 485 employees, including 8 of their 10 division managers. However, determining the type of incentive plan to implement is difficult since little is known about how frequently incentives must be provided, what percentage the incentive should be of base pay, and what minimum standard of work should be required before incentives are paid.

In the United States as well as many other countries, the 30% incentive system is the traditional figure used;[27] that is, 30% of the base pay may be earned

TABLE 6-2

Tasks Completed per Week,
Before and After Intervention

Average Number of Tasks Completed

Employee	During Baseline	During Intervention
1	22	180
2	47	89
3	30	99

In the 10 months prior to the intervention, $10,836 was spent on overtime and additional part-time help. In the next 18 months only $6,132 was spent on those two types of expenses.

as an incentive for increased productivity. Although the 30% figure is commonly used, it is not based upon systematic research according to one review which summarized the studies on the incentive system and production.[28]

1. Pay is more closely associated with performance as the incentive percentage of pay increases. But there may be a level where productivity reaches its maximum and greater percentages are not more effective.

2. Lower percentages may protect the worker from decreases in production that cannot be controlled by worker behavior; for example, machine breakdown.

3. Lower percentages would appear to make personnel costs easier to estimate for the organization.

An analogue study—a simulated work situation in the laboratory using college students—was conducted to examine the effect of different percentages of base pay as incentives.[29] Parts were assembled by placing nuts and colored washers on bolts in a particular order; for example, nut—red, washer—black, etc. The correct order of securely tightened nuts was required for credit as an assembled "widget." Researchers then paid the different groups of "workers" 0%, 10%, 30%, 60%, or 100% of base pay as incentives. The higher the incentive percentage, the lower the base pay received. Thus, the 0% group received $4 for a work period assembling parts, but the 30% and 60% groups received $3.07 and $2.50 base, respectively, and 0.13 and 0.021 for each "widget" over 50 in the work period. "Employees" were allowed to take breaks at any time during their 15 workdays of 45-minute work periods each.

APPLICATION 6-3

Bucks for Bankers

The Union National Bank is said to be typical of such institutions, 22 stories of glass and marble, but it is unique in its application of the behavior-centered leadership style. The proof department employees encode machine-readable numbers on the bottoms of checks. Accuracy is essential. Here are some interesting facts about the use of the ABC approach with the proof department:

1st Baseline: 1,065 items per hour (industrial norm: 900–1,100)

Intervention: Posting graph of results of praising high performance

Results: 2,100 items per hour

2nd Intervention: Posting graph and bonus based on output up to 2,500

Results: 2,800 items per hour

3rd Intervention: Posting graph and bonus based on output with no maximum.

Results: 3,500 items per hour. Workers earn incentives bonus of 50 to 70% of their base salary.

The authors report that while proof departments are often the biggest problem area in a bank, the Union National proof department became the smoothest operating unit in their organization. Turnover had been 110%, but after the intervention, it was 0%. Absenteeism went from 4.24% to 2.23%. Employees were reduced from 11 full-time and 3 part-time to 3 full-time and 6 part-time. Overtime was reduced from 475 hours to 13 hours and savings by processing checks faster was about $100,000 a year.

Behavior-centered management was tried with the tellers as well. The goals of the program for tellers were to increase the number of customers who open new accounts, increase transactions, and reduce daily differences on cash outages.

Intervention: assignment of points for specific performance levels in each category with points calculated each day and then a bonus based on the weekly average. Note that the incentive would automatically be reduced by absenteeism during the week.

In addition, while customer volume increased 67%, teller staffing decreased. The remaining tellers received increased compensation, recognition for outstanding work, and well-defined work goals, among other benefits.

	Points Earned	New Accounts	Cash Out	Transactions
Baseline	32	102/year	$15,961	17.9/hr
Intervention	71	4,300/year	$13,772	29.5/hr

100   MANAGING BEHAVIORS TO AFFECT OUTCOMES

The results showed that, even on the first day, the incentive groups out-produced the no-incentive group. Across the last 5 workdays, the 0% incentive group averaged 69 parts per day while the incentive groups assembled an average of 85 to 89 parts per day with no systematic or significant differences between them. As in the research done on productivity in real factories, monetary incentives significantly increased productivity in this simulated work setting. Incentive groups assembled an average of 17 to 20 parts more per session than those in the base-pay-only group. However, although all incentive groups assembled about the same number of parts daily, their pay was not equal, since neither their base pay nor the amount of money paid per part was equal. The greater the incentive, the less total pay they earned. Thus, paying high percentages of base results in no greater gains in productivity than paying lower percentages of 10 and 30%. Also, the higher rates could result in union complaints because of the lower guaranteed pay.

The analogue study of the type described above allows us to examine the effects of different variables such as incentive percentage of base pay over short time periods at low costs. But we must be more cautious about developing plans to initiate incentive programs in actual work settings based on the results of analogue or artificial studies. However, the evidence described in Chapter 4 allows us to say that incentives do increase productivity.

Schedules of Reinforcement

In Chapter 4, we discussed the advantages of schedules of reinforcement. Instead of reinforcing the person for every correct behavior, we reinforce her for every fifth correct behavior or for being "on task" after a certain amount of time has elapsed. Schedules of reinforcement are very useful for maintaining behavior at high rates and, if introduced gradually, for preventing worker slow-down when the supervisor is not around. Sometimes, schedules of reinforcement will produce higher rates of performance and add interest for the worker as is seen in Application 6-4.

Quantity of work and quality of work go hand in hand. When a certain class of behaviors affects an outcome, we are interested in increasing the frequency of those behaviors. Sometimes that increase in quantity also affects quality as perceived by the customer. For example, sales behaviors of retail employees directly influence sales and can affect the satisfaction of the customer. Thus, retail store managers encourage store clerks to (a) approach potential customers, (b) smile, (c) greet customers, (d) ask customers if they need help, and (e) suggest that customers look at or consider certain

APPLICATION 6-4
Trapping the Beaver Trapper

In this study the effects of a continuous reinforcement (CRF) schedule were compared to those of a variable ratio (VR) schedule on beaver trapping.[30] The trappers worked for a forest products company trapping mountain beavers, and all belonged to a strong international union. They were paid $7 per hour throughout the study, and in the 4 weeks prior to the intervention they were averaging 0.52 beavers per hour each. The trappers were divided into two groups and then alternated on a weekly basis on a CRF or a VR-4 schedule of reinforcement for the remaining 12 weeks of the trapping season. When on the CRF schedule, a trapper received $1 for every beaver. When on the VR-4 schedule, he received $4 for each beaver if he could correctly predict twice to the supervisors whether the roll of dice would yield an even or odd number. Thus, he would get the $4 on the average for every fourth beaver he trapped (dice probability = 0.25, 1/2 x 1/2). When on the CRF schedule, they averaged 0.78 beavers per hour but when on the VR-4, they averaged 1.08, increases of 50% and 108%, respectively, over the schedule rates. Furthermore, their answers to a questionnaire at the end of the trapping season indicated that their reactions to the VR-4 schedule were significantly more favorable than to the CRF schedule. The results suggested that the VR-4 schedule added excitement to their work and gave them strong feelings of accomplishment.

The beavers were not questioned. There were no measures of the changes in mountain beaver behavior and probably too few left to obtain a reliable measure of attitude.

merchandise. Of course, as any highly successful salesperson can tell us, each of those behaviors is tailored to the customer.

Successful selling is an art with many "rules of thumb"; some are reliable, and some are merely superstitions. Much time is devoted to training salespersons, especially those who sell big items such as real estate and automobiles. One of the many rules of selling is that customers will more often purchase an item if they believe they are receiving good service. They are also more likely to purchase an item if it is suggested to them than when it is not. The first rule deals with quality and the second deals with quantity. The same behavior may serve both quantity of sales and quality of service. We see this effect in the family-style restaurant described in Application 6-5.

The authors of the suggestive-selling study believe that the measurement of outcome (sales of targeted items), rather than behaviors (suggestive sales behaviors), may have masked some of the other effects. During the study, servers often complained about how often the customers ignored or declined their suggestions. Recall in Chapter 4, which described schedules of reinforcement, there is always a danger of ratio strain occurring when reinforcement is thinned too fast or when it occurs too seldom. A behavior occurs less and less often if there is too little reinforcement. Ratio strain may have occurred for the hostesses because so few customers ordered the target items following suggestive selling.

Summary

Productivity begins with specificity; in this case, specificity about the behaviors related to increased output on the worker's part. Sometimes managers ask employees to identify desirable behaviors, and other times managers identify critical tasks and behaviors themselves. In either case, the end goal is to determine what actions productive workers take so that other workers can learn to do so as well. Methods for training employees in these desirable performances include videotapes demonstrating the correct methods, instruction with positive feedback, and practice with reinforcement.

Specificity and productivity go together in yet another way. When workers understand the rules governing certain behaviors such as socializing, they can avoid behaving inappropriately. In other words, they can quickly determine that socializing is acceptable under certain conditions (in the breakroom at break time) and unacceptable under other conditions (at the workstation during work time). Of course, managers must be careful to follow their own rules and socialize under appropriate conditions as well.

Other antecedents that have positive effects on productivity include reorganizing into work teams, involving employees in setting goals, and inviting workers to suggest ways to solve productivity problems. When coupled with incentive systems (which serve as both an antecedent and a consequence), these strategies become even more effective. Management should not, however, forget the power of feedback as well, but not the typical type of quarterly or annual feedback. Workers need frequent individualized feedback and coaching that tell them not only what their output is, but what they can do to increase that output.

Use of incentive systems, while shown to improve work quantity, raise interesting questions that require additional study. Research has shown that the incentive need not be very large relative to the base pay, but what minimum standard of work should be required before incentives are paid?

APPLICATION 6-5
Tips Are Not Enough

Let's see what happens when goal setting, feedback, and positive reinforcement are applied to the behaviors of suggestive selling by six waitresses and two waiters in a family-style restaurant.[31]

Management had decided that the best way to increase profits was to increase sales per customer. There had been a decline in business and sales, which may have been due to the lack of advertising dollars and the time of year (summer).

The effect of suggestive selling on three targeted items, alcoholic drinks (cocktails, beer, and wine), appetizers, and desserts, was measured by counting the sales of the items as recorded on the checks daily. After a baseline of 3 weeks, during the routine monthly meeting, suggestive selling techniques for alcoholic drinks were discussed with warnings not to sell drinks to teenagers. The group-set goal was 45% of customers purchasing alcohol. The potential for increased tips was also discussed. Graphic feedback to the staff was presented every 3 days, and verbal feedback, including praise, was given by the two managers daily. In addition, choices of two free movie tickets,

three free games of bowling, or 1 hour of billiards were given to those who exceeded the goal. Cash awards of $25 were also given to the server who had the highest overall percentage of sales of the item for the month. After 4 weeks, a similar procedure was put in place for appetizers and after 3 more weeks, for desserts. The goals set for those items by the staff were 25% for appetizers and 12% for desserts. The managers attempted to reduce those goal levels because they were so high, but the staff were confident they could do it. Notice how the percentage of the target items increase as the behavior-centered approach is introduced for each. The program was terminated when the assistant manager resigned to return to school. Note, too, the resultant drop in sales when the ABC approach ended. During the intervention, the increased sales of target items amounted to approximately $1,260 per month for the restaurant.

Even though staff would receive more tips (est. 15% of check) and about $24 on the average per month when sales of those items were up, that promise did not maintain the suggestive selling behaviors.

Although we still have questions about how best to use certain techniques to increase work quantity, we do know that the ABC approach is effective. When management trains the employee, sets attainable goals with employee participation, gives frequent feedback and coaching, and reinforces productive behaviors, the work force responds with higher rates of output. Best of

FIGURE 6-2

Percent of Tickets Including the Target Item

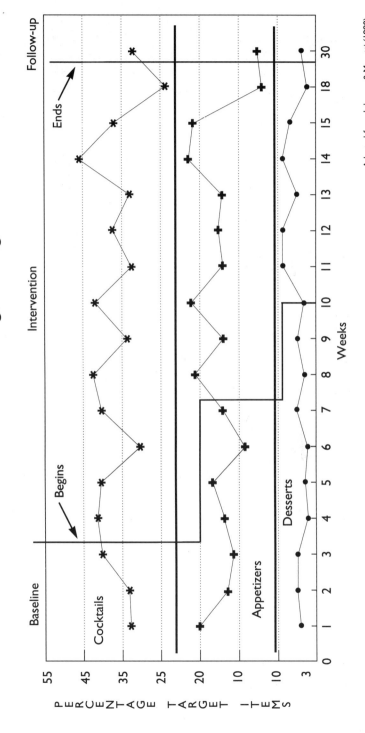

Adapted from Johnson & Masotti (1990)

all, significant reductions in the work force and increases in profit accompany the gains in productivity.

NOTES

1. Katzell & Guzzo (1983); Guzzo & Bandy (1983).
2. Katzell & Guzzo (1983); Nicholas (1982).
3. Schneider (1985) has described the military financial programs reported by Broedling & Hubb (1983); Oliver, van Rihn, & Babin (1983); and Ginnett (1983), as well as those in other federal programs.
4. Oliver et al. (1983).
5. King, Lau, & Sinaiko (1983); Broedling & Hubb (1983); Oliver, van Rihn, & Babin (1983); Ginnett (1983).
6. Marks, Hackett, Mirvis, & Grady (1986), p. 68.
7. Fisher (1981).
8. Walton (1976).
9. Those interested in developing work teams will find an excellent review of procedures and considerations in their development in Sundstrom, De Meuse, & Futrell (1990).
10. Paul & Gross (1981).
11. Hughes, Rosenbach, & Clover (1983).
12. Miller & Phillips (1986).
13. Allenspach (1972).
14. See Owen (1976).
15. Narayanan & Nath (1982).
16. Golembrewski, Yeager, & Hilles (1976).
17. Nollen (1979).
18. Wikoff, Anderson, & Crowell (1983).
19. Fellner & Azaroff (1984).
20. Pritchard, Jones, Roth, Stuebing, & Ekeberg (1988).
21. Pritchard et al. (1988).
22. Wikoff et al. (1983), p. 123.
23. Locke (1982).
24. Dierks & McNally (1987).
25. Wilk & Redmon (1990).
26. Perry (1988).
27. Fein (1970).
28. Frisch & Dickson (1990).
29. Frisch & Dickson (1990).
30. Saari & Latham (1982).
31. Johnson & Masotti (1990).

CHAPTER 7

Improving Production Quality

Production errors, whether they result in unacceptably high rates of waste, damage, or cash shortages, are very costly. First, there is the cost represented in the damaged materials. Second, the time required for corrections results in decreased quantity of work produced. Finally, the business loses customers who will not tolerate substandard performance or poor-quality products. Hence, employers prize workers who have the capabilities to meet both quantity and quality standards in their work.

By monitoring their own work output, detecting errors when they occur, solving problems as they arise, and asking for help only when it is needed, productive individuals enable an entire team to produce higher quality work. Because they need little supervision, these workers also free their superiors for other supervisory activities.

Problems in work quality often result because the individual does not recognize the mistakes he makes, or he does nothing about them when he does notice them. These behaviors are products of his past learning history.

As a child and an adolescent, the error-prone worker seldom had to notice his errors or correct them. Other people corrected his errors for him, depriving him of the opportunity to learn that poor performance has many negative consequences. When he wiped his dirty hands on his shirt, his mother washed it. When he tracked mud in the house, somebody else mopped it up. When he lost his spending money because he could not remember where he had put it, his mother replaced it.

His parents or his girlfriend corrected the spelling errors in his homework, and, when he put a dent in the family car, his parents paid the deductible. Moreover, when they yelled at him or scolded him for his negligence, if they ever did, the punishment occurred long after the careless act.

He never connected the problem behaviors with aversive consequences, and, just as important, he never learned that detecting and correcting errors on his own could spare him considerable negative feedback.

People who have never or seldom experienced aversive consequences for their actions continue to commit errors on the job with the expectation that someone else will take care of the problem. Managers must supervise these workers so that they understand work expectations and experience the consequences of meeting or not meeting those expectations. But, poor work quality may occur for a variety of other reasons:

1. Many people will choose immediate small rewards over delayed larger rewards. Spending money on impulse items rather than saving for a larger, more expensive item is one example. Patronizing the local bar with co-workers after work instead of staying after work for an hour to complete one of the company's training programs is another example of opting for the short-term over the long-term reinforcer. The additional training would not only improve the worker's accuracy and productivity in her job, but also would improve her chances when it comes time to bid for a new position within the company.

2. Many people will avoid small, immediate punishments even though this may result in large delayed punishments. An example is the person who leaves tools dirty, even though it causes the tools to rust or wear out earlier, or fails to put his tools away at the end of his work period, so that he can clock out on time. Because he fails to clean or put away his tools when he completes one job, he must spend even more time on his next job simply preparing to start work.

3. Many people will choose a small, immediate reward even when the action usually results in a large delayed punishment. Sleeping in or taking the time to drink a second cup of coffee in the morning, even though it makes them late for work and may result in a loss of pay, is an example of that principle.

All adults have, of course, learned to recognize and correct some errors immediately because they have had to suffer negative consequences. For example, to avoid obvious negative consequences, they check the parking brake when parked on a hill and put the dog out before going to bed. Yet, they continue with many of their old habits, especially at work. They approach each new situation with their old habits, indicative of the following perspectives on their work:

"If there are no immediate negative consequences, don't worry about it."

"If there are no immediate rewards for correcting an error, don't do it."

The key, therefore, to discouraging unproductive habits and to encouraging quality requires effective use of basic antecedent and consequence techniques by management.

This chapter presents behavior-management strategies that encourage workers to improve their production quality. In the sections to follow, specific behavioral strategies are described in relation to target behaviors typical of the employee who produces high-quality output.

Produces sufficient quality of work. Everyone's work varies in quality from time to time. Sometimes a person produces error-free output; other times the person's work has an unacceptably high error rate. Of course, that is the reason that manufacturers hire inspectors. The inspector's job is to monitor the quality of the work. When a particular employee's error rate is higher than that of other workers, a supervisory intervention is required.

Prompting and reinforcement. Some employees have legitimate complaints that supervisors never tell them about the 88% of their products that are of high quality, but only about the 12% falling below acceptable standards. In this case, the manager is overlooking opportunities to use the technique of positive reinforcement. If reinforcement is given more regularly to employees for their achievements, they are more likely to produce better quality products.

Initially, the supervisor shows the worker the products that she has produced that are of acceptable quality and reinforces her for them. Then he shows her the products that are unacceptable in quality and specifies exactly what the product's imperfections are and what the worker did that resulted in the errors. To pinpoint the steps in which the worker is making errors, the supervisor asks her to demonstrate the creation of the product. As she completes each step, the supervisor should reinforce her for proper procedures and correct improper procedures. At the end of the session, the supervisor prompts her by telling her that he will expect a lower rate of errors in the future. When the number of errors decreases, he should quickly and regularly reinforce her for this improvement in quality.[1]

A large error rate may also be due to working too fast. Instead of attending to the quality of the product, the person attends to the number of products being completed. Observation of the employee will reveal the steps in which carelessness occurs due to working too quickly. Prompting individuals to work more slowly and reinforcing them for the slower rate and the improved quality of the product will often reduce the errors.

Changing the antecedents. When the worker has control over the speed of production, changing of antecedents may be a particularly effective strategy for improving the quality of work.[2] Chapter 3 describes the use of signals to control behavior. For example, a signal light on a timer might be used to direct the worker when to start working on a product. If the signal light is timed to slow production, workers learn the habit of producing at slower rates with the expectation that their errors will decrease. If they hurry through the work, they should be directed to wait until the signal light illuminates before they can start on their next product.

Negative contingencies.　When prompting or controlling antecedent stimuli are impossible or ineffective, the supervisor may elect to impose penalties, provided that sincere positive reinforcement is given for improvements.[3] Penalties can be in the form of decreased pay for unacceptable products, or the individuals can be required to repeat the work until it is performed without error. Thus, a person who cleans a work area inadequately would reclean the untidy areas a number of times (overcorrection positive practice, see Chapter 5). If breakage is the problem, individuals should clean up each broken object before starting on a new item. If paid on a piece rate, the workers lose pay because clean-up time decreases the time available to produce work. If the person must complete a certain number of items before taking a break or leaving for lunch or home, the clean-up time interferes with the worker's ability to complete the product quota within the necessary time span.

Identifies Own Mistakes

When the supervisor decides that a high error rate is due to the worker's failure to notice the errors, the supervisor may choose to implement such interventions as (a) a team meeting to determine how to teach the person to identify and correct mistakes, (b) discrimination training, and (c) positive reinforcement with feedback.

Team meeting.　In the team meeting, the supervisor brings together all of the employees working on the product and explains to them that errors are costing the company money and causing unnecessary work. She gives them specific examples of the types of errors and asks them to suggest other examples of errors.

Examples of errors should be listed on a blackboard or flip chart that can be seen by everybody. Then she asks the workers to describe the causes of the errors and relates each suggested cause to a specific error. After summarizing the causes, she asks for suggestions as to what each worker does or could do to reduce errors. Employees with lower rates of errors are often able to explain the steps they take to reduce their own error rates.

As individuals describe what they do to reduce errors, the supervisor reinforces the responses. She finishes the session by asking them what they should do when they see they are making an error. Again, the supervisor reinforces the responses. Thus, in the team approach, she is asking workers who have lower error rates to describe their work procedures. In this way, the team meeting teaches more error-prone employees to recognize errors and to identify what other workers do to control errors. She finishes the session by telling all of the employees that they are expected to reduce their errors. Application 7-1 provides an example of how the team meeting can help employees identify and correct errors. Clearly specifying the tasks, assigning responsibility, and providing feedback saved the pub!

The authors of that study concluded by reiterating one of the most important themes in this book. "Behaviors that clearly had been intractable to change by more standard aversive management practices seemingly were readily altered by but two of the interventions that are available to OBM (organizational behavior management) practitioners."[4]

Feedback. Feedback is another technique that can be used with or without the team-meeting procedure. To use feedback, the supervisor gives employees in a section information daily on the number of errors or the number of items manufactured without error.

Feedback may be given in a variety of ways. The total number of flawed items can be graphed and posted so that every person in the section can see it. Or, the average number per person can be graphed and posted. In Application 7-1 ("Clean It or Close It!"), management graphed and posted the percentage of targeted cleaning outcomes achieved by each of the student workers.

In addition to posting publicly the total number of errors per group or the average per person, the supervisor may decide to provide each individual with daily information on his or her performance relative to the performance of the rest of the group. The individual graphs or feedback should be made available privately because groups are liable to tease or taunt those who have the most or least number of errors. If the person is teased or criticized for making the most errors, even though he is trying to improve, he may give up and act as if he does not care. The person who is harassed for having the least number of errors may purposely increase his error rate to decrease the negative consequences he receives from the group or the one or two persons who are making the disparaging remarks.

Private feedback can be given orally or by placing the graph in an envelope that is kept at the workstation or in the office. The supervisor might add a feedback system for the whole group by posting daily the number of quality and flawed products. A simple, but effective, use of feedback is illustrated in Application 7-2. Notice what happened when feedback was discontinued.

APPLICATION 7-1

"Clean It or Close It!"

The citation from the state board of health for the campus bar's lack of cleanliness was the last straw for the university administration. They called in the management of the student-operated university pub and gave them a mandate. "Run the campus bar legally and profitably and clean it up or close it."

The authors of this study[5] did not mince any words in describing the conditions of the bar: ". . . conspicuous, pervasive accumulation of grease and various sticky materials on virtually every surface." The "garbage areas were strewn with debris. Beverage and food leftovers often remained uncovered."[6]

With the help of the behavioral consultants, management discussed possible solutions and decided on a combined antecedent and consequence approach. They would utilize (a) task clarification to communicate what needed to be done (antecedent) and (b) graphed feedback to inform student workers as to how well they were doing (consequence).

"Task clarification" simply meant that management divided the bar into 11 areas and determined the cleaning tasks involved in each area. Examples of tasks or response products needed in the 11 areas included "put bar stools up," "clean beer garden of garbage," and "wipe off all games."[7]

Management first called a general staff meeting. During this team meeting, they presented the 11 areas of the bar, complete with the cleaning tasks in each of those areas (task clarification). The student workers discussed the overall problem of cleanliness, including specific details such as the cleaning behaviors required to accomplish tasks in all 11 areas. Thereafter, an unscored checklist was posted in each area to remind students of their jobs.

Before introducing the feedback technique, the investigators determined that the team meeting produced an increase of 13% more cleaning tasks being completed. Graphing and posting of feedback charts resulted in even more significant increases in completion of cleaning tasks—and for the customers, a clean campus bar.

Discrimination training. For workers who continue to have a high error rate, the supervisor may need to provide training in error detection.[8] He should choose a training time that does not interfere with the flow of work. The employee is asked to examine the work she has produced during the previous hour or during the morning. The supervisor then asks the worker to divide the product into two piles, those that do not have errors and those that do. He then reviews the products that she considers error-free and identifies any that contain flaws.

After pointing out flaws to the individual, the supervisor explains that the person's assembly process caused the flaw. He asks the individual to explain the nature and cause of the error in each flawed piece, reinforcing the person for describing the error and the cause. The supervisor then mixes the perfect

FIGURE 7-1
Effects of Feedback on Typing

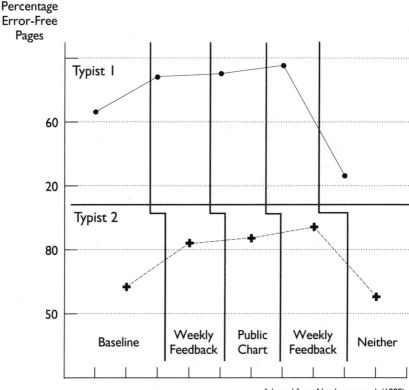

Adapted from Nordstrom et al. (1988)

and flawed materials and asks the worker to identify those with errors and those without, reinforcing her for correctly identifying irregular pieces. Again, he asks what in the manufacturing process caused the error. Correct answers are reinforced. Before ending this discrimination training session, the supervisor informs the person that another training session will take place if errors continue to occur at a high rate.

If many pieces have errors in the future, another practice session is scheduled. After a few repetitions of this discrimination training, the employee will anticipate and avoid production mistakes. Of course, some employees will show significant improvement after the first training session, while others will need more practice. Even adults with mental retardation have been shown to eliminate errors in discrimination tasks with repeated practice during training.[9] Regardless of how many training sessions are required, improvement should be quickly reinforced publicly or privately, depending upon the person.

Having two employees inspect each other's work twice a day is another way to improve error discrimination. The supervisor tells both workers that she is initiating a method to improve the ability of employees to notice and correct errors. She informs them as to when and how they are to use this quality-control procedure and reinforces any suggestions as to how the procedure might be improved. By occasionally checking their review of each other's work at the time it is occurring, she is able to reinforce the procedure and the outcome. By teaming one employee who makes many errors with one who makes few errors, the supervisor provides the error-prone worker with a desirable model as well as an incentive to decrease the number of flaws.

Goal setting. To use goal setting, the supervisor posts at the person's workstation the number of flawed items the individual has produced.[10] He then either tells the worker that the error rate should be reduced to X amount or asks the person how much the error rate can be reduced on the next day or week. X should be an amount that is definitely attainable by this particular worker, but is not necessarily the final amount of improvement that is desired. It is more important for the worker to believe that he can do it and for the supervisor to reinforce him for improvements than it is for the supervisor to berate him for his failure to reach an acceptable level immediately. On the next day, the supervisor posts the number of irregular items produced and reinforces the individual for any improvements. The supervisor continues to post the error rate, while at the same time reducing the number of errors allowed and continuing to reinforce progress. With consistent application of the technique, the manager will enable the worker to achieve the accuracy goal and maintain an error rate comparable to that of workers who are doing acceptable work. We will see how well that goal-setting strategy worked in Application 9-3 on safety. It is very important that the improvement be sincerely reinforced.

Often the techniques of goal setting and feedback are linked in an intervention designed to reduce production errors. Interestingly, the two strategies offer managers an alternative to punitive and authoritarian methods of influencing performance. They are also applicable to professionals such as scientists and engineers. In Application 7-3, we describe the use of goal setting and feedback to decrease the number of design errors and missed project due dates on the part of three engineers in a light truck manufacturing company.

Positive reinforcement. Previous strategies for reducing error rate have stressed the importance of positive reinforcement for error-free production.

APPLICATION 7-3
Engineering Engineers

If you were managing a small group of production engineers in a light truck manufacturing company,[11] you would be very interested in finding answers to the following questions:

1. How can I decrease errors in drafting plans?

2. How can I increase the number of projects that are completed on time?

3. How can I "engineer" engineers' performance in a less authoritarian and punitive manner to achieve those outcomes?

The three engineers worked on a variety of projects, most of which required timely preparation of production designs consistent with customer specifications. They custom-designed plans for walk-in vans, parcel delivery vans, cargo haulers, and flat-bed carriers; and the accuracy and timeliness of those plans were of great concern.

In the past, management had adopted, what seemed to them anyway, a very logical approach for directing the engineering staff. Without consulting with the individual engineers, the manager simply assigned projects and due dates, giving some consideration to the engineers' current workloads and schedules. Unfortunately, the strategy had several negative byproducts. Planning errors and missed project due dates resulted in inaccurate cost estimates, the purchase of incorrect material, and serious production delays.

Engineering staff rarely had the opportunity to volunteer ideas about project scheduling, and they felt that they were often given unfair assignments. In addition, the manager often overextended himself by assuming primary responsibility for too many projects. To make matters worse, although the manager required each engineer to maintain daily records of the amount of time devoted to each project, he checked the record infrequently and then only to discuss "excessive usage of time." Contacts with the manager, therefore, were to be avoided; you were either going to be chastised for being behind schedule or be assigned more work. Is it any wonder that the engineers often missed due dates, and in hurrying to catch up, made even more errors in their plans?

With the help of consultants, the manager devised a goal-setting and feedback strategy. They tracked two outcomes—the number of errors in plans submitted and the number of missed project completion dates. During a 10-week baseline period, which included 5 weeks of practice in participatory goal setting, the number of errors and missed project due dates fluctuated widely. With the

continued on next page

continued from previous page
goal-setting and feedback techniques in place, the number of errors dropped from 4 to 6 per week during baseline to fewer than 2. Missed completion dates disappeared almost entirely over the 10-week follow-up period, decreasing from about 2 per week during baseline to 0 for most of the follow-up period.

Next, the manager constructed an Engineering Project Scheduling Board (EPSB) which was placed in a prominent spot in the engineering department. The board displayed information on the various projects underway; for example, name of project, date begun, expected completion date, and name of chief engineer. The board contained columns to indicate whether each project was on schedule, past due, or completed on time. To implement the goal-setting strategy, the manager met individually on a weekly basis with the three engineers. They negotiated which projects met the criteria for inclusion on the EPSB and who should have responsibility for the various designs. They also arrived at an agreement as to when the project would be completed, given the engineer's other duties. Situations requiring renegotiation of due dates were also clarified.

The department secretary updated the EPSB on a daily basis and noted plan errors and missed due dates in a separate record. The frequency of errors and missed due dates had stabilized at a lower level. Now the engineers were more involved in setting their own schedules and better informed as to the outcomes of their efforts. The manager was so impressed with the results that he added two other engineers to the plan.

One of the most basic strategies in management, positive reinforcement, follows the timeless adage, "Catch them doing something right." Managers must remember not to take positive performance for granted: witness what happened to the typists' performance when feedback and recognition were withdrawn.

Another study of the importance of reinforcement in improving quality was done in an industrial setting.[12] Although the assembler had completed several sessions of training, he continued to make mistakes above the standard of 2 rejects per 100. So the manager decided to follow a shaping strategy whereby she used performance feedback, attention, and praise for desirable behavior.

At first, the supervisor reinforced the employee for any work samples containing fewer than 5 rejects per 100. Then, the manager faded out the reinforcement after the worker demonstrated a steady improvement. Now the supervisor provided attention and praise for work batches with 4 or fewer rejects, then 3, and, finally, 2 rejects or fewer. The use of positive reinforcement resulted in the worker rapidly reaching the criterion of 2 rejects or fewer per 100.

Initiates Action to Correct Mistakes

Sometimes individuals detect errors but do nothing to correct them. In this case, the person either does not know how to decrease errors or has no incentive to do so. When the person lacks the proper knowledge, the team-meeting approach, previously described, can be used to teach the person how other workers decrease their errors. The supervisor should ask the employee to repeat aloud what he learned from the team meeting about how to reduce his error rate. The supervisor reinforces the employee's description of the corrective behavior. Should motivation be the problem, the supervisor might institute an incentive plan or a response-cost procedure. Also, see chapters 11 and 12 for intervention programs directed at problem behavior of the individual employee.

Incentive plan. Equipment breakdowns due to careless maintenance cost companies a great deal of money. A simple incentive plan can decrease unnecessary mechanical failures. For example, workers can be notified that their machines will be inspected on an irregular basis (see Variable Interval Schedules in Chapter 4). Equipment in good working order will be tagged. Workers whose machines have received a tag will earn either a small monetary bonus, an extra break, a longer lunch break, or a shorter workday.

The cost to the organization of small incentives is more than compensated for by the decreased costs of machinery repair or replacement. Workers can also be encouraged to reduce their errors if they receive small bonuses for error rates below a specified amount. During periodic inspection of products, the supervisor can reinforce workers by compliments that are heard by other workers or by time off as rewards for producing high-quality work. Points can be used as rewards for well-maintained equipment or error rates that are below the average. Workers can accumulate points to purchase back-up reinforcers such as time off, gift certificates, or merchandise.

Strategies employing negative consequences are often used to encourage workers to correct their own mistakes. Negative consequence techniques result in careless workers paying for their mistakes.

Some, if not most, people strive for high-quality production because they take pride in their work. They have had a long history of receiving frequent external reinforcement for high-quality work and have come, over time, to reinforce themselves for excellence. Other people, however, have experienced no consequences for carelessness in the past. They have no reason to improve the quality of their work. Two procedures, both requiring careful supervision of the workers, can be implemented to reduce carelessness. Workers must learn that the probability of paying one of these two consequences for carelessness is much greater than the probability of having no consequence for errors.

Response cost. The response-cost procedure results in a reduction in wages or an increase in the amount of time a person must work for each flawed product or error produced. Workers who pay a response cost for their carelessness should also receive reinforcement for their improvements as the consequences begin to take effect. If they are sincerely reinforced for improvement, they strive for quality because the consequences are positive instead of negative; that is, they begin working to earn reinforcements rather than to avoid punishment. An example of a response-cost solution is presented in Application 7-4. The authors of that study noted that response-cost strategies should not be used when they violate contractual arrangements made with the union or individual workers.

Overcorrection positive practice. In positive practice, the consequence is practice in doing the job correctly (see Chapter 5). Thus, the person who is careless in cleaning his tools or machinery is supervised as he practices cleaning tools. The person who does not put the new prices on all items on the shelf is given extra pricing assignments. The person who did not count the merchandise in stock before reordering is assigned to do an extra inventory of stock.

In each instance of practice, the person is told the reason for the assignment is because he is negligent in cleaning the tools, pricing the stock, or checking the merchandise in stock. The practice should take him approximately two or three times as long as it would have if he had done the work properly the first time. At the end of the practice, the supervisor reinforces him for the completion of the assignment and informs him that he will practice again if the problem reoccurs. Note that the overcorrection procedure will be successful only if the practiced behavior is not a preferred behavior and if the probability of practice when not doing it right the first time is very high.

Seek Help When Help Is Needed

Two types of help-seeking problems that affect work quality commonly occur in the workplace. Some workers do not seek help when it is needed; others seek help when it is not needed. In fact, some workers seek help almost continuously.

Practice in seeking help. When not seeking help results in serious problems such as a breakdown in machinery or a serious loss of production, a list of those situations in which assistance should be requested should be posted

APPLICATION 7-4
Sharing the Losses

Frustrated by the continuing incidence of cash shortages, the manager of a small family restaurant, open from early morning to late in the evening, decided that "it was time for a change."[13] Restaurant staff simply had to pay more attention to the task of giving customers correct change. Moreover, the manager also recognized that not all of the mistakes were due to errors; some of the lost cash resulted from theft. The question of what to do weighed heavily on the manager. Installing surveillance equipment, hiring private detectives for additional security, or subjecting employees to "lie detector" tests seemed too heavy-handed. Moreover, those techniques could lead to excessively punitive responses—the manager would have to fire anyone apprehended while dipping into the till.

A behavioral consultant suggested that the cash shortage problem was an excellent opportunity to use a response-cost strategy that affected all of the cashiers. A group response-cost strategy was selected because it was not possible to identify the specific staff responsible for the errors. The group response-cost contingency was preceded by explaining to the employees how the new system would work. On any day that cash shortages exceeded 1% of that day's receipts, the total shortage, divided by the number of cashiers working that day, would be subtracted from each cashier's salary for that day. In other words, the manager gained the attention of the cashiers; they realized that "it is time to make a change." Of course, the authors quickly added that response-cost strategies should not be used when they violate contractual arrangements made with the union or individual workers.

Using a reversal design in which he measured the shortages before the intervention, during, after, and again when he restarted the intervention, the manager achieved some excellent results, without embarrassing or terminating anyone. As can be seen in Figure 7-2, the first use of the group response-cost strategy resulted in a decrease of 3.5% in cash shortages, with only 2 days out of 12 exceeding the 1% standard.

Following removal of the response-cost consequence, shortages soared to their previous mark. The average increase in shortages was 3.73% over the intervention level. Results of the second implementation of the strategy again demonstrated the connection between group response cost and cash shortages.

One final note—the manager achieved the goal at only a minimal discomfort to the employees. Response-cost fines were assessed only three times throughout the entire experiment for a total of $8.70 per cashier.

FIGURE 7-2

Cash Shortages and Response Cost

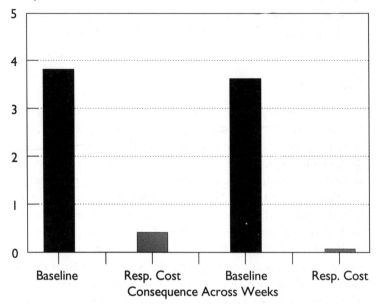

Average Percent
of Daily Receipt

Consequence Across Weeks

Adapted from Margolin & Gray (1976)

where it can easily be seen by those operating the machinery or working at that station. The supervisor should also review each of those situations with the person who was at that station when the shutdown occurred, and she should explain the importance of asking for assistance.

The situation and the appropriate response to the situation should be explained in specific terms; for example, "When the feeder line put too much material at your station, you did not inform anyone of the problem. Pretend that happens again, how can you tell that there is a problem and show me what you would do?"

If the person demonstrates no knowledge of the proper procedure, the supervisor should provide instructions such as, "Inform me or the person controlling the feeder." The worker should then walk through the correct procedure. The supervisor reinforces the worker and says that he is expected to seek help the next time that type of problem occurs. The supervisor should seek opportunities to reinforce the worker when help is sought or to repeat practice sessions if necessary.

If the problem is one of machinery breaking down because the maintenance crew was not notified, the supervisor has the individual describe the signs indicating that the equipment is not working properly, then asks the worker to explain the necessary action. The worker should rehearse the procedure of asking for help. Reinforcement of the rehearsal and of future help seeking is critical. Notice that this coaching method includes training the employee to recognize the problem and coaching him on what to do.

Summary

Production quality problems such as high error and damage rates, failure to recognize errors, typing mistakes, and cash shortages represent significant costs to businesses. Improved quality of work output is a function of increases in desirable employee performance such as identifying mistakes, initiating action to correct mistakes, and seeking help when help is needed.

Behaviors characteristic of the productive worker respond well to the behavior-centered approach to management. The practice of feed-forward control is important in that antecedents such as goal setting and task clarification are effective as strategies to increase the quality of work output. Similarly, feedback and consequences for work products are effective management procedures for reducing errors, waste, and costs. Positive contingencies in the form of praise or incentives are essential for improvement of quality. Negative contingencies in the form of restitution, repeated practice, and response cost have also been shown to be efficient means of reducing errors by employees. Finally, research evidence has shown that the behaviors that cause high error rates return very quickly when expectancy, accountability, and reinforcement are discontinued. Thus, implementation of the behavior-centered procedures has a significant impact on work quality and the discontinuation of those procedures results in a return of careless behaviors.

NOTES

1. Nemeroff & Karoly (1991).
2. Brown (1982).
3. McKelvey, Engen, & Peck (1973).
4. Anderson et al. (1988), p. 86.
5. Anderson, Crowell, Hantula, & Siroky (1988).

6. Anderson et al. (1988), p. 77.
7. Anderson et al. (1988), p. 77.
8. Rettig (1975).
9. Close, Irvin, Prehm, & Taylor (1978).
10. Komaki, Waddell, & Pearce (1977).
11. McCuddy & Griggs (1984).
12. Luthans & Kreitner (1985).
13. Marholin & Gray (1976).

CHAPTER 8

Improving Attendance and Punctuality

In this chapter, we discuss methods for improving the attendance and punctuality of workers. The focus is on both the target behaviors that contribute to attendance and punctuality and the antecedent and consequence techniques that influence those behaviors. Although tardiness and absenteeism are the focal points of the chapter, several related behaviors were discussed in the previous chapters on work quantity and quality; for example, "begins work without prompting," "works steadily during work period," and "continues work until work period ends."

A wide variety of antecedent and consequence strategies are presented for the reader's consideration. Typical antecedents suggested include behavioral contracts for improvements in attendance, job enrichment, modeling of target behaviors, self-instructional and self-management training, and prompting and instruction. Consequence techniques include both positive reinforcement in the form of compliments, tokens, and incentives and negative contingencies in the form of corrective feedback, the behavior-analysis form, and overcorrection/positive practice.

Before we examine the specific management ABC strategies, consider the study described in the reinforceability section of Chapter 5. Who were the employees who showed up for work on the day after the big storm in Chicago, even when there was to be no penalty for absenteeism?[1] Generally, it was the employees who had indicated previously that they were most satisfied with their supervision. People who like and respect their supervisors want to please their supervisors. If their boss wants them there on time, they will make the extra effort to be there on time.

Arrives at Work on Time and Returns from Breaks on Time

Productivity begins with punctuality. Time lost due to arriving late for work or overextending work breaks is time lost for production. Unlike absenteeism and in spite of its importance, tardiness is *not* often the subject of research, and few of the studies reported deal with any type of intervention.[2] Nevertheless, effective methods for teaching individuals to be on time are available. They include behavioral contracts, modeling,[3] incentives, response cost,[4] and prompting and reinforcement.

Prompting and instruction.   It is best to start with the simplest method of all, reminding (prompting) the worker to be on time. At the close of the workday, the supervisor compliments the frequently tardy Cathy on some aspect of the day's work. Then she prompts Cathy about arriving at work on time tomorrow morning and might even suggest that Cathy think about the importance of being on time the next day before she goes to bed that night. If that is not effective, we move to the next strategy.

Prompting and self-analysis.   Often individuals have not formed the habits at home that will enable them to leave for work on time. In such cases, the supervisor or personnel manager might call the person in and ask the person why he is late so often. The manager then asks what the person will do differently in the future to make sure that he is on time. If the person gives an unsatisfactory answer such as, "Get out of bed when the alarm rings, instead of just shutting it off," or "Go to bed earlier," say "Obviously, your plan has not worked for you in the past; what can you do to make sure that you will get up on time?" The manager finishes the interview with a *brief* statement about the importance of arriving on time, positively reinforces any stated workable plan, and informs the person that he is expected to be there on time in the future.

Behavioral contracts.   As described earlier in this book, behavioral contracts are based on the simple notion of "You do something, and I will do something." In this case, the agreement centers on the employee agreeing to reach certain intermediate and long-range goals to improve her attendance and punctuality. The agreement is entered into in writing between the supervisor and the worker with both parties signing the contract.

The contract specifies the actions and deadlines for the worker as well as the agreed-upon responses by the supervisor. For example, reaching the first goal of no absences or tardiness a month results in the person being recommended for advanced training or for a better job. Two months obtains a raise in salary. The contract represents a formal agreement between the two parties that increases the probability that the worker will modify her behavior and maintain the improvement over time.

Controlling antecedents: Setting your own schedule.   Flextime increases the control that employees have over their own schedules without detracting from the productivity of the organization.[5] In one study, employees determined their own starting and ending times for work within parameters set by management.[6] Participating employees also agreed to adjust schedules so that an adequate work force would be on hand during all work hours.

There were 173 secretaries, technicians, and drafters in one division of this large multinational corporation that designed high-technology products. Personnel set their work schedules between the times of 7 A.M. and 7 P.M. A significant gain was reported in the area of decreased absenteeism. Following implementation of flextime, an average of 1.7 employees were absent per day, a significant improvement over the 5.7 employees absent per day before flextime. Improvements were also reported in the quality of work-group relations and supervisor-employee relationships. All of these improvements occurred without any decrease in the level of productivity.

Modeling.   Following the principle "Do as I say and not as I do" is as counterproductive in a business as it is in a family. If they see supervisory staff or experienced employees arriving late for work, workers quickly follow the examples set by these highly visible employees. Therefore, the easiest way for new employees to learn to be on time is for their models to be on time. For this reason, employers have found it helpful to instruct senior employees to model punctual behavior; that is, demonstrate by their actions the importance of punctuality. They might even say loudly and clearly, "Well, it's time to go back to work; let's go."

An effective example of modeling in the construction business was cited in Chapter 3. The manager who supervised six carpentry teams in building apartment complexes instructed his senior carpenters to return from breaks promptly so that the other workers would do so as well. In a retail setting, the store manager should open the door in the morning, sharing a smile and a friendly welcome with arriving employees.

Job enrichment as an antecedent.   Enhancing the challenge and importance of functions performed in a job can also have a positive impact on attendance. A job-enrichment strategy was implemented in a government agency with 90 clerical workers. The experimental group participated in a wider variety of tasks that they considered more meaningful and more significant than some other functions. They also received more feedback on the quality and outcomes of their performance. Absenteeism and turnover declined in the group receiving the job-enrichment approach. No differences were found after 6 months in the quality or quantity of performance between the two groups.[7]

Incentives. One study of tardiness reported over 750 instances of lateness for 131 workers in 1 year.[8] As an initial response to this problem, the plant implemented an incentive program that rewarded workers who had the best *annual* attendance and punctuality records. Dissatisfied with their results, plant managers began to question the wisdom of an *annual* incentive plan. Their "new and approved" approach is described in Application 8-1.

The outcome of the "Pesos for Punctuality" application is easily explained by a basic principle of behavior management. Reinforcement must follow the target behavior as immediately as possible; otherwise, individuals do not associate the reinforcer with the specific target behavior. An end-of-year incentive is too far removed from the day-to-day behavior of arriving at work on time.

Another interesting incentive plan was also demonstrated in an industrial setting. Based on the concept of drawing a poker hand, the technique allows each worker who arrives on time to draw a playing card. At the first break, each individual who returns from work on time draws a second card and so on through the lunch break and the afternoon break.

At the end of the day, workers with four cards qualify to draw a fifth card. The person with the best poker hand wins a prize or a slip of paper that can be exchanged for money at the end of the week. To discourage cheating, cards should be recorded as they are drawn. The only way that a person can play and win is to have five cards at the end of the day. The only way that the worker can have five cards is to be on time at each of the different times during the day. An individual could win as many as five times a week, depending upon the luck of the draw.

The poker hand technique could also be modified to fit a weekly schedule in which workers draw one card a day for a specific incident of punctual behavior such as arriving at work on time in the morning. One such study gave each employee who came to work on time a playing card from a deck of cards. At the end of the week, the person with the best poker hand won $20. Not only did the procedure significantly reduce absenteeism, but the improvement continued after termination of the program.[9]

Another incentive plan enables workers who arrive on time to select the jobs that they would like to do that day. Individuals who are continuously on time are the ones who receive the most desirable workstations and tasks for the day. The advantage of this type of "activity reinforcer"[10] is that it involves no additional cost to the employer.

APPLICATION 8-1
Pesos for Punctuality

In this study, tardiness among workers in a manufacturing plant in Mexico was the targeted behavior. Prior to the introduction of the positive reinforcement system, the U.S.-owned company had rewarded punctuality with annual bonuses. Once a year, they gave 500 pesos to the 10 workers who had the best attendance and punctuality records, 10 prizes of 400 pesos to workers with the next best records, and prizes of 300 pesos each to the 20 workers with the third best records.

If a worker was tardy more than three times within a period of 30 days, he was suspended for 1 day without salary. The suspension occurred at varying times from 1 to 3 weeks after the third tardiness.

Twelve workers were selected from 131 blue-collar employees for this study because of their chronic tardiness, 10 or more in the previous year. Six were assigned to the treatment group, and the others to the nontreatment group. The treatment group was informed that, by arriving on time daily, each person would receive a slip of paper that could be redeemed at the end of the week for 2 pesos (10 per week). Guards already assigned to time clocks verified that nobody punched another's card, and they handed out the punctuality slips. The treatment condition of 8 weeks was followed by a no-bonus period for 4 weeks, a return to bonuses for 9 weeks, another no-bonus period for 9 weeks, and a final return to bonuses for 32 weeks. The results can be seen in Figure 8-1.

The results indicate that the daily reinforcement procedure is much more successful than the annual bonus and punishment system in reducing tardiness among those who have chronic problems with punctuality. The authors of the study believe that the success of the procedure was due to the immediacy of the reinforcement as compared to the delayed bonus at the end of the year. At the time of the study, 2 pesos were worth 16 cents in United States currency, and the workers were being paid an average of 50 pesos per day.

A lottery program was another approach used to improve attendance in response to several disturbing trends in the performance of employees of an electronics firm.[11] After reviewing the records, the production manager determined that absenteeism and tardiness were on the increase. He also learned that larger numbers of employees were receiving sick-leave benefits under the firm's short-term disability insurance program.

FIGURE 8-1

Bonuses for Punctuality

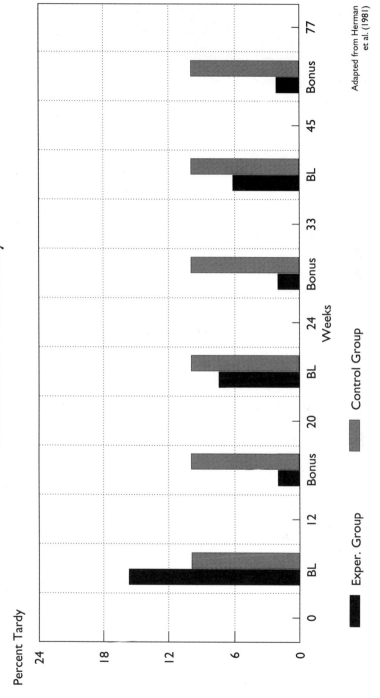

Adapted from Herman et al. (1981)

A program was started under which employees could qualify for a monthly drawing provided that they had a perfect attendance and punctuality record for the month. Any absence or incidence of tardiness precluded eligibility for the month, a policy that eliminated decisions as to the legitimacy of reasons for absenteeism or tardiness.

The description of the plan printed in the company bulletin represented the antecedent. Several reinforcing consequences were used. The names of all office and production personnel who were eligible were posted on the plant bulletin board (public recognition), and a $10 award was given to the winner of the lottery.

An analysis of sick-leave expenditures for the 11 months prior to the program and the first 11 months after the lottery showed a total savings of $3,109.11 compared to the program cost of $110, an impressive 30 to 1 cost-benefit ratio. Moreover, there was a 31% decrease in total sick-leave expenses. The authors of the study suggest that a similar program might produce comparable gains in safety and production.[12]

Although the electronics manufacturing firm experienced many benefits, they did caution future users of the approach about the following:

1. When only one name is drawn, many employees are not rewarded. Improvement in attendance and punctuality is more likely to be maintained if more names are drawn and rewarded.

2. If a person is late by 2 minutes in the first week of the month, there is no incentive to not be late or miss a day of work for the rest of the month. Greater gains in punctuality and attendance are likely if (a) there is a second drawing for half of the monetary award for persons late only once, (b) the winner of the reduced reward must be present for the drawing which is held on a randomly selected day, and (c) all employees whose names are in the drawing receive a playing card to keep or give away. The best poker hand at the end of every five drawings wins another award.

Group contingencies.   Managers of a large rehabilitation facility decided to attack the problems of organizational inefficiency and increased costs stemming from high employee absenteeism.[13] They adopted a group contingency strategy (consequence) for any work shift (10 to 15 people) that maintained absences below a criterion level for a 4-week period. The group contingency was an altered work schedule for 4 weeks so that all staff persons on the shift received days off on every other weekend. Usually, staff received only every third weekend off.

Although the change in weekend scheduling was only a small incentive, it was sufficient to mobilize peer pressure not to be absent. As a result, significant decreases in absenteeism were reported for five of the six shifts. A similar peer-pressure technique has been found to be successful in decreasing absenteeism in industrial settings.[14]

Self-management training. Techniques also exist whereby much of the control for modifying behavior is transferred to the employees themselves. Self-management training is illustrated in a large business where the tradespeople were found to be working about 32 to 33 hours per week even though they were hired to work 40 hours per week. Application 8-2 describes how the consultants and maintenance supervisors solved the problem.

Notice that self-management training incorporates both antecedent and consequence strategies that are under the control of the person. Setting short- and long-term goals and writing contracts are examples of antecedent strategies. Anticipating problems and solutions is a useful application of rehearsal, another antecedent technique. Self-monitoring attendance behavior

---

APPLICATION 8-2

This One's for You

Two consultants had a theory about job attendance. They believed that employees who exercised more control over their own behavior would improve their job attendance records. They involved a small group of carpenters, electricians, and painters in self-management training for 1 hour a week for 8 weeks. The trainers also met with participants for 30 minutes a week on an individual basis when necessary. The 8-week program taught group members to

1. Set immediate and long-term goals for improved job attendance.

2. Complete a behavioral contract that included self-selected reinforcers and punishers for dif-

ferent levels of goal attainment.

3. Self-monitor their attendance behavior.

4. Administer the consequences as specified in the contract.

5. Brainstorm problems and solutions for situations that might interfere with adherence to their contract.

Results supported the value of the training. Average hours per week of job attendance increased significantly for participants, outcomes that were clearly demonstrated in 3-, 6-, 9-, and 12-month follow-ups. Here are the results for two groups of workers who were assigned at random to a training or control condition.

continued on next page

---

continued from previous page

Number of Hours Present Per 40-Hour Work Week

Groups	Pretraining	3 mos.	6 mos.	9 mos.	12 mos.
Training	33.1	35.7	38.6	38.2	38.4
Control	32.3	30.0	31.6	30.9	34.9

Costs of the self-management training in time and money proved to be a wise investment when the impact on production is projected based on the additional hours of job attendance. But, improved job attendance was only one outcome of the study. Participants in self-management training

1. Applied self-management techniques in other areas of their lives; for example, weight loss and smoking cessation.

2. Maintained their improvements in attendance over a 12-month period.

3. Increasingly used sick leave for legitimate reasons (medical appointments and illness) rather than for reasons related to failure to solve family, co-worker, or transportation problems.

Because of the success of the self-management training group, the control group was given similar training by a different instructor and also showed significant reductions in absenteeism.[15]

which produces feedback and self-administering reinforcers and punishers are two consequence strategies. These self-management skills enable employees to organize and control their own behavior.

An important aspect of self-management training is teaching employees that they have more control over their behavior than they think.[16] This change in workers' understanding about their ability to control their own behavior is seen in Application 8-3.

Quality circles. The establishment of quality circles in industrial settings as an antecedent strategy was described in Chapter 2. Small groups of workers engaged in similar work meet once a week for about an hour to identify and, possibly, to solve work problems. Data from one study indicates that training, sharing new ideas, and participation in work decisions as part of a quality circle also can reduce absenteeism. Figure 8-2 shows a comparison of those who participated in quality circles and those who didn't in the manufacturing division of this large multidivision corporation. As can be seen, although those who participated in the quality circles did not differ in number of days absent per month from those who didn't at the beginning of the study, there were large differences during the last 3 months of the study.

APPLICATION 8-3
Get Yourself Under Control

Frayne and Latham (1987) conducted self-management training for 20 unionized state government employees who had used 50% or more of their sick leave. The intervention included the basic steps of self-management described in Application 8-2, but also emphasized problem identification and development of coping strategies. When compared with results of the control group, self-management trainees maintained better records of attendance, a finding even more characteristic of those trainees who reported increased confidence in their own ability to overcome barriers to attendance.

One interesting premise of this study was as follows: People who do not come to work may be unable to cope with personal obstacles in their home or work life. Therefore, an important part of self-management training involved participants in identifying personal obstacles to attendance in order to overcome those obstacles.

Before the training, participants typically responded to obstacles by simply defining themselves as ineffectual, that is, "I guess we are the delin-

quent bunch." As a part of the training, they learned to define barriers in terms of problem situations (e.g., difficulty with supervisor), to clarify conditions maintaining the problem, and to specify and practice coping behaviors.

Coupled with the other steps of self-management training, the problem definition/coping strategy ensured that participants not only knew what the obstacles were, but also knew how they could respond effectively to those obstacles. Sometimes people fail to solve problems for a very simple reason—they do not know how to behave in the problem situation. This simple step of problem identification and development of coping strategies fills their behavioral void.

By the way, the nine most frequent reasons given for using sick leave were (a) legitimate illness, (b) medical appointments, (c) job stress, (d) job boredom, (e) difficulties with co-workers, (f) alcohol- and drug-related issues, (g) family problems, (h) transportation difficulties, and (i) employee rights ("they owe me sick leave").

Response cost and punishment. Strategies for decreasing undesirable behaviors are also appropriate for influencing punctuality. Workers who continually arrive late for work may be penalized in a variety of ways. Common sanctions include oral warnings, written warnings, placing an employee on probation, and termination. Implementation of punishment and response-cost

FIGURE 8-2

Absenteeism and Quality Circles

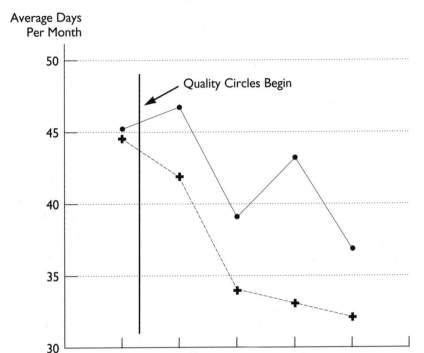

Adapted from Marks, Mirvis, Hackett, & Grady (1986)

techniques requires careful recording of the worker's behavior coupled with appropriate administration of negative sanctions following the behavior.

Negative sanctions can be important aspects of good management. While generally accepted as important in shaping behavior, positive reinforcement is often viewed as the only appropriate approach. Some managers believe that negative consequences for undesirable employee behavior should be avoided. This conclusion is erroneous for several reasons.[17] Management use of negative sanctions for inappropriate behavior has been found to strengthen employee commitment to follow norms for desirable performance, to clarify group goals, and to increase group commitment to the goals. Failure to administer negative sanctions, when appropriate, has the opposite effect.

It produces feelings of inequity among workers and serves to reinforce, in the long run, undesirable behavior.

In the case of tardiness, the supervisor should note each incident and the amount of production time lost in the worker's personnel file. The initial incident of tardiness might result in corrective feedback (oral or written) from the supervisor, which also clarifies the nature of the sanctions that will be applied. On the other hand, the supervisor may wait until the worker accumulates a specified number of late marks before introducing negative sanctions for the performance. In addition to termination for chronic tardiness, two other types of penalties are possible, a behavior-analysis form for tardiness (response cost) and limited access to information on career advancement.

Figures 8-3 and 8-4 provide examples of a behavior-analysis form for tardiness and absenteeism. The response cost occurs when the worker is required to complete a lengthy form explaining why he was late for work. In response to the page of questions, the worker explains where he was instead of at work, why he was late, whether he has been late for similar reasons in the past, what he will do to avoid the same problem in the future, etc. The worker soon decides that it is much easier to maintain a better record of punctuality than it is to complete the form. Forms of this type, when used consistently, have proven to be very effective consequences for changing behavior.

When the behavior-analysis form for tardiness is used, the employee should complete the form before clocking in, clock in, and turn in the form so that the supervisor can check and sign it. The supervisor should read the responses to make sure they are not sarcastic or "cute," sign the form, and inform the person that the form will be kept on file. Although it may be used only for those individuals who have demonstrated habitual tardiness, the form is most effective if used when anyone in the department or section is late. Those who aren't late won't have to complete the form.

The overcorrection behavior-analysis form has been routinely used to decrease tardiness in many retail stores and distribution centers; its effectiveness in treating problems of absenteeism is still unclear. When it was used in a Wal-Mart distribution center, it had no effect on an absenteeism rate of approximately 3%.[18] However, its use coincided with the skiing season in this resort area where a high percentage of the center's part-time employees were college students. The form might be more effectively applied with blue-collar workers or in settings where less attractive reasons than skiing exist for missing work.

The manager must reinforce improvements. If a worker has been on time only 3 days out of 5 in the past, a positive remark should be made when there

FIGURE 8-3

Overcorrection Behavior Analysis
Tardiness at Work

1. How late were you today?
2. When did you realize that you might be late for work?
3. How far from work were you when you *realized* you might be late?
4. When did you *know* that you would be late for work?
5. What did you do then?
6. How far from work were you when you *knew* you were late?
7. What were you doing then?
8. What could you have done?
9. When did you inform your supervisor that you would be late?
10. On what other occasion(s) were you late for work?
11. What could you have done before leaving for work to make sure you wouldn't be late?
12. What could you have done last night to make sure you wouldn't be late today?
13. What is the effect on your co-workers of your being late?
14. What is the effect on your work of your being late?
15. Describe your plan to avoid being late for work in the future.
16. What assistance do you need from management to avoid being late in the future?
17. What action would you recommend management to take if this problem recurs?

_____

Name

_____

Signature   Date

_____

Supervisor's Signature   Date

have been 4 consecutive days of on-time behaviors. The manager should not wait for 2 weeks of on-time behaviors before acknowledging the improvement if he wants continued improvement. In fact, some research indicates that recognition and praise for other on-the-job accomplishments have a positive effect on job attendance. Application 8-4 describes how a pat on the back is as good as a full house.

FIGURE 8-4

Behavioral Analysis of Absenteeism

1. Which day (date) did you not come into work?
2. What was the reason for missing work?
3. When did you first know that you would not be in to work?
4. When did you notify your supervisor that you would not be in to work?
5. What types of work would you have done if you had come in on that day?
6. What was the effect on your co-workers of your not coming in to work?
7. What was the effect on your job of your not coming in to work?
8. What could you have done on that day to make sure you wouldn't miss work?
9. What could you have done before that day to make sure you would not miss work?
10. What else could you have done?
11. What do you plan to do to avoid missing work in the future?
12. What assistance do you need from others to avoid missing work in the future?
13. What assistance do you need from your supervisor to avoid missing work in the future?

Name

Signature   Date

Supervisor's Signature   Date

A supervisor might implement another system for penalizing the late worker. In some business settings, the supervisor is the one who distributes information on new opportunities for advancement or training available in the company. These announcements may be distributed initially only to those individuals who have maintained a good record of attendance. When workers realize that they have not received such information by a certain time, they may inquire as to the reason. This interchange between the employee and the supervisor provides an ideal time to discuss the importance of on-time behavior. Of course, the manager should resume informing the worker of new opportunities just as soon as the worker demonstrates an acceptable level of on-time behavior, thereby positively reinforcing desirable behavior.

APPLICATION 8-4

Thanks, I Needed That!

Many factors such as job satisfaction affect turnover and absenteeism in an organization. However, the relationship between job satisfaction and turnover may be somewhat more complex than many people think. There appear to be different reasons for job turnover for poor performers than for effective performers.[19]

In a study of 295 hospital employees from clerical, service, nursing, and administrative sections, it was found that poor performers are more likely to stay with their jobs if they are satisfied with them. For high performers, turnover remains relatively unchanged as their job satisfaction increases. An unexpected finding? Maybe not.

The authors of that study reasoned that poor performers have no other reason than job satisfaction to stay. They may even experience organizational and co-worker pressure to look for another job. Good performers, on the other hand, receive many tangible and intangible consequences that encourage them to stay regardless of their level of job satisfaction. They seem to respond more to praise, recognition, advancement, and pay increase, which is contingent upon good performance. So don't overlook the power of positive reinforcement as a tool to encourage your best performers to stay with you. It may make the difference in the good performer's decision to stay or leave.

Where possible, other types of response-cost strategies may be tried. For example, the late worker might be informed that 15 minutes is deducted from her paycheck for any part of 15 minutes late. Another approach may involve expecting the worker to stay late to make up for the time lost. Both of these techniques prove to be more effective than sending the person home for the day whenever she is late. Of course, response-cost strategies are not feasible for all settings; for example, settings in which additional time on the job, loss of pay, or loss of break time either violates labor laws or union contracts or results in additional overtime costs.

Summary

Chapter 8 stresses the importance of positive reinforcement of desirable behavior to modify tardiness and absenteeism. Use of positive reinforcement creates a work climate that encourages punctuality and attendance. And yet, negative sanctions must also be a part of the manager's approach. If the manager fails to address undesirable behaviors, he leaves the impression that the behaviors may be acceptable. Employees come to doubt his commitment to certain goals, such as improved attendance, and to the behaviors required to achieve those goals. Therefore, the negative performances model actions that other workers may adopt when they see that no negative consequences result from tardiness or absenteeism.

The chapter also describes a wide variety of antecedent and consequence techniques. Antecedents, such as reminders to arrive on time for work or personal goals to improve one's attendance, either prompt or suppress targeted behaviors. Consequences were described in one of two general categories—negative sanctions (behavior-analysis form) or positive reinforcement (attendance incentives).

Some strategies such as self-management combine antecedent and consequence techniques in one approach. They also require active participation of the employee in administering the technique as well. In self-management of attendance, the worker identifies problem situations and coping strategies, sets personal goals, and self-monitors and reinforces progress toward the goals. A self-instructional technique was used to help an employee identify and list the steps that she needed to follow in order to leave the house on time in the morning. The worker memorized the steps and practiced them at home on her own.

In short, the literature on improving attendance and punctuality indicates that the behavior-centered management approach can have a significant effect on being there, on time, all the time.

NOTES

1. Smith (1977).
2. Leigh & Lust (1988).
3. Miller (1978).
4. Iwata & Bailey (1974).
5. Allenspech (1972).
6. Narayanan & Nath (1982).
7. Hackman & Oldham (1975).
8. Hermann, De Montes, Dominguez, & Hopkins (1973).
9. Pedolino & Gamboa (1974).

10. Brown (1982).
11. Wallin & Johnson (1976).
12. Wallin & Johnson (1976).
13. Reid, Schuh-Wear, & Brannon (1978).
14. Sheridan (1972).
15. Latham & Frayne (1989), p. 415.
16. Frayne & Latham (1987).
17. O'Reilly & Puffer (1989).
18. Brandt (1992).
19. Spencer & Steers (1981).

CHAPTER 9

Improving Safety in the Workplace

Attempts to increase the quantity and quality of work are of little avail if the safety and health of employees are at risk. In this chapter, the behavior-centered approach is applied to safety in work settings. In the next chapter, the high cost of employee health problems is addressed with the ABC approach.

Safety has been a very important concern for employers because of the humanitarian, economic, and legal implications of accidents on the job and practices that put the employee at risk. Despite the deaths, disabling injuries, and legal repercussions resulting from unsafe practices in work sites, few well-controlled studies of safety programs in work settings have been conducted.

Safety Interventions

Antecedents described in chapters 2 and 3 are applicable to problems with safety. Strategies whereby managers identify behaviors, state clear and specific directions, train, and use stimulus-control procedures are important. Unfortunately, the usual antecedents in industrial settings such as safety posters, slogans, or standardized safety audits are not very effective as evidenced by the fact that so many accidents continue to happen.

Posting signs to prompt people to have safe attitudes toward their work is like telling our children to have better attitudes toward their parents, their homes, or their rooms. It may impress visitors, but it is a waste of time and effort as far as changing behavior is concerned. Pinpointing safe practices on signs or in directives, on the other hand, is helpful. Thus, antecedents directing employees to report spills to their supervisors immediately, to wear goggles when cutting wire restraints from boxes, to walk *around* conveyor belts are effective in improving safety. Similarly, stimulus-control procedures of painting red lines on the floor around dangerous machines, placing flip-up covers over the start-up switches of dangerous machines, and arranging for a whistle to automatically sound when the temperature or radiation approaches dangerous levels are also very effective methods of producing safe behaviors and decreasing accidents.

Pinpointing safe behaviors when giving directions, training employees how to perform tasks in a safe manner, and setting safety goals can be very effective in reducing accidents. They are, however, more effective when followed by regular feedback about the employee's use of safe practices. Specific safe behaviors were identified, safety goals were set, and feedback was provided on a regular basis in the study described in Application 9-1.[1] Note the improvement in safety as shown in Figure 9-1.

Feedback is one method of applying consequences to behaviors in the behavior-centered management approach. Information is supplied to the employees so that they can continue or change their behaviors depending upon the content of the feedback. Feedback by management also gives confirmation to the worker that there will be follow-up on training or directives.

The more consistent the feedback, the more predictable are the self-corrections by the employee. If the chef never hears how much the customers like his pies, his pies will never improve. If he always gets feedback, he can begin to predict the customers' response when he varies the spices or the baking time. But sometimes feedback is not enough. If after he adds more spice, the waitress informs him that the customers thought the pie was very spicy, what does he know? Should he continue to make it that spicy, or should he reduce the spices? But if she returns and says the customers thought the pie was very spicy and very good, he knows what to do in the future. Reinforcement is needed. Positive reinforcement is needed not only by chefs, but also by bakery workers as we see in this next study of the ABC approach in safety.

Safe behaviors were targeted in two departments in a large bakery where there had been a long history of unsafe behaviors resulting in serious accidents.[2] Application 9-2 describes how workers were first trained to identify safe and unsafe behaviors and were given feedback. Again, slides were made to assist the workers during training to identify safe and unsafe behaviors.

How do you like our title on Application 9-2? One of the authors of this book treated a lady who had suddenly developed a phobia for flour after she had found a piece of meat, about the size of a finger, in her newly opened bag of flour. Whereas before the discovery she had loved to bake for her husband, children, and grandchildren, she not only could not bake anymore, but also she became nauseated if she saw flour on a counter or walked down a store

The ABC of Safe Outcomes

Antecedents and consequences were used to reduce accidents in a heat-exchanger manufacturing plant with 58 male workers who were equally divided into day and night shifts. The safety outcome measure was the percentage of all workers who had a perfect score on a safety checklist during a 30-minute observation period. Safety performance behaviors were determined from 5 years of accident reports and interviews with employees and supervisors. Specific safe behaviors were then described, "Keep your hands and fingers out/away from places such as pinch points and other places where injuries could occur" and "If oil, grease, or other slippery substances are spilled within a five-foot radius of where you are working . . ." Each of the 35 safe-behavior rules included examples. These were listed on the safety checklist.

Slides of each rule showing safe and unsafe behaviors were made. After 10 weeks of baseline, training meetings were held, and the slides where shown to each shift. A goal of 95% of employees with perfect scores on the checklist was set, and this goal was posted on a sign in a prominent location. After 6 weeks of the training and goal-setting intervention, a once-a-week feedback intervention period was begun. For 7 weeks, a bar graph showing the goal (95%) and the average safety performance level of the previous week was posted. Next, the feedback was changed to every second week for a period of 4 weeks before the feedback signs were removed for another 4 weeks (the goal-setting sign removed). Figure 9-1 shows how the safe performance level changes after the antecedents of safe-behavior training and goal setting were introduced and changes again when feedback was introduced and reintroduced.

aisle where flour bags were displayed. We are happy to report that the case was treated successfully using behavioral therapy procedures. But we could have titled Application 9-2 "No More Fingers in the Pie."

Earlier, we said that the chef needs to know not only that the customers can tell his pies are spicier, but that he also needs to know that customers like the pies. Some might claim that a good chef doesn't need feedback or approval from the customers; he can taste the pies himself. "Don't tell me; I know how I'm doing!" is what some people say. But is that a valid way to obtain information? Let's see what happens when workers rate their own safety performance.

FIGURE 9-1

Training and Feedback in Manufacturing

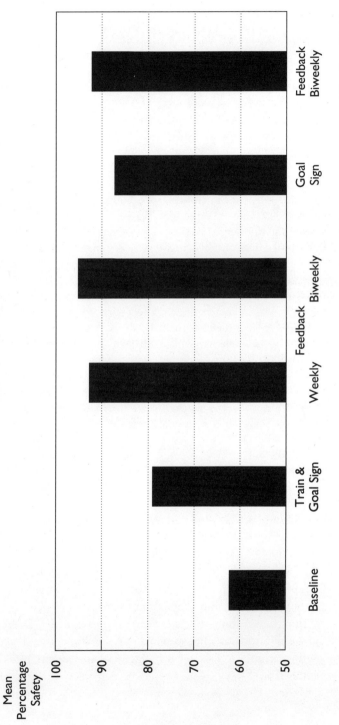

Adapted from Chhokar and Wallin (1984)

MANAGING BEHAVIORS TO AFFECT OUTCOMES

APPLICATION 9-2

No Blood on These Cookies

In this study, we see the effect that pinpointing behaviors and reinforcement have on occupational safety. Two departments working the second shift were selected for the interventions because over two-thirds of the accidents had been occurring then. Bakery goods were manufactured in one department (make-up); packing, bagging, sealing, and stacking (wrap-up) occurred in the other. Prior to intervention, it was observed that little or no positive reinforcement was given for safe practices in either department.

Very specific descriptions of unsafe practices were made; there were 15 in wrap-up and 20 in make-up. Two examples are "When cutting wire bands from stacks of boxes or spacers, employee cuts with one hand and holds the metal strap above the cut with the other hand"; and "Roll pans are stacked no higher than the rear rail of the pan rack."

On the first day of intervention in each department, at a 30-minute session, employees were shown slides of safe and unsafe behaviors for each of the targeted items; for example, climbing over a conveyor belt versus walking around it. Employees were then shown a graph of the percentage of acts performed safely during the previous 5 (wrap-up) or 13 (make-up) shifts so that everybody could see the seriousness of the problem. When a 90% target level was suggested by the employees, a line was drawn on

the graph, and the graph was placed where workers would be able to see it daily. In addition, supervisors were directed to increase their reinforcements of observed safe practices.

Next, a multiple baseline design was used in which the target behaviors were observed in both departments for 5 weeks, but the behavior intervention of feedback and reinforcement was begun only in the wrap-up department. Although the graphs were in place for both departments, the graph in the wrap-up department was updated weekly showing the percentage of safe practices observed the previous week. Safety behaviors continued to be observed in both departments for another 8 weeks before graphs were updated weekly, and supervisors were instructed to reinforce the safe behaviors observed in the make-up departments. After 3 more weeks of reinforcement in both departments, a reversal phase of no feedback and no reinforcements for safe behaviors was begun.

Table 9-1 shows the effects of the reinforcement on the safety behaviors practiced by workers in each department as interventions began and after the intervention.

Because only 15% of the wrap-up supervisors and 54% of the make-up supervisors reported giving recognition (reinforcement) to workers for safe practices, the authors of the
continued on next page

continued from previous page
study believe that the improvements were due to the feedback procedure of graphing safe practices. It was noted that when the president of the company saw the results of the reversal phase, an employee was appointed and trained to post data not only for the targeted shift but also for the other shift. Within a year, injuries had stabilized at less than 10 lost-time accidents per 10 million hours worked, which resulted in the plant moving from last to first place in safety in the company rankings. Their plaque indicated no disabling injury over a period of 10 months.

TABLE 9-1
Feedback and Reinforcement to Improve Safety

	Make-up Department		Wrap-up Department	
	Duration in Weeks	Mean Percent	Duration in Weeks	Mean Percent
Baseline	5.5	70	13.5	78
Intervention	11.0	96	3.0	99
Reversal	8.5	71	8.5	72

Adapted from Komaki, Barwick, & Scott (1978)

Goals set by management without participation by employees were communicated to workers in four different plants.[3] In one plant, the work group rated their own safety performance on pre-prepared forms on a weekly basis but did not receive feedback or praise from their supervisors. In the second plant, supervisors provided feedback, but no praise, and employees did *not* rate their own safety performance. In the third plant, employees were given feedback from their foremen, were individually praised, and were asked to rate their own performance. In the fourth plant, they did *not* rate their own performance, but did receive feedback weekly and were praised for their individual safety achievements.

Safety performance improved the most in plants three and four where weekly feedback and praise for successful attainment of safe goals occurred. Satisfaction with their jobs was also significantly higher only in those groups receiving feedback and reinforcement. Thus, evaluating one's own performance does little to improve safe practices.

In Application 9-2, we also saw that goal setting by the employees was one of the first steps taken to improve safety. What happens when the sub-goals are progressive (become higher each week) and when they are imposed by management with no worker input? What happens when the safety-relevant behaviors of each level of management are pinpointed as well as those of the workers? Let's see what happens when we examine these questions in a large corporation over a longer period of time than in the previous illustrations. Also, what is the *cost* or *savings* of such an extensive program? The answers to these questions are revealed in Application 9-3. One of the advantages of implementing the behavioral interventions in this large corporation was that many of the managers had been trained in performance management, a management model that includes pinpointing behaviors; measuring performance before and during interventions; and using feedback, goal setting, and positive reinforcement.[4]

The success of the ABC methods in that large industrial organization was attributed to a number of factors. Subdividing the large departments into smaller work units and tailoring the target behaviors to the work performed in those units were important. Starting the interventions in departments where there are many safety violations is also a helpful procedure when safety managers need to show rapid improvement with these safety interventions. Gathering safety information not only from accident reports, but also from all levels of management and employees got everybody involved. And, certainly, pinpointing behaviors at every level contributed to the great improvement in safety and cost savings. That is, supervisors were not just told to compliment the workers when there was improvement, but were told how, when, and where to compliment them and received training in this important part of the intervention.

As we teach in our behavior-centered management workshops, if we wait until a child is getting a passing grade of 70% before we praise her, we may wait forever. But if we are willing to start reinforcing her when she gets one more spelling word right, 4 out of 10, than she ever got correct before, we have a very good chance of turning our poor speller into a very good speller. She has learned that spelling words correctly produces reinforcement. Similarly, Application 9-3 illustrated a changing-criteria procedure. As the work teams reached each subgoal, they were reinforced enthusiastically and given a new subgoal that was higher, but still attainable.

Safety outcome measures can usually be obtained in relatively short periods of time. Behavioral methods are applied; safety behaviors are observed; and accidents are recorded. However, many unsafe behaviors may have

The ABC of Safety and Savings

In this study, three departments which operated on two shifts were identified as having the highest accident rates.[5]

Department 1: 100–130 workers producing printed circuits by using punch presses, laminating, and applying patterns to boards and plating.

Department 2: 47–63 workers assembling and testing electrical components with boards, using manual and automated methods.

Department 3: 40–45 workers partially assembling and wrapping large circuit boards.

Departments were supervised by managers and divided into subunits of approximately 25 workers with supervisors. Each subunit had its own unique set of safety-performance targets. After types of accidents had been determined from records, interviews with safety personnel, managers, and workers, as well as from direct observations, safe alternative behaviors were specified. These included such behaviors as "sort no more than one or two boards at a time," "load carts without overhang," "label containers," and "pivot instead of twisting body when carrying a load."

Each subunit was observed for approximately 10 to 15 minutes weekly to determine percentage of behaviors performed safely and per-centage of zones in areas scored "safe." These were combined to give "percentage of safety achievements."

Following the baseline period measurements in each department, employees were told how to perform safely using the pinpointed safe behaviors. A chart was posted within each unit, listing the safe behaviors and showing graphs of the percentage of safe achievements for that unit. Feedback and reinforcement procedures were also described. Each new weekly data point was fed back through department managers and supervisors, accompanied by a message from the safety manager that summarized the accomplishment, suggested improvements, and added congratulations. The messages were personalized to the units which had selected names for themselves. For example, "Great, 92%! (Supervisor's name) Lions are over their goal again." Each unit supervisor had been directed and trained in how to give feedback and reinforcement. Workers were shown the new data point on the chart and praised in an enthusiastic manner. Individual examples of unsafe behaviors were handled individually.

Subgoals were revised and plotted on the graphs every 4–5 weeks. These were set above the previous performance levels. In addition, low-cost ($2–$5) rewards such as luncheons,

continued on next page

continued from previous page
tape measures, pens, ice scrapers, etc., were given to all members of the team when they reached their first major goal. And when a unit reached 100%, they were given a free luncheon, plaques, a ceremony, or a group photograph.

Figure 9-2 shows the improvement in safety in each department across time. Further evidence of the improvement is revealed by the fact that, in all departments, the Office of Safety and Health Administration recordable accidents (required medical treatment) decreased from 47 in the 6 months prior to intervention to 30 in the 6 months during intervention. Similarly, lost-time accidents decreased from 14 to 1 during the same periods. Meanwhile, a very conservatively calculated estimate of net savings produced by these interventions was $55,000 for the year (1988), even though interventions covered only half a year.

delayed, long-term effects. Outcomes from such behaviors are of special concern to the United States National Institute for Occupational Safety and Health (NIOSH). For example, exposure to toxic substances is particularly dangerous to the long-term health of workers.[6] The usual approach is to keep workers and toxic substances separated by well-developed physical and chemical-engineering methods.[7]

One such toxic substance is styrene, a chemical commonly used in the manufacture of automobiles, tires, boats, plastic furniture, and paints. It has multiple toxic properties. Besides irritating the eyes, it can produce neurological damage, cell mutation, and cancer when exposures are over 100 parts per million (ppm). It has been estimated that over 30,000 workers in 1,000 plants are exposed to it full time, and over 300,000 periodically contact styrene-containing compounds.[8]

Common methods to control exposure to styrene are primarily engineering controls such as the use of booths to contain it and exhaust ventilation to both remove and dilute it. In the study reported in Application 9-4, the ABC methods of pinpointing, training, and reinforcing safe behaviors were used to control styrene exposure.[9]

In the study illustrated in the previous application, when training was initiated, one of the trainers stated that he absolutely would not wear a respirator. The discomfort and inconvenience of some devices that protect the worker are frequent problems encountered by management. The problem is that the payoff for healthful or safe behaviors is delayed, and the punishments for unhealthful behaviors are often remote. In other words, the long-term benefits of wearing respirators around toxic substances are outweighed by the

FIGURE 9-2

Safety Performance Within Departments

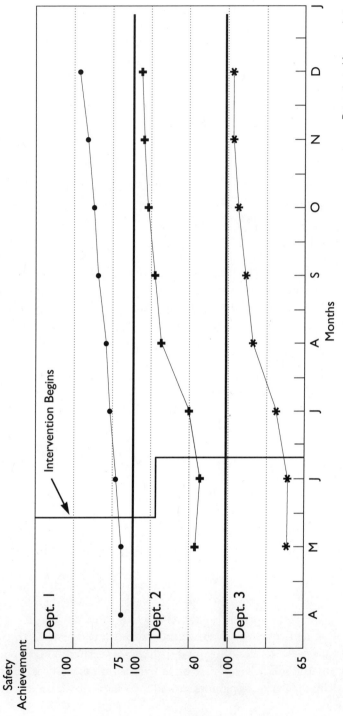

Data estimated from graphs in
Sulzer-Azaroff et al. (1990)

immediate discomfort or inconvenience. Similarly, wearing earplugs at noisy workstations is avoided by many workers. One method of overcoming the problem is to increase the payoff, and another is to make the payoff for safe behavior more immediate. We see one method of overcoming the resistance to wearing safety equipment such as earplugs in the study described in Application 9-5.[10]

APPLICATION 9-4

Pinpointing and Praise for Prevention

LA-B-CONCO, a manufacturer of laboratory equipment with fiberglass-reinforced plastics, decided to examine the effects of behavioral methods as a further means to reduce styrene exposure.

First, the research staff, after observing the behaviors of a number of workers, pinpointed nine that would reduce exposure. These included (a) place molds to be sprayed in the airflow created by the fan (molds), (b) spray in the direction of airflow (airflow), (c) cover hands with gloves and wear long sleeves (skin cover), and (d) close booth doors when working with styrene (doors).

Data were collected on targeted behaviors, exposure to styrene, production rates, and amount of time working. The last two were important in showing that increases in the target behaviors would not affect productivity. Exposure to styrene was measured by air samples, drawn through charcoal filters at a rate of 50cc per minute, from a location 10cm from the worker's mouth. These samples were taken by activat-ing pumps, worn by the workers, whenever they were near sources of styrene. Styrene exposure was found to range from 2 to 280ppm momentary concentrations.

Following baseline measurements across several days, individual workers met with a trainer who described and, sometimes, modeled each of the recommended behaviors and explained how each might be useful to reduce styrene exposure. Twice a day, visits by the trainer were accompanied by praise for the recommended behaviors and by suggestions for improvement when the targeted safe behaviors did not occur.

Figure 9-3 shows a representation of the improvements in some of the targeted behaviors.

Styrene exposure was reduced by 36% for the chopper, 42% for the rollout worker, and 57% for the gel-coater. The significance of these gains is revealed by the pre-intervention exposures of 150, 121, and 210ppm, respectively, when the federal standard time weighted average was 100ppm at the time of the study.

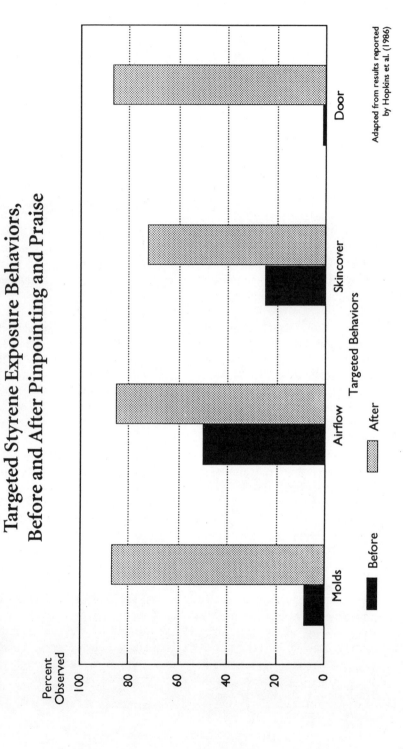

FIGURE 9-3

Targeted Styrene Exposure Behaviors, Before and After Pinpointing and Praise

Adapted from results reported by Hopkins et al. (1986)

No More Ringing in My Ears

Wearing earplugs is often viewed as a nuisance by workers even when they know that repeated exposure to intense noise causes a permanent hearing loss. It is difficult to get workers to wear the earplugs because there is an unpleasant adaptation period, the earplugs require regular cleaning, and they cause increased sweating around the ears. Prior to the intervention, even supervisors stated that "one's hearing is his own business,"[11] and that they only supplied them to those who wanted them.

The average noise level in this Israeli textile factory was 109 decibels, which is above the recommended noise level for industrial environments. A token economy was introduced to modify the earplug-wearing behaviors of three shifts of weavers in the factory. During the baseline, the average usage by the weavers and maintenance workers was 70% and 30%, respectively. Starting with Group A, tokens were dispensed daily for wearing earplugs on a variable interval schedule, random times, by the supervisors during their inspec-

tion tours. Workers could not see tokens being dispensed because of their dispersion in the factory. Group B began receiving tokens 1 week later, and Group C 2 weeks later. Tokens, numbered notes bearing the company's letterhead, could purchase consumer products which were put on display with their token price tags when the intervention began for each group.

After 1 week of intervention, all three groups had improved to over 87% and continued their improvement to 95% of the time wearing earplugs across the next 3 months. After the 24th week, tokens were no longer given for earplug use. Instead, it was agreed that the supervisors would try to maintain the earplug utilization level by requiring earplug usage, praising use, and reprimanding workers who did not use them. As a result, there was no decline in utilization across the next 3 months or 6 months later, even though there were 14 new workers in the weaving department who had not been present during the token intervention.

Consequence techniques described in Chapter 5 such as overcorrection positive practice and overcorrection behavior analysis are also applicable to safety concerns. The reader is cautioned not to use the overcorrection positive-practice procedure as a punishment for inappropriate behavior. The purpose of overcorrection positive practice is to change the behavior; that is, to stop the practice of an unsafe behavior and to encourage the practice of the safe behavior instead. To prevent the employee from seeing overcorrection positive practice as demeaning and then reacting in a hostile manner, the manager should present it as a retraining procedure.

Thus, when the forklift operator does not engage the brake or remove the shift from forward before raising the fork, the load strikes a pallet and tears open a carton, damaging the merchandise. The supervisor tells him that he needs retraining. Thus, for a 15- to 20-minute period, the forklift operator is required to practice carrying empty pallets and stacking them as he brakes and disengages forward before operating the lift lever. The cost in retraining time is outweighed by the savings in time not lost in future accidents. If all the forklift operators discover that they must complete such a retraining procedure every time an accident occurs, they will be much more careful about their behaviors while operating forklifts.

Overcorrection behavior analysis is being used when the person who has an accident is required to complete the behavior-analysis form. Figure 9-4 shows one type of behavior-analysis form as it would apply to accidents. Such a form would be given to the person who had committed the accident, who would then be required to fill it out, sign it, and return it to the supervisor. The form takes approximately 7–10 minutes to complete. If the person cannot read or write, the questions are read to her, and she supplies the answers so they may be written down by the foreman or supervisor.

Because some safety managers want to encourage employees to report near-accidents as well as those that actually occur, the overcorrection behavior-analysis form could be replaced by a behavior-analysis form that does not include the overcorrection components. Such a form might include only four questions:

1. What happened?
2. What caused the accident to almost happen?
3. What prevented the accident?
4. What suggestions do you have to prevent this from happening in the future?

The ABC approach could also be used to increase the number of individuals who reported near-accidents. The antecedent strategy is to notify employees that accidents may be better prevented if workers report near accidents to their supervisors, and that those who do will be eligible for a prize, a bonus, or a day off with pay. A safety team could then choose monthly or quarterly winners based upon the answers to questions 3 and 4 on the forms.

Summary

Safety and health have direct effects on many outcomes of concern to employers and employees alike. Productivity, tardiness, absenteeism, and turnover have been found to be related to unsafe and unhealthful behaviors of workers. There is a need to change these practices, and Chapter 9 presents a number of behavior-centered management procedures that can improve safety practices.

Demonstrating use of the ABC approach to improve safety behaviors of workers, the applications illustrate a variety of antecedents and consequences in factories and other companies, ranging from the control of injuries in bakeries to the production of safe behaviors when handling toxic substances. Illustrated were the use of training procedures and the promotion of specificity when describing safe practices to workers—and when demanding changes in supervisory behaviors that trigger and reward those safety practices. When safe behaviors are increased, unsafe behaviors have to decrease. Likewise, when unsafe behaviors decrease, accidents and workers' compensation payments also decrease.

NOTES

1. Chhokar & Wallin (1984).
2. Komaki, Barwick, & Scott (1978).
3. Kim & Hamner (1976).
4. Daniels & Rosen (1986).
5. Sulzer-Azaroff, Loafman, Merante, & Hlavacek (1990).
6. Bingham, Niemeer, & Reid (1976).
7. NIOSH (1983).
8. NIOSH (1985b).
9. Hopkins et al. (1986).
10. Zohar & Fussfeld (1981).
11. Zohar & Fussfeld (1981), p. 49.

CHAPTER 10

Improving Health in the Workplace

The psychological effect of work is a 2-sided coin. Although work may promote psychological health, it can also contribute significantly to stress and emotional illness. To the extent that unfavorable conditions at work cause stress, emotional illness, and accidents, they also cause work quantity and quality to suffer. Other work outcomes discussed in this book—for example, errors, absenteeism, tardiness, turnover, and net profit—are directly related to the physical and emotional health of the worker as well.

Employee Health: A Big Business

Health care of the American worker is a big business. The amount of money spent on health care by private sources, primarily employers, tripled between 1975 and 1985 to an estimated $40 billion.[1] Upon becoming chairman of Chrysler Corporation, Lee Iacocca was surprised to learn that Chrysler's primary supplier in terms of dollars spent was Blue Cross/Blue Shield.[2] Current statistics documenting rising health-care costs are believed to be signs of the future as the labor force ages and as benefits for the retiring worker continue for longer periods of time.[3]

Investments in the health of the work force are wise. Turnover and absenteeism are both reduced to the extent that employers pay more attention to the health of the worker.[4] As a result, wellness or occupational health promotion has become a major goal of many organizations in North America and Europe.[5]

The target behaviors of wellness programs include eating, drinking, smoking, substance abuse, and exercise. Positive changes in the frequency of these target behaviors are directly related to desirable changes in a number of unsatisfactory and costly outcomes.

Another factor that must be considered when evaluating health costs is the emotional state of the worker. Mental disorders were the third most disabling condition among Social Security Administration disability allowance recipients (musculoskeletal injuries and circulatory diseases were first and second in 1975–76).[6] By 1988, mental disorders had become the most prevalent, accounting for 21% of all allowances.[7] The term *gradual mental stress* (GMS) refers to the "cumulative emotional problems that stem mainly from exposure to adverse psychosocial conditions at work."[8]

The facts to follow underscore the gravity of GMS:

1. Over 364 thousand psychiatric claims were received by the state of California alone in 1979;[9] one-half of these resulted in monetary awards. GMS is one of the major categories in psychiatric injury claims.

2. When disabling injuries were generally declining from 1980 to 1982, GMS claims more than doubled.

3. Workers' compensation costs for GMS surpassed the average cost of claims for other occupational diseases.

Compensation costs are only the "tip of the iceberg." According to a number of studies, the costs of emotional disorders among workers extend to outcomes such as medical services delivered, lost work time, and decreases in productivity, all of which adds up to losses that run in the tens of billions of dollars annually.[10]

Efforts by management to reduce worker stress are, therefore, beneficial to the employee and cost effective for the organization. A wide array of health-promotion programs exist. For example, proposals developed by over 1,000 professional and lay persons to prevent leading work-related diseases and injuries have been published by NIOSH in a 2-part document.[11] In the remainder of this chapter, we discuss the application of the behavior-centered management approach to some of these health-related behaviors.[12]

Stress Reduction at the Workplace

Although considerable research exists showing that stress is a major contributor to employee ill health, less evidence is available to support the assertion that programs initiated by employers are effective in decreasing stress in the workplace.[13] One such program examined the three classes of stress: (a) psychological, such as anxiety, depression, and irritation; (b) somatic complaints, such as migraine headaches, dizziness, and nausea;

and (c) physiological, such as levels of epinephrine and norepinephrine.[14] Levels of epinephrine and norepinephrine (physiological measures) are considered indicators of stress because they are released into the bloodstream when the body responds to a stressor. Application 10-1 describes the intervention program and results.

In this study of 230 employees in a public agency, 99 of the employees volunteered to participate in the stress-reduction program. These social-service employees determine eligibility of clients for benefits, provide counseling, and handle emergency cases. Heavy caseloads, inadequate resources, and the frequency of crisis situations were often cited by the workers as sources of stress.

Although all employees were promised—and given—treatment, the 40 who were first to receive the instruction on stress control were randomly selected by a lottery. All were administered the tests for the emotional indices of stress, filled out questionnaires about their somatic complaints, and gave urine samples. All measures were again taken after the first group was trained and after the second groups had received similar instruction.

An experienced stress-management psychologist taught the cognitive interpretation and control methods across eight 2-hour sessions in consecutive weeks in a room provided by the agency. Employees were taught how to recognize their own stress-producing thoughts and how to replace self-defeating thoughts with more adaptive "can do" cognitions. The last four sessions taught them how to use progressive muscle-relaxation techniques when events at work occurred that were stress producing and how to combine these methods with the adaptive thinking (see Meichenbaum, 1983).

The results of these efforts were a qualified success. As the groups received the training, the urine tests revealed a reduction in the physiological measures of stress, although these were not clearly significant in some cases. There were also decreases in the anxiety, depression, and irritation for the first group receiving the treatment, but only reported anxiety decreased for the second group of workers after treatment. Four months after treatment, the stress indices continued to be lower than the pretreatment measures but were higher than they had been immediately after the therapeutic training sessions.

Note that the authors of the study (see note 14) recommended caution in adoption of such stress-management programs. They rightly fear that employers might turn to the ubiquitous 2-day stress seminars or 3-hour training films that are being offered by many consulting firms. In fact, the authors stressed that their 16-hour, 8-week program was too brief to produce more long-lasting effects on stress, even though their program was conducted by highly trained specialists.

Given that carefully planned stress-management programs conducted by well-trained professionals benefit the workers physically and psychologically, what are the benefits for the company? This question was partially answered by a 5-year study of the cost-benefits of worksite health-promotion programs.[15] Twice yearly since 1978, all employees of Blue Cross/Blue Shield of Indiana were invited to participate in an on-site health-risk identification and reduction program. Besides risk screening by questionnaires and physical measures, group programs were offered for nutrition and weight reduction, smoking cessation, and fitness. Individual therapy at the worksite was given for alcohol and drug abuse.

Participants, those who enrolled in one or more programs and attended at least three sessions, were compared with nonparticipants on health-care costs across the 5 years of the study. Health-care costs consisted of health insurance benefit payments as determined by claims records. Short-term cost analyses showed that the participants responded to the risk screening and advice to seek medical care by filing more claims. Long-term cost analysis showed the pattern reversing itself dramatically with payments per participant being only 76% of the nonparticipants. The reduction in health-care costs across the period of the study was $519 per participant. Even when start-up costs of the program were included in the calculations, the company saved approximately $50 per employee per year.

A very successful physical fitness program was also developed by the Prudential Insurance Company for their 1,400 employees in the southwestern home office in Houston in 1978.[16] Their new building had a rooftop exercise area with "first class" facilities, including a quarter-mile running track, exercise platforms, gymnasiums, stationary bicycles, etc. Over 650 workers participated in the 5-year study. Although participants had higher major medical costs than the 4-year average of the home office for the year prior to the study, in the year after entering the program, they reduced their costs 39% below those reported by the home office. The pre-program figure suggests that the participants were not drawn to the program because they were healthier.

In general, Prudential found that the lower the fitness level, the higher the medical costs both before and after the program was begun. Once the physical fitness program was in place, disability absences decreased by 20%, disability cost of absences dropped by 32% (savings of $91.24 per participant), and major medical costs dropped by 46%. These impressive decreases in health-care costs occurred at the same time that national health-care expenses were increasing annually at an average rate of 14% (see note 16).

Besides the cost effectiveness of fitness and stress-reduction programs, what other benefits do companies derive from fitness programs? The impact of a fitness program on productivity, absenteeism, and turnover, as well as fitness, is illustrated in Application 10-2.

As can be seen in the fitness application, the management antecedent behavior of organizing and offering a fitness program has a significant effect on such outcome measures as turnover, absenteeism, productivity, and

---

APPLICATION 10-2

Is Fitness Worth It?

Two large Canadian assurance companies agreed to participate in this study of the effects of a program on fitness, productivity, and absenteeism.[17] Of the test company's 1,281 employees, 34% enrolled in the fitness program but only 27% completed all physiological and psychological evaluations. Of the 577 employees in the control company, 24% completed all evaluations across the 15 months of the study.

Volunteers were recruited using a display booth outside the cafeterias of each company. At the test company, after the fitness testing and measurements of worker satisfaction, a 6-month fitness program was initiated. Fitness classes consisting of 30 minutes of rhythmic calisthenics, jogging, and ball games were held three times weekly, with a slow progression to

increasing endurance. Participating employees in the test company soon sorted themselves into nonpartici-pants, dropouts (started but did not continue fitness programs), low adherents (attended occasionally), and high adherents (two or more classes per week). Comparing the different groups before, during, and after the fitness program was in place, we see differences in physiological state, turnover, productivity, and absenteeism. For example, although all showed decreases in body fat, increases in oxygen intake, and gains in flexibility (sit and reach), those in the high-adherence group showed the most improvement in each case.

Over the course of the study, there was a 4% increase in productivity in the 30 departments of the control

continued on next page

---

continued from previous page
company but a 7% increase in the 23 departments of the test company. Absenteeism decreased by 42% in the high adherents to the fitness program, which was a 22% advantage relative to the others in the test company. Total days absent dropped by 76% for males and 50% in female high adherents when postfitness was compared to prefitness program data.

The turnover results are of special interest. Although the average lengths of service with the company were similar for all groups (over 8 years), both the high and low adherents to the fitness program had significantly less turnover than nonparticipants and dropouts. Whereas the turnover rate was only 1.5% for the program participants, other employees of the company had a 15% turnover rate across the same 10 months of the program. The authors of this study calculated the cost of hiring and training a new employee at $6,250 (see note 17). The reduced turnover annual saving was projected at $273,000 for the company. The decrease in absenteeism was estimated to produce direct savings of $88,000. Net savings of the program would be $231,000 at the time of the study and, if the other employees enrolled in the program, 5% of payroll.

economic benefits for the participating employee. However, 80% of the employees chose not to participate. One survey by the U.S. Public Health Service indicated that 66% of worksites with more than 50 employees offered at least one health-promotion activity; 22.1% offered fitness programs.[18] Only a small percentage of the employees participated in these programs. Furthermore, the evidence from that survey suggests that those who *do* participate do not need the programs as much as those who *do not* participate. White-collar workers, prior to participation, were less likely to smoke and weighed less than nonparticipants.

Participation rates vary by employee classification, too. Gebhardt and Crump (1990) reported in one study that 15 to 30% of the white-collar workers chose to participate, whereas only 3 to 5% of blue-collar workers did so. Different ABC strategies may be necessary to increase the participation of blue-collar workers. For example, blue-collar participation in a fitness program in a pharmaceutical company increased to 36% when the program was taken to the worksite.[19] Although some blue-collar workers will state that the reason for their nonparticipation is because they get enough exercise on the job, many remain seated most of the day with repeated motions in limited planes of movement. Others have very strenuous demands during emergencies but little regular exercise most of the time; for example, firemen and police. Let's see what happens when management uses the antecedent strategy

Fighting Fires With Fitness

In 1970 the Occupational Health Service of the County of Los Angeles began a program to (a) increase muscular strength and endurance, (b) reduce the magnitude of coronary heart disease, and (c) reduce insurance claims for orthopedic and cardiovascular injuries and illnesses of its 1,800 firefighters. Exercise programs and fitness plans were prescribed individually following physical examinations. Physical fitness manuals and stationary exercise bicycles were distributed to the 163 fire stations where group nutritional counseling was also presented to the firefighters and their spouses. After the periodic physical and exercise examinations (average: every 3rd year), individualized counseling by an exercise physiology technician was given. Figure 10-1 shows the change in physical work capacity before the physical fitness program was begun in 1973 and after 10 years of the program.

In addition to the improvements in work capacity, the authors of the study examined the firefighters in different fitness categories for flexibility, strength, exercise diastolic blood pressure, exercise heart rate, and physical work capacity. For each measure, those who were most fit showed the best score (healthiest), and those the least fit showed the worst. There were proportionately more back injuries and more heart attacks for those firefighters who were least fit compared to those in the middle or highest fitness categories across the years of the program. Workers' compensation costs have decreased 25%, and no firefighter has suffered a heart attack while fighting fires.

of *requiring* participation as illustrated in Application 10-3. In this study, firefighters in one county in California were directed to participate.[20] Imagine the grumbling when it was announced.

Again, we see the savings produced by a fitness program, especially when efforts are made to evaluate every worker and to prescribe individual fitness programs through counseling. However, there still were problems in getting some firefighters to adhere to their programs, as shown by the fact that those who were least fit had more back injuries and heart attacks. Putting the exercise bicycles at the worksite was important, but workers often need incentives to use the bicycles. Antecedents to promote participation in fitness programs and consequences for continuing in the programs are needed. Both were used in the health program of Southern New England Telephone Company, and

FIGURE 10-1

Work Capacity Before and After Counseling for Fitness

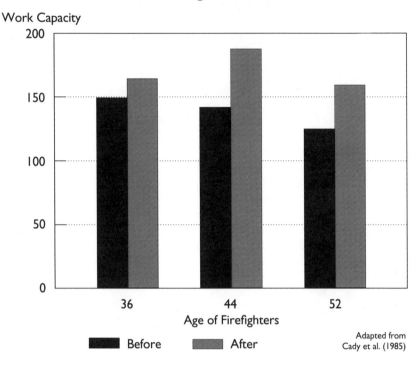

Work Capacity

Age of Firefighters

■ Before   ▨ After

Adapted from
Cady et al. (1985)

they resulted in a dramatic increase in participation. Over 50% of the blue-collar men and over 70% of the clerical women were involved in the health program. Their approach is illustrated in Application 10-4.

The low cost of the incentives are impressive. T-shirts and coffee mugs do not cost much when compared to the savings in health costs. Even greater participation and savings are probably possible if some of the other ABC methods discussed and illustrated in other chapters are used. The lottery system that was used to decrease absenteeism[21] could be extended to participation in health programs by giving prizes to the three names drawn weekly or monthly in the lottery where only those who attended every session were eligible. Costs of such back-up reinforcers are negligible relative to the gains in fitness and health that result from participation. The use of a token economy as illustrated in Application 9-5 might also be effective.

APPLICATION 10-4
Incentives for Healthful Behavior

"Reach Out For Health" was initiated by Southern New England Telephone in 1983 for their 14,000 employees.[22] It was unique in the variety of approaches used in achieving the objectives of building awareness, increasing knowledge, and providing skills to maintain behavior change.

First, a health screening was conducted on site on company time. Occupational nurses and health providers questioned each employee about medical history, self-care, and exercise habits and then took a number of health measurements such as blood pressure, pulse, body fat, lung function, and flexibility. An individual health profile, which included a diet and fitness plan, was generated for each employee. One week later, each employee was counseled about the initial results of their health plans.

The antecedent promotional strategies and consequence rewards for participation are noteworthy elements of this company's program. The antecedents included 45-minute health talks that included a free lunch, an opportunity for a group of 10 or more employees at any site to request a class on any topic of health education, health fairs, and featured articles on health care in the company newspaper. A variety of 18 different health courses were regularly offered on topics related to weight control, aerobics, nutrition, and stress (parenting, teens, aging, relaxation, and assertiveness). Also noteworthy was the use of consequences to maintain participation and behavior changes. These included gift certificates to purchase another course, T-shirts, gym bags, and coffee mugs.

The ABC procedures resulted in over 7,000 employees voluntarily participating in the health screening and in the health and exercise courses. Of the female participants, 73% were nonmanagement (office and clerical), and of the male participants, 50% were nonmanagement (craftsmen) employees.

What if choice of jobs or work shifts were contingent upon regular participation? And what if we try to solve two health problems at one time by making a stress-reduction procedure dependent upon participation in a fitness program? Such a solution becomes possible if we consider a suggestion made by Oregon senator Mark Hatfield (1990).[23] He points to the stress on the millions of workers who worry daily about the day care of their young children and elderly parents. Over 6 million families in the United States in which both parents work have children under the age of 6, and 24% of all workers are providing some care for at least one elderly parent (U.S. Bureau of the Census, 1990). If reduced cost for day care or access to the company day-care facilities was partially dependent upon regular participation in a health program by the worker, we could reduce workers' stress and improve their fitness at the same time.

Summary

The costs of gradual stress syndrome and mental health problems of workers as well as other stress-related problems involving cardiovascular and musculature diseases have increased dramatically in recent years. We have described the evidence that shows the economic benefits to the employer when health programs are initiated at the workplace. Also illustrated are other benefits of reducing absenteeism and turnover as well as improving productivity and worker satisfaction.

Behavior-centered management directed at healthful behaviors includes promoting health and fitness through free health-screening programs and health fairs, prescription and education, and incentives for participation. The cost savings have been documented, and the procedures to produce participation have been illustrated. Everybody wins when health and safety become targeted outcomes at work.

NOTES

1. Polankoff & O'Rourke (1987).
2. Iacocca (1984).
3. Ilgen (1990).
4. Johns & Nicholson (1982); Smulder (1980).
5. Glasgow & Terborg (1988).
6. Fischbach, Dacey, Sestito, & Green (1986).
7. Social Security Bulletin (1989).
8. Sauter, Murphy, & Hurrell (1990), p. 1148.
9. Lublin (1980).
10. For an excellent review of these studies, see Sauter et al. (1990).
11. NIOSH (1985, 1988).
12. For more extensive reviews of approaches to health in the workplace, we recommend the excellent reviews by Ilgen (1990), Everly & Feldman (1984), and Rodin & Salovey (1989).
13. Newman & Beehr (1979).

14. Ganster, Mayes, Sime, & Tharp (1982).
15. Gibbs, Mulvaney, Henes, & Reed (1985).
16. Bowne, Russell, Morgan, Optenberg, & Clarke (1984).
17. Cox, Shephard, & Corey (1981).
18. Christenson & Kiefhaber (1988).
19. Gebhardt & Crump (1990).
20. Cady, Thomas, & Karwasky (1985).
21. Wallin & Johnson (1976).
22. Kaplan & Burch-Minakan (1985).
23. Hatfield (1990).

Improving Individual Employee Performance

CHAPTER 11

Correcting
Deficit Behavior

In our workshops on behavior-centered management, we have heard more than a few managers describe behavioral deficits directly related to survival at work. Some workers may not use proper hygiene procedures; others fail to control their tempers or obey rules. When such concerns do occur, they require immediate attention from all involved—the manager, the employee, and co-workers. Not only do these behavioral deficits adversely affect an individual's ability to maintain a job, but they also interfere with the person's ability to develop positive co-worker relationships. Antecedent and consequence strategies for influencing the performance of individuals in relation to these job survival tasks are described in this chapter.

Maintain Satisfactory Personal Hygiene Habits

Personal hygiene habits are generally developed well before a person reaches adulthood. In fact, parents are expected to teach a child acceptable grooming practices early in his or her development. However, in some families, children are not taught how to maintain regular patterns of bathing, brushing their teeth, combing their hair, and using deodorant. In other cases, people may have learned these habits at home but have failed to maintain them over time due to carelessness or depression (a symptom requiring professional help). Some manager actions can create improvements in an individual's hygiene habits if the problem is one of insufficient knowledge or concern.

Prompting.   Prompting is an effective manager action that occurs before the target behavior. The manager should follow several steps when using the prompting strategy: (a) begin the session by stating one positive work performance of the individual, (b) describe the problem behavior to the person, (c) provide a rationale for why it is a problem behavior, and (d) explain how to maintain acceptable personal hygiene.[1]

Using one approach to prompting, the manager calls the employee into a private office and states some aspect of the person's work behavior that is positive. "John, I want to tell you how much I appreciate that you arrive at work on time every day. It's nice to know that we can depend on you." Thus, the manager clearly specifies one behavior that John does well before moving to the problem behavior.

The manager next mentions that John needs to make one improvement to become an even more effective worker, "John, you have a problem with body odor. People just don't find it pleasant to work around you. But you can do something about the problem. You need to bathe and use a deodorant each morning before you come to work." John should be asked if there are any reasons why he comes to work this way, and the manager should respond appropriately to any needs that John may have for personal counseling or other types of professional help.

In describing the rationale for the behavior change, the manager may wish to discuss (a) the worker's personal health, (b) the negative effects on other workers or the supervisor, and/or (c) the impression the worker makes on visitors and customers. Should John react angrily to this good advice, the manager should not fall into the trap of arguing with John. Instead, the manager should reiterate John's positive work behaviors, the need for a change in one area (personal hygiene practices), the rationale for the change, and the specific practices that John should institute. The manager should close the session by informing John that he is expected to change and that the manager will monitor his progress. Improvements in the target behaviors should be noticed and positively reinforced immediately by the manager.

Contingency interventions.   Prompting and contracts occur before the behavior and serve to elicit its occurrence. Contingency interventions or manager actions after may also be applied to decrease or increase the frequency of target behaviors. In a behavioral contract, John could choose a work activity that he prefers (reinforcer) which will be delivered following maintenance of good hygiene for a week. Involvement in the chosen activity reinforces John for maintenance of good hygiene practices. Therefore, even in an antecedent strategy, the behavioral contract, the manager also uses a contingency intervention such as positive reinforcement. Contingency interventions using negative consequences are possible as well.

John might experience some penalty for not correcting the problem, such as writing out an explanation for his poor hygiene (response cost[2]) or losing some privilege such as driving the forklift (time out[3]). Whenever punishment-oriented techniques are used, the manager must be doubly vigilant in noting any improvements in the target behaviors. In such cases, the manager should use the technique of shaping; that is, positively reinforcing gradual approximations of improved hygiene on John's part. Research indicates the efficacy of shaping or differential feedback (praising only performance improvements), particularly when the praising is accompanied by good instructional practices.[4] Reinforcement should be gradually reduced (thinned) until the appropriate positive behaviors become habits. Any return to inappropriate personal hygiene behaviors should have immediate negative consequences.

Dress Appropriately for Work

Learning what clothes to wear and how to wear them is another task easily accomplished by most workers. Typically, the employer informs the new worker of the clothing recommendations or requirements when the person is hired. Moreover, the new worker can observe the other workers' attire (models) to learn about appropriate dress. The new worker is expected to obtain the clothes, wear them, and maintain them over time. Although most people are aware of the importance of proper dress and know how to maintain their clothes, some people may have never actually done it for themselves. A simple prompt about the condition of the worker's outfit and the need to take the clothes to a laundromat may suffice.

Another type of clothing problem may arise due to personal preferences of the worker. The person selects clothes to express his or her preferences, but the choice may cause some difficulties. For example, beads or shirttails may become entangled in machinery; canvas or sport shoes do not protect the feet from injury; or, low-cut dresses may result in sexual overtures from other workers. Improper dress habits resulting from lack of knowledge or skills may be dealt with by confrontation first, followed by contingencies if necessary.

Confrontation. The manager may choose to confront the apparel problem by calling the worker into a private office. First, the manager reviews the worker's positive work habits and then reviews the dress code required for the job. In the review, the manager clearly explains how the worker's attire is not meeting those guidelines. If the problem is the result of lack of knowledge about clothing maintenance or repair, the manager should refer the person to a family member or, possibly, even a co-worker who could explain procedures to follow or could arrange for the person to receive instruction.

If the apparel problem is the result of a lifestyle preference, the manager must provide a rationale for why the clothing is not acceptable on the job. Safety concerns and customer expectations are but two reasons why a change in dress may be required. In closing the discussion, the manager stresses that inappropriate dress will not be tolerated and that any future deviations will result in a negative consequence which is explicitly described. The manager ends the confrontation session by restating the worker's appropriate work behaviors and by stressing that she has confidence in the worker's willingness and ability to dress appropriately in the future. Appropriate dress behaviors should be sincerely and positively reinforced in a discrete manner when next observed by the supervisor.[5]

Contingencies. If the worker continues to dress inappropriately for work, the supervisor should institute the consequences previously explained during the confrontation session. For example, the supervisor may choose to make the first written record of the problem in the employee's file. This written record may initiate a more formal disciplinary procedure which would result in termination given additional infractions by the worker. The worker must be notified immediately of the addition of the comments to the personnel file. Again, the manager should explain the specific nature of the infraction and the likely consequences of continued abuse of the dress policy.

Behavioral contract. In essence, a behavioral contract clearly spells out who is to engage in what behaviors, what the consequences will be for the contracted behaviors, and who will provide the consequences. Several guidelines that were presented in an earlier chapter about developing contracts bear repeating:

1. Select only a few meaningful behaviors for the contract.
2. Include reinforcers (contingencies) that are important to the worker.
3. Write out the contract and provide places for signatures of both parties.
4. Include the desired behaviors, the actions the worker will adopt, not the problem behaviors in the contract.
5. Provide attention and immediate reinforcement whenever the targeted behaviors are demonstrated.
6. Renegotiate aspects of the contract if necessary.
7. Record and share progress made by the worker.[6]

In the case of contracting for compliance with the dress code, the employee and the manager should identify several critical behaviors for the employee to follow. They should then explore potential reinforcers (contingencies) for the behaviors and select those that are meaningful to the employee and practical from the supervisor's perspective. Included in the contract, these reinforcers are administered by the manager when, and only when, the employee demonstrates the target behaviors in the agreed-upon manner.

The details of the contract should, of course, be developed privately between the manager and the employee. Similarly, the reinforcers in the contract should be administered discretely in accordance with the plan set forth in the contract. For example, the person might be informed in the contract that only on those days when he is in compliance with the dress code will he be allowed to work at the job or station he prefers. Otherwise, he will be assigned to work elsewhere or will be sent home to change.

Temper Control

People who anger easily are very disruptive in the workplace. First of all, they are a constant source of tension for other employees. Equally important, they may cause serious customer-relations problems. Just a few employees with problems controlling their temper can result in continual complaints to the manager, which interfere with the manager's ability to do her job. Finally, the actions of such people—glaring at others, pounding tables or desks, throwing objects, shouting at others, or striking others—are certainly disruptive, if not dangerous, to other workers as they do their jobs. Any behavioral intervention must include the message that displays of temper in front of customers are disruptive and will not be tolerated.

On-the-job contingency. The first step in dealing with aggressive workers is to describe the situation and the problem behavior to them. The manager then provides a rationale for the change needed and specifies the consequences for future aggressive behavior. Depending on the seriousness of the offense, the manager may be required to remove the worker from the workplace and to institute due-process procedures.

If the infraction is disruptive, but not dangerous to others, the manager may implement a 15-minute "cooling off" period. Prior to his return to the work area, the employee may be instructed to write a 1-page description of the situation, the factors leading to the disruptive behavior, and what must be done so that the problem will not recur. After discussing this report with the worker, the manager specifies the consequences of the next disruptive behavior. The reasonably detailed reporting requirement serves as a mildly aversive consequence that should result in decreased disruptive behavior in the future.

The worker might also be assigned a position on the loading dock for a brief period of time (30 minutes) as a consequence of the disruptive behavior. Several ground rules should be followed in administering such a "timeout" procedure. The supervisor should state the rules in advance as to the consequences for unacceptable behavior. When administering the timeout—that is, timeout from social reinforcement or desirable activities—the manager should use a calm tone of voice and display no signs of anger. The manager should disregard objections and arguments from the worker and proceed with the penalty, following a clear restatement of the behaviors that the worker must cease.[7]

Preventive strategy. Some workers may simply not know how to respond to frustrations in an appropriate manner. In such cases, the manager may find that it helps to explore some alternative problem-solving strategies with the worker.[8] Possibly, if the worker knew some other response to make in the situation, he would be less likely to endanger or disrupt others. When the manager does not have the skills for this type of coaching or counseling, she should refer the employee to a personnel officer who does or to a psychologist.

The manager might first help the person identify and describe the events (when, where, who, and what) that cause him to become angry. Together, they could develop a list of these situations and discuss them in some detail. Next, the manager should provide a rationale for change by explaining why the worker's disruptive behaviors cause problems and what is likely to happen if the behaviors continue.

Discussing rationale and consequences sets the stage for the next step—helping the employee develop acceptable behavioral responses in anger-provoking situations. Because the anger is real, the person must express his feelings either by saying to himself, "This makes me angry," or by saying to the other person, "You make me angry when you use my tools and supplies without asking. In the future, please ask me before you use something of mine."

The manager and employee should role play the situation, focusing particularly on how the employee expresses his anger and his perception of the problem and its solution. To facilitate learning, the supervisor may model the problem-solving behaviors for the worker. The worker then role plays the performances, receiving reinforcement and corrective feedback as appropriate from the manager. Occasional reinforcement of the new behaviors on the job is also an important part of the manager's responsibilities.

Many of us may have heard the following from our parents, "Now, when you feel yourself getting angry, count to 10 before you do anything." That simple piece of advice helped to suppress more than one temper outburst. But, there are some other things that we need to know, such as problem-solving skills and social skills that help us better cope with our daily problems. Problem-solving training to help people control their tempers is described in Application 11-1.

APPLICATION 11-1
Things Their Parents Never Taught Them

In this study, cognitive and social skills were taught as methods of overcoming problems.[9] For example, the training included how to respond effectively to on-the-job stress rather than to lose one's temper when frustrated and walk off the job. First, the person must develop some new thinking skills. When confronted with a problem situation, the person must consider the consequences of any planned actions. Next, she should review the alternatives available in the situation and evaluate how each of those alternatives would affect others. Finally, the person needs to practice communicating the best coping response, particularly in situations involving nonpeers such as a supervisor.

Although referring to teenagers in their study, the authors described some skill deficiencies typical of some adults in the work force. According to the authors, the young people in their study lacked social skills and acceptable assertive behaviors. They tended to behave impulsively with little consideration about how their actions affected others.

The results of the problem-solving and social-skill training were that instructed students (a) generated more alternatives to problem situations in school and at work, (b) responded more effectively in nonpeer interactions such as job interviews, and (c) experienced fewer incidences of tardiness, absenteeism, and misconduct referrals. It does not take much imagination to see how this same program could help many people achieve meaningful outcomes at work.

What is involved in the training? First, the students, teachers, and employers were interviewed in order to identify problem situations and skill deficiencies of the students. Then they scripted responses to the typical problem situations that illustrated problem-solving cognitions (thoughts) and behaviors. These scripts were used in approximately 11 hours of live and/or videotaped modeling and role-playing training sessions. Participants saw the scripts enacted either on videotape or by live actors, discussed the skills used, and practiced the recommended cognitions and behaviors.

So, what are some of the things that parents may never have taught? Things one can do while counting to 10 include:

1. Assessing the problem from the other person's viewpoint.

2. Considering the possible effects of your first reaction.

3. Thinking of several alternatives before responding to the problem situation.

Obey Rules and Regulations

Rules at work are of two types. Some rules are task specific; they direct the employee's behavior so that tools are used safely, inventory controls are practiced, or production standards are met. Often referred to as informal rules, other rules pertain to functioning effectively in on-the-job social relationships. Informal rules instruct workers in proper ways to behave with their supervisors, co-workers, and subordinates.

Existing in every work setting, informal rules function to (a) proscribe or suppress certain behaviors by serving as antecedents to remind the employee to avoid actions resulting in negative consequences and (b) prescribe or activate other behaviors by serving as antecedents to remind the employee to perform actions with a high probability of producing positive reinforcement. Therefore, it is very important to inform (instruct) employees as to how informal rules either prescribe or proscribe certain on-the-job actions.

Failure to follow rules and regulations may stem from several causes: (a) being uninformed about the expectations, (b) forgetting the regulations, or (c) knowingly ignoring the rules. Several behavioral strategies apply to these different situations.

Instruction. When a person first takes a job, the manager should clearly explain the rules of the employment setting to the worker. Even then, some of the rules may be forgotten during the early phases. When the person is observed breaking a rule, the manager should approach her, ask her to stop work, describe the rule that is not being followed, and explain why it is important to follow the rule. For example, the worker may have forgotten to place a safety guard properly. A simple reminder and demonstration of the proper procedure may suffice. At the same time, the manager should remember the "catch her doing something right" rule and reinforce her occasionally for proper safety procedures.[10]

Sometimes the rules in question are very specific and address proper ways to handle material, use equipment, or record break time. In other cases, the rules are more general and speak to proper behaviors for maintaining positive on-the-job relationships with co-workers and supervisors. Managers may orient new workers to these rules and commend them for following rules in an instruction/positive-reinforcement strategy. One set of rules that can help employees get along with others at work was developed on the basis of a survey of adults about what behaviors of others help to reduce conflicts, maintain good relationships, and achieve goals: (a) accept fair share of work,

(b) cooperate in task activities, (c) help when asked, (d) cooperate despite dislike, (e) don't criticize co-workers to supervisor, (f) ask for help and advice, and (g) don't be overly inquisitive about private life.[11]

Prompting and fading.   The supervisor may also recommend that the worker develop a list of rules for operating the machinery. The list could be posted on the wall or near the machine to remind the worker of proper procedures. The worker could consult the list prior to operating the machine. With time, the manager could help the worker reduce the amount of steps on the list to a single terse reminder such as "use safety guard," or simply "SG." Hence, the worker gradually fades out the amount of information to review.

Self-instruction.   Self-instruction training is another effective method for teaching workers to follow rules and regulations regarding work-related situations. The technique typically involves several steps, such as defining problem situations, modeling of appropriate responses by a trainer, and instructing workers in self-statements conducive to following prescribed procedures. Examples of typical worker self-statements are as follows: (a) "this is an example of the problem situations that we have discussed"; (b) "in this particular situation, the proper response is to . . ."; (c) "now that I have responded, my action resulted in . . ."; and (d) "I did a good job." Application 11-2 describes how self-instruction was used to increase the ability of two workers to follow rules for responding to work-related situations.

Contingency management.   In cases where the worker is familiar with the rule but chooses to ignore it, the manager may implement a contingency management approach. In other words, the manager explains the consequences to expect for not following the rule and then follows through on such consequences whenever the problem behavior is observed. Application 11-3 illustrates how a response-cost procedure can be successful when threats are not effective.

Another type of consequence would be for the employee to complete an overcorrection behavior-analysis form. If he was not using a safety guard, he would have to complete the lengthy form explaining why the guard was not in place. The use of that form, which was first described in Chapter 5, is illustrated for safety violations in Chapter 8. After completing a few such forms, the employee will probably decide that it is much easier to be more alert in the future about use of the safety guard. The behavior-analysis form is adaptable for use as a consequence for other problem behaviors such as high error rate or absenteeism (see chapters 7 and 8 for other applications).

APPLICATION 11-2
"You've Got Me Talking to Myself"

In this approach to self-instruction training,[12] two employees were taught to do the following:

1. State the problem they need to solve, such as "The drain is clogged."

2. State the correct response, such as getting the tools necessary to do the job and using them correctly.

3. Report the response and its effects, such as "fixed it" or "drain works now."

4. Reinforce themselves for the proper response, such as "good job."

First, they were taught to identify and define the work-related problems that usually caused them to stop working or to continue working without considering the consequences of their actions (e.g., pack defective products). Simple problems, but ones with serious consequences, were described: for example, a clogged drain, misplaced materials, a slick spot on the floor, and improperly packed products.

While modeling the proper response to the problem situations, the trainers spoke to the two trainees about each of the steps involved. Next, each worker practiced the responses with corrective feedback from the instructors. During this practice, the trainers also instructed the workers in the use of self-instructional techniques. First, the workers spoke aloud the self-instructional steps, then they repeated the steps silently to themselves.

Employees learned one proper response to each of five common job-related problems and practiced "talking to themselves" using the four self-instructional statements while solving the problems. Results provided support for the value of self-instructional training. The workers performed more effectively on random presentations of the problem situations over time. More important, they used the 4-step self-instruction strategy to solve related problems, but ones on which they had not received specific training.

"Talking to yourself" is not such a bad idea after all, particularly when it enables workers to improve their abilities to follow rules and regulations while promoting independence from constant supervision.

The supervisor might also request that an experienced co-worker praise the employee occasionally when she uses the safety equipment properly. This type of intermittent reinforcement from a "significant" other at the worksite encourages the worker to maintain the behavior. It also shifts some of the reinforcement responsibility from the manager to a person in the natural setting.[13]

APPLICATION 11-3

Happiness Through Response Cost

In this study, five cleaning duties were targeted for the attendant who worked 35 hours a week in a large game room located in the downtown area of a city.[14] The room contained 40 game machines and a change counter. The attendant had been threatened with loss of his job on numerous occasions for not carrying out the cleaning duties; for example, sweeping, cleaning the light fixtures, etc. The first attempts to initiate new interventions to modify the behaviors were refused. The attendant declined to record instances of his own working behavior; the owner of the business declined to consider increased pay, time off with pay, longer lunch periods, or social reinforcement. The owner did agree to make take-home pay correspond to the percentage of cleaning duties completed.

Before the response-cost procedure was introduced, the attendant averaged 67% of duties completed. After the consequence contingency was applied, the attendant lost less than $15 from his clocked pay on the first day (the response cost), and then averaged 93% of duties completed over the next 2 weeks. The owner then informed the employee that he was doing so well that he would receive full pay regardless of performance. The attendant's performance then averaged only 62% over the next week. When the contingency was reinstated, performance increased to 97%. Customers were now receiving change promptly; machine malfunctions were being reported promptly; and the premises were being cleaned daily. Informal observations revealed a smiling, whistling attendant and a pleased manager. There also were no shortages in the change fund during the intervention phases.

Summary

Chapter 11 presents a variety of behavior-change strategies which address different aspects of complying with the requirements of the work role. Some of the techniques use antecedents or "manager actions before the behavior" (e.g., training in problem solving) to influence the frequency and strength of certain performances. Others use consequences or "manager actions after" techniques (e.g., reinforcement or extinction) to influence the behavior in question. In a few cases, both the antecedent and consequence approaches are incorporated for an even stronger intervention.

Some examples of antecedent strategies are very simple to implement, such as the prompting and rationale technique used with the target behavior "maintain satisfactory personal hygiene habits." After receiving feedback about a positive performance, the worker is reminded of what the problem behavior is and of the rationale for why it is a problem. In many cases, a brief explanation is all that is required to influence the worker to make a change.

Straightforward examples of consequence techniques are also given, such as use of positive reinforcement to encourage a worker to use safety equipment properly. The supervisor stops by the workstation and briefly mentions his appreciation of the worker's use of the safety guard. It was even suggested that some of this reinforcement could be provided by a co-worker, an important person in the worker's natural setting.

Finally, several strong interventions were described that incorporate both antecedent and consequence techniques. One effective strategy involves the use of instructional techniques, which clarify the behaviors to be learned, and the use of differential feedback, which provides reinforcement for learning gains and corrective feedback for errors.

The behavioral contracting approach also includes both A and C methods. First and foremost, the contract specifies the positive behaviors to be adopted (antecedent), such as improved hygiene practices (bathe daily and use a deodorant), and elicits the commitment of the worker to adopt those behaviors. The contract also spells out the positive consequences which will result from adoption of the behaviors. Administration of the consequences represents use of the C approach.

NOTES

1. Marr & Roessler (1986).
2. Winkler (1970).
3. Kazdin (1972).
4. Van Houten (1984).
5. Cuvo, Jacobi, & Sipko (1981).
6. Hall & Hall (1980a).
7. Hall & Hall (1980); Hall & Hall (1980b).
8. D'Zurilla (1986).
9. Sarason & Sarason (1981).
10. Blanchard & Lorber (1981).
11. Henderson & Argyle (1986).
12. Hughes & Rusch (1989).
13. Van Houten (1984).
14. Komaki, Waddell, & Pearce (1977).

CHAPTER 12

Correcting Excess Behavior

Survival skills at work also include the ability to control certain behavioral excesses—that is, doing something too much. In this chapter, we describe behavioral surpluses that cause employees to have difficulties with their supervisors. At work, they may seek attention from their supervisors too often, complain to their supervisors too frequently, argue over directives, swear at tasks or others when corrected, play practical jokes, exhibit bizarre or highly idiosyncratic behaviors, or sexually harass others. Some excesses described may be redefined as behavioral deficits. When that is possible, we apply some of the same procedures that we covered in chapters 1 through 5 and Chapter 11.

Behavioral excesses may produce frustration, impatience, and even anger in other employees as well as the supervisory staff. Supervisors of such employees must not take personally behaviors directed at the manager, because the employees' behaviors are habits developed in past experiences with other authority figures. The employees would behave in a similar fashion with almost anyone in authority over them. Instead, a behavior-centered approach is recommended.

Seeking Attention

Some workers stop working whenever their supervisor approaches their work area. If they merely smiled, nodded, or waved and then resumed their work, we would be pleased with their friendliness. But when they leave their workstation to talk, tell a joke, or otherwise socialize with the supervisor every time he enters their work area, their work suffers and the supervisor's time is wasted. Any attention we give to this person on such occasions is only reinforcing the inappropriate behaviors. Therefore, extinction of the attention-seeking behaviors is the first intervention that should be considered.

Extinction of inappropriate attention-seeking behavior requires the manager to ignore the person totally. If ignored whenever he stops working and given attention only when he stays on-task, the employee will soon associate work with attention and reinforcement. Off-task employee behaviors will also extinguish.

Reporting Trivia

Some employees do not inform the supervisor of important information or of critical events when they occur; others constantly provide the supervisor with information. For the former, procedures described in Chapter 7 regarding "Seeking Help When Needed" are applicable. In addition, prompting with positive reinforcement is useful. Employees who give too much information too frequently are often seeking attention. Extinction and negative-practice procedures can be very effective.

Prompting with positive reinforcement. The supervisor first lists the information she desires from the employee; for example, notification of machine breakdowns, defective tools, or equipment; insufficient work materials; or specific interpersonal problems such as fighting or arguing. She stresses to the employee who has not reported these types of information that these events should be reported whenever they occur.

The supervisor must describe each item on the list in very specific terms, supplementing the explanation with demonstrations whenever necessary. After the employee indicates understanding of the points and of the reporting procedure, she should post the list somewhere near his workstation so that he may refer to the list in the future.

If the list pertains to all employees, it can be presented on a large poster visible to everyone. Subsequent reports of relevant information should be praised. Systematic reinforcement for reporting relevant information will yield long-term positive results. Note that this procedure was very successful in the study reported in Chapter 9, where safety practices were posted in the bakery and positive reinforcement by the supervisors significantly reduced accidents and workers' compensation payments.

Extinction. Extinction combined with positive reinforcement[1] is effective with the employee who is constantly reporting unnecessary information. Whenever the person reports irrelevant information, the manager should ignore the message and the employee. On the other hand, she should reinforce reports of relevant information.

Consistent applications of this procedure will help the employee discriminate between irrelevant and relevant information and report only that which is relevant. If the worker persists in inappropriate contacts, the manager should say, "That information is irrelevant. Do not leave your workstation to tell me that type of thing. Return to work." Such a response will decrease the employee's trips to the supervisor's desk.

Negative practice. Employees who seem compelled to report everything may be on a high reinforcement ratio for doing so in other settings; that is, most of the time they get attention whenever they gossip or report information, no matter how irrelevant. To suppress this behavior, the supervisor may implement a strategy in which the negative consequences of the behavior outweigh the positive consequences of attention. For example, the employee should be required to write irrelevant information on a sheet of paper or a form whenever she comes to the manager with unimportant information. Thus, if the person persists in reporting the gossip and trivia, the supervisor acts like a broken record, saying, "Go write it down. I don't want to hear it. Go write it down, and bring it to me," repeating those phrases as often as necessary.

After the employee completes the form and submits it, the supervisor puts it aside and sends the employee back to work. It is important that the employee not see the supervisor reading the information. The effort required to fill out the form, combined with the lack of immediate attention, should quickly result in the person suppressing the behavior of reporting trivia or gossip.

Complaining

Some people seek attention by complaining to their supervisors about anything and everything. They complain about their workstation, the machinery, their working hours, other employees, customers, assignments, and their physical discomforts. These complainers differ from other employees by the sheer frequency of their complaints. Sometimes all they seem to need is attention, and sometimes they demand immediate action. Although supervisors should respond to legitimate complaints, they must also decrease the frequency of complaining behaviors that are attention seeking in nature. A negative-practice procedure with delayed attention may be used in such instances.

Negative practice with delayed attention. When the frequent complainer approaches and starts to complain, the supervisor interrupts him and tells him that the complaint must be recorded. She hands the employee a sheet of paper, a pad, or a complaint form and directs him to write it down. Ignoring any protests about the complaint not being that important, she says, "It must be recorded. Write it down, put the pad (paper or form) on my desk when you are finished, and I will read it later." She then walks away. Later, she reads it, possibly takes appropriate action, and informs the employee that she has read the complaint and taken steps to remedy the situation or not, depending on the nature of the complaint.

If the negative practice with delayed attention procedure is followed every time the person makes a complaint, the complaints should significantly decrease in frequency. Although the employee is continuing to get attention by complaining, the immediate reinforcement has been removed, and the extra work of writing out the complaint becomes aversive. In the case of the employee who only makes complaints in meetings, a very similar procedure should be followed in which he is asked to submit the complaint in writing. Application 12-1 demonstrates the use of negative practice and other behavior-centered strategies to decrease the frequency of an employee's complaining behaviors.

We have wondered what would happen if the employees in those departments in a company where everybody has a computer were directed to make their complaints to the computer. When the employee calls up the complaint program, the computer responds in the following therapeutic manner:

Computer: What is your complaint?

Employee types in answer.

Computer: Could you be a little more specific about it?

Employee types in answer.

Computer: How does that make you feel?

Employee types in feelings.

Computer: It must make you angry when nobody does anything about that problem. What suggestions do you have for changing the situation or solving the problem?

Employee types in suggestion.

Computer: Hmmmm. That's interesting. Would that make you feel better?

Employee answers.

Computer: Maybe we should run your suggestion up the flag pole and see if anyone salutes. Would you like your suggestions stored and sent to your supervisor's computer station? Yᴇs or Nᴏ?

Note that such a computer therapist might also handle the problem of the employee who is afraid to make complaints directly to the supervisor.

APPLICATION 12-1

Programming a Programmer's Complaints

This study described how a manager dealt with one common behavioral excess,[2] "complaining too much about conditions at work." It seems that the employee found something wrong with almost everything. Part of a computer software development team, the employee complained to the manager about "working conditions, the company pension plan, the poor quality of work of other employees, the weather, the cost of gasoline, and a host of other issues" (p. 3).

The manager had been doing his best to satisfy the employee by quickly attending to every complaint and trying to resolve every problem. However, the harder he tried, the more the employee complained. When he finally realized that all his attention and efforts were just reinforcement for complaining, he took a different approach.

First, he obtained a baseline of the number of complaints, and he then developed a program of alternative consequences to the "sympathetic ear/ready response" approach,

1. Listen to the employee but provide no reassurance.

2. Request a written description of the complaint.

3. Suggest that the programmer solve the problem himself.

4. Ask for written recommendations on problem solution.

Some of the results of these new consequences were a significant reduction in complaints over a 2-month period, complaints that addressed business concerns instead of extraneous matters, and useful documentation and/or recommendations. Reassurance and encouragement from the manager continued but only when the programmer followed the new program for complaints.

Fear of Supervisor

Previous experience with punishing parents and teachers can inhibit some behaviors that are needed on a job. Once when we were giving a workshop on stress-reduction methods for office workers, a secretary said that she was afraid of her boss. A number of the other clerks and secretaries stated that they also were afraid of their bosses.

We asked for examples of stressful situations. One secretary experienced significant stress when her boss walked into her office about 15 minutes before quitting time with some letters that had to be typed. The fact that he had taken a long lunch break or had talked with his buddy about some basketball game when he could have been writing the letters upset her. As a result of his assignment, she had to stay an hour late with no warning and type the letters. Did she ask whether the letters could be typed the next day? She said she didn't dare.

We then asked her what she did do. She said with a smile, "I cry a lot." When her boss saw her crying, he would ask her "what's wrong?" and she would tell him. Sometimes he would let her go home and type the letters the next day. Sometimes she had to mope for a couple of days before he would notice.

When we suggested that she ask for a meeting to explain the difficulties it caused her to get such assignments so late in the day, she again said she was afraid. She had worked for this supervisor about 8 years, and, according to her, he had always given her good evaluations. He never threatened her or even criticized her work. Yet she feared him.

Was it fear of him or fear of authority figures in general? It was probably the latter, and her behavior of crying was the only one that had worked part of the time with previous authority figures. Although we could not give her assertiveness training during our short workshop, we did recommend that those who were afraid of their bosses for no reason receive such training.

Some employees have a history of receiving so much criticism from authority figures that they freeze from fear when a supervisor is near, stop working for fear of making a mistake that would be criticized, or make numerous mistakes. If the employee is a productive worker otherwise, the basic behavioral procedure is one of demonstrating to her that the supervisor's presence is not a signal for punishment. Frequent interaction characterized by reinforcement, not criticism, will usually solve the problem. In more severe cases, the supervisor may implement a desensitization procedure.

Desensitization. When an employee stops working when the supervisor approaches her work area, but does not look up as if seeking attention, the supervisor should praise the employee's appropriate work habits and then leave. If she stops working the next time, the manager should ask her to demonstrate how she does her job and then reinforce her performance. Talking with her at the start or end of the workday may solve the problem by showing her that she need not fear him.

For more severe cases, a method of desensitization might be used. To start, the supervisor stands within 20 feet of the employee. If she continues to work, he moves away and later returns to within 15 feet. If the employee continues to work but looks up, he nods his head in a reinforcing manner and moves away. The manager continues this procedure until he is within 10 feet, then

5 feet, and then beside the employee, while the employee continues working. He reinforces the person for continuing to work in each of the instances previously noted.

Poor outcomes may also result from a management climate that breeds fear and mistrust in employees. To create such an atmosphere, managers typically violate a great many of the behavior-centered principles. For example, they misuse antecedents by not clarifying what is expected of employees or by constantly changing standards. They may fail to recognize good performance when it occurs and instead rely on punishment as a means of setting an example. The end result is that employees do not believe that they are treated well and, as a consequence, they do not produce. Application 12-2 provides data in support of the positive impact that behavior-centered management has on employees who do not fear their supervisors.

Resisting Supervision and Criticism

People with a habit of responding to supervision or correction by denying and arguing are especially difficult to manage. In fact, they may react as if every statement made by the manager is a criticism of their work. Such oversensitivity is usually due to a history of parental criticism which they could only escape by arguing and defending themselves.

When employees argue only when their work is criticized, a reinforcement and fading procedure can be effective. When individuals argue regardless of what is said to them, an instruction and practice procedure should be used.

Reinforcement and fading. Upon approaching the employee, the manager provides some nonthreatening or positive information and makes a reinforcing statement such as, "I appreciate the way you listen to the information I give you. It makes my job easier when people listen carefully." The supervisor continues this practice of giving positive or neutral information about the workplace (work hours, work conditions, employee's production rates) and reinforces the individual in a sincere manner for listening carefully to what the supervisor says. If the employee asks questions about what the supervisor has said, the supervisor should answer his questions as completely as possible. When the manager believes that the employee is accustomed to the supervisor approaching and giving positive comments, he then approaches the employee, says something positive about the person's work, then makes a very brief, minor criticism of an aspect of the person's performance. Following this mild criticism, the manager should immediately reinforce the employee for listening.

APPLICATION 12-2

Do Unto Employees as You Would Have Them Do Unto Customers

Quality in retailing is the function of two factors—product and customer service differences. Product differences are easily and quickly copied by competitors. Customer service, however, is another matter. It results from the priorities and actions of managers.[3]

If, for example, employees are afraid of their supervisors, then the quality of customer service declines. Poor customer service results in decreased sales volume. Unfortunately, some managers give little thought to the way in which they treat employees, concentrating more on factors "such as store environment, product selection, and the generation of customer traffic . . ."[4]

In this study, three factors were found to predict store sales volume (sales per payroll hour): employee support, employee incentives, and quality customer service. Employee support is the key term for understanding how to relate more effectively to the sales staff. High levels of employer support as perceived by employees were described in terms of two categories, the quality of employee treatment by management and timely support by other parts of the company such as distribution. Quality employee treatment by management not only decreases fear of management but increases sales volume. Employees defined quality treatment by endorsing positively such items as

1. The employees are treated fairly.

2. The company has enough employees to meet customer needs.

3. The company's policies are consistently followed.

4. Employees are trusted by upper management.

5. Employees are paid enough for the time they spend in public relations for the company.

6. The tasks employees are asked to do are not too physically demanding.

If you want good customer service, "Do unto your employees as you would have them do unto your customers."

When he next approaches the employee, the manager should give neutral or positive information first, then make some necessary critical comment, followed quickly by reinforcement to the employee for listening without becoming defensive. On every second or third approach, the supervisor should only present positive or neutral information so that the employee does not associate the supervisor's presence with criticism. As critical comments are introduced gradually, the manager prefaces them with positive or neutral comments and reinforces the employee for listening carefully. If the employee becomes antagonistic, the supervisor has faded in the criticism too fast. If done systematically, reinforcement and fading-in can result in the employee learning to accept criticism appropriately.

Instruction and practice. Instruction and practice can be used with persons who become argumentative about almost anything that the supervisor might say to them. First, the supervisor discusses the problem privately with the person. After praising the employee for positive aspects of his work, she explains that the individual has a habit of not listening to constructive suggestions and of reacting defensively to constructive criticism. If the person argues this point, the manager should respond in a neutral fashion, listening to the person until he finishes. She then repeats the individual's positive work qualities but re-emphasizes that this problem of constant arguing is a habit the employee needs to change.

Ignoring any arguments or hostile comments, the supervisor demonstrates an acceptable way for the employee to respond to supervisory correction. Before the demonstration, she repeats that the person is argumentative and then describes how the employee should respond to criticism.

Following a description of the problem situation and desirable behaviors, and if the argumentative tone has decreased, the supervisor leads a practice session with the employee. "Let's pretend that I am criticizing the way you turn your machine on in the morning." (Select an activity that the person does correctly.) The manager criticizes the employee and then compliments him for paying attention. She then asks the person to respond to the criticism and reinforces the appropriate response. The employee should practice receiving criticism on some other matter with the supervisor reinforcing him for responding properly.

Finally, the manager should choose a third situation that is related directly to the employee's duties, again reinforcing appropriate responses. The supervisor closes by stating that the employee has demonstrated the ability to handle criticism well, that she expects the employee to handle criticism better in the future, and that she will appreciate seeing that change.

Later on the same day, the manager should make a neutral comment to the employee and reinforce him for paying attention as described in the previous section. On the next day, she should mildly criticize the employee and then reinforce the individual appropriately. The remainder of the procedure is as described in the previous section.

Changing Work Behavior Consistent With Criticism

When employees acknowledge supervisory criticisms but do not change their behavior, the manager should use the overcorrection procedures described in Chapter 5, such as response cost, or the "Initiates Action to Correct Mistakes" section in Chapter 7. For those who complain and argue while directions are given, the supervisor should use treatments such as the ones described above for teaching the person to accept criticism.

Interference With the Supervision of Others

An employee may interfere with supervision in several different ways. Some individuals attempt to usurp the supervisory role and direct their co-employees' activities, resulting in resentment and, often, production problems. A practice and reinforcement procedure or a self-instructional training approach should be scheduled to deal with this problem.

Some individuals may interject comments of criticism into the supervisor's effort to instruct, teach, or correct other employees. A combination of extinction, prompting, and negative practice procedures should be used to decrease interference with supervision.

Practice with reinforcement. Initially, the individual is confronted with the fact that he has been attempting to direct others. Should the person deny this type of activity, the supervisor should be prepared to provide specific examples. If the denial continues, the manager should ignore it and initiate the following instructions: "Pretend that another employee in your area is working in a way that you think is wrong. What would you do?" The manager should reinforce such replies as, "I would continue working and not say anything" or "I would report the incident to the supervisor." Of course, the supervisor should determine the appropriateness of reporting the problematic behavior of the other employee. Practice of appropriate responses reinforced by the supervisor should be repeated. One to 2 hours following instruction, the supervisor should reinforce the individual for not directing or "bossing" others. Reinforcement of positive instances of not interfering with others will suppress "bossiness" and increase appropriate responses.

Extinction, prompting, and overcorrection behavior analysis. When the supervisor is correcting or directing another person and an employee interrupts, comments, or complains, she should first ignore the individual (extinction), hoping that the person's inappropriate comments will extinguish. If the individual does not stop, she should be reminded to return to work (prompting), and the manager should talk to her privately about not interfering in the future. For extinction to be successful, the supervisor must persist in ignoring the employee's comments across a number of days. Improvements on the employee's part should be reinforced.

If the individual persists in interfering, the manager should implement an overcorrection behavior-analysis solution. Following the next interruption, the supervisor instructs the employee to complete in writing the familiar form with the numerous open-ended questions: "What was occurring when the incident began?" "What did the other employee do that was inappropriate?" "What should she have done?" "What will you do in the future when this occurs?" If required to complete this form for each interference, the person will quickly learn to suppress this irritating behavior.

Horseplay and Practical Jokes

Generally speaking, the worksite is no place for practical jokes or horseplay. Still, to relieve apparent boredom with their jobs, some workers may initiate such behavior. Several reactions to horseplay on the job are possible.

Overcorrection restitution. In this procedure, the worker is expected to correct for the effects of the horseplay or practical joke.[5] The manager first describes the inappropriate behavior to the worker and the negative effects it had on other workers. Next the worker is instructed to take action to "correct" for the prior negative effects. Both manager and worker may need to determine what those corrective actions should be, such as cleaning up the work area or restocking supplies. It should take the worker about 15 minutes to correct for the inappropriate behavior. After the worker completes the clean-up or restocking, the manager should restate the problem behaviors and the consequences to expect if the worker demonstrates the inappropriate behavior in the future.

For maximum impact, the overcorrection-restitution procedures must be used immediately and consistently after the occurrence of the problem behavior. The manager should also remember that horseplay is one means that the worker has for gaining attention. Hence, the incidence of the problem behaviors may increase during the initial stages of the procedure. However, with consistent application of the overcorrection-restitution consequence, the worker will soon decrease the frequency of the behavior.

Two additional points should be made in reference to application of this procedure. First, workers should be sincerely reinforced when they decrease the frequency of a problem behavior. Second, the manager should remember that the problem behavior was an effort to gain attention. Other, more appropriate, ways exist to gain attention on the job. To provide attention to the worker, the manager needs to provide sincere positive reinforcement to the worker for productive work behaviors. Hence, the supervisor applies a balanced behavior-change strategy in the situation. She decreases the positive reinforcement previously provided for inappropriate behavior, while also applying negative consequences to those same actions. Loss of attention is, however, balanced by provision of attention (positive reinforcement) for desirable performance, thereby coupling a reinforcement approach with the overcorrection strategy.

Other consequences. The manager may add any one of several negative contingencies to the situation immediately following the problem behavior. In addition to the restitution in the previous example, the manager may require the effects on the work environment be corrected during the worker's break time or at the end of the workday. The worker might also be informed that the incident will be recorded in his personnel folder. The supervisor must explain very clearly what the implications are of the first written notation and of any future instances of the behavior.

Obscenities and Vulgarities

To deal with a worker who is cursing at others or at objects in the work environment, the manager may apply several techniques previously described regarding control of temper or decreasing horseplay. However, the manager must first confront the worker with the fact that obscene and vulgar statements or gestures in the workplace are unacceptable. The specific situation in which the behavior occurred should be described along with the rationale for why the behavior is unacceptable. The supervisor and worker should discuss alternative responses to the situation in order to identify appropriate responses for the worker to make.[6]

Modeling and role playing may be used to help the worker acquire alternative, more acceptable, responses to the situation. Contingency management may be needed to decrease the frequency of the cursing. Finally, by monitoring the worker's conversational behavior in the future, the manager can reinforce decreases in obscenities and increases in socially appropriate language and responses. As a result, workers will show considerable improvement in their language on the job.

Bizarre Behaviors and Personal Eccentricities

Some employees have developed habits while working that can be very disruptive in the workplace and, therefore, must be suppressed, if not eliminated. These include continuous humming, whistling, slamming doors and file cabinet drawers, eating potato chips (loudly), letting off gas—at both ends—loudly, or mimicking others. Some of these behaviors, although irritating to other employees, are ignored. Some are dealt with by the employees themselves, "Will you please stop whistling? I can't concentrate on this report which is due." But sometimes, even though the "bothered" employees have asserted themselves, the offender ignores them or takes an oppositional position that he will do as he pleases. It is not his problem if his "knuckle cracking" or "operatic singing" bothers anyone. Instead, he says it's their problem, "Just cover your ears if you don't like it."

When the problem has been brought to the attention of the supervisor, he or she must deal with it. He cannot hope that it will go away, because most of the time it won't. He loses the respect of his employees if he brushes it off with some comment like, "That's just the way he is. Ha, ha. Just ignore him." Even if the supervisor is not bothered by the idiosyncratic behavior, he is the boss and must deal with it in some fashion.

If the complaining employee is one who complains frequently about the behaviors of others, see the earlier section in this chapter on complaining, and talk to the complaining employee about the need for more tolerance of people who do things in different ways. Increase the reinforcement for appropriate work behaviors of the complaining or bothered worker when she is not complaining.

When the behavior is obviously one that bothers other employees and is or can be disruptive to communications or work if it continues, the supervisor has alternatives:

1. Teach the complaining employee to be assertive. Be positive, empathetic, and supportive. Teach the person what to say, how to say it, and even when to say it. Follow up and reinforce.

2. Call in the accused worker if the complaining employee has already asserted herself to no avail, or if the problem is so serious that it is probably causing problems for others also. As described in chapters 11 and 12, first be positive about the employee's appropriate behavior at work and then tell him why he is a valuable employee. Don't ask him whether or not he does the inappropriate behavior. Tell him that it has come to your attention that he is doing it or tell him that a complaint or complaints have been made about his behavior. Inform him that the behavior must cease. If he states that is just a bad habit or that he doesn't realize that he is doing it, tell him that it is understandable and that many people have habits that irritate others, but this one must stop. Ask if he needs help in stopping and reinforce him for any verbal agreement to stop. Within the week, follow up. Don't hesitate to call the person in to reinforce him for his improvement, to ask him how his efforts to stop the behavior are going, or to refer him for help if he is having difficulty with his problem.

Supervisors should be trained and encouraged to refer workers for help when those employees have personal problems or habits that are disruptive. Referral to the personnel department where there may be professionals on the staff or trained counselors should be encouraged. If there is no in-house expertise, the supervisor should have available the names, addresses, and telephone numbers of at least two psychologists, psychiatrists, drug and alcohol counselors, or social workers. Sometimes the employee is more prone to seek help if the supervisor makes the call and then lets the person talk to make the appointment. Sometimes the person needs the support of another, a relative or co-worker, to go for the first appointment.

Occasionally, a behavior is so noticeable that it not only bothers other employees, but it also interferes with the person's ability to acquire and retain a job. Such was the case described in Application 12-3.[7] What do you do with a person who drives a big truck everywhere—an imaginary truck?

Sexual Harassment

Some people use the workplace as a stalking ground to find others who will satisfy their sexual needs. And sometimes they use their sexual overtures as a way to exercise their power over others. Probably no surplus behavior on or off the job can cause more anger, fear, and feelings of helplessness in employees than being subjected to sexual harassment. When such behavior is brought to the attention of a supervisor, he must act to eliminate it with haste because it can cause all kinds of problems in communications, productivity, and absenteeism, and can cause serious legal repercussions as well. The

---

APPLICATION 12-3
He's Still Trucking Along

The counselor at this rehabilitation facility requested consultation on a method to reduce the behavior of driving an imaginary truck by a 17-year-old student. Tony was about to graduate and seek employment. His counselor felt that Tony's visual impairment might make it difficult for him to get a job and his "motoring" behavior might make it impossible.

"Motoring" consisted of driving an imaginary vehicle by making loud motor and transmission noises as he shifted gears (it was an 18-wheeler and required much shifting). He steered the truck down hallways and across the campus. When stopped for a conversation, he would turn off the engine, talk with the person, climb

continued on next page

continued from previous page

back into the cab, restart the engine, and drive away. Although lectured to and scolded by teachers, and teased by his peers, he persisted, claiming he had been trying to stop the motoring for 3 years but when angry, he just wanted to jump in his truck and "smoke 'em." The seriousness of the problem was revealed by a number of brief observations across each day of the baseline. He averaged 47 motoring incidents out of 50 observation periods.

Not wanting to take driving away from this young man who would never be able to obtain a driver's license and who seemed to derive a great deal of pleasure out of "driving his truck," the consultants devised an ABC intervention to reduce the imaginary truck driving by reducing the truck. In the counselor's office, he was again told that his habit of motoring in the big truck would interfere with employment. He agreed that he should stop but that it was a habit. He was given a model sports car in a match box that was labeled "garage." Putting the "garaged vehicle" in his pocket, he practiced removing it from the garage to his hand in his pocket. He then drove it around the office while being reinforced. Next, he was taught to lower his motoring sounds in proportion to the size of the vehicle (a barely audible hum). After mentioning the improvement in Tony's appearance when "motoring" with the small vehicle, his counselor encouraged Tony to practice motor-

ing in the hallways, across campus, and in the dorm. By the fourth week of intervention, driving the imaginary truck had been reduced to 15 of 50 observations.

After contracting to reduce daily driving of the semi-truck to below 6 (goal setting) in exchange for getting a free bowling pass or going to a teenage hangout for an ice cream, Tony reduced driving of the imaginary truck to 2 of 50 observations. By this time, he was choosing daily between a model sports car or a model truck to carry in his pocketed garage. Finally, another incentive was added. Zero imaginary truck driving would earn him a "real" steering wheel and a cassette tape containing the sounds of a "real" 20-gear semi driving across country with accompanying CB chatter, directed at him in his "truck." The steering wheel and cassette were to be used in his room. Don't laugh; it's within the range of other normal but unusual weekend hobbies, such as collecting and playing with model trains, parachute jumping, or listening over and over again to a favorite rock group.

By the way, a year later when the manager of the laundry in another city where Tony worked and his foreman were asked what kind of a worker he was, they replied that he was the best—hard working, cheerful, always there and on time. His foreman then said—he does have this one strange habit. He puts his hand in his pocket and hums loudly when he's hurrying to the bathroom."

behavior-centered management procedures described in the section on bizarre behaviors and personal eccentricities are also applicable to the behaviors of sexual harassment. The manager should be aware that when he confronts the harasser, he may get vehement denials, laughing and joking, accusations that the complainer was asking for it, "I didn't mean anything by it," and even apologies. Regardless, the manager does not need proof of such harassment to say, "If it is occurring, it had better stop right now." Don't get into an argument with an employee, and make sure you follow up as described previously.

Summary

The information in this chapter shows how to enhance on-the-job survival of employees by reducing their behavioral excesses, particularly those excesses that negatively affect the relationships among employees and between employees and their supervisors. An important balance is maintained between (a) decreasing the surplus behaviors with such methods as extinction and negative practice and (b) increasing deficit appropriate behaviors with approaches such as prompting and positive reinforcement.

Punishment by itself is not recommended. It only tells people what behaviors to decrease, not what deficits to increase. Other techniques that clarify expectations and reinforce desirable behaviors are needed to activate and maintain productive behaviors in the workplace.

Many of the behavioral excesses are the products of learning histories in which those behaviors worked for the employees sometimes and in some places. Yet consistency in the application of the behavior-centered management procedures will eliminate or at least bring the behaviors down to an acceptable level. As a result, "everyone wins"—the employee keeps his job, and the manager gets rid of those behaviors that interfere with work.

NOTES

1. McKelvey, Engen, & Peck (1973).
2. Brown (1982).
3. Weitzel, Schwarzkopf, & Peach (1989).
4. Weitzel et al. (1989), p. 29.
5. Foxx & Bechtel (1982).
6. D'Zurilla (1986).
7. Marr, Hinman, & Bush (1979).

ABC From
Top to Bottom

CHAPTER 13

Managing Management Behavior

It should be clear by now that the behavior-centered approach has been used to make very significant changes in the behaviors of employees in business, industry, and human-service delivery organizations. The behaviors targeted for change directly affect outcomes that are not only the goals of organizational leaders but also the measures of their success. Examples of such outcomes influenced by the behavior-centered approach include the number of products produced (Chapter 6), the quality of work (Chapter 7), absenteeism and tardiness (Chapter 8), safety (Chapter 9), and health (Chapter 10).

Throughout the book, we have stressed that the ABCs of the behavior-centered approach focus on behavior. Additionally, we have demonstrated the importance of the manager in delivering these ABCs. In other words, the antecedents (A) that affect the behaviors of employees are behaviors of managers. The consequences (C) that affect employee behaviors are behaviors of managers, too. Manager behaviors, employee behaviors, manager behaviors. Behaviors, behaviors, behaviors.

If It's Good Enough for Me

In our institutes on the behavior-centered approach, it is not difficult to convince the manager participants that the ABC methods are effective and that the A's and the C's are the responsibility of the manager. They will also agree that if they change the behaviors of the employees, the targeted outcomes will change in the desired direction as well. Outcomes that were unsatisfactory become satisfactory, and those that were satisfactory become superior whether those outcomes address accident rates, low productivity, customer complaints, turnover, absenteeism, or profit. But, at the end of our workshops, managers often raise a very serious issue. They say that their management behaviors have changed or will change, but how about the behaviors of their own bosses? "So we go back and use these procedures and even train our assistant managers and department supervisors to be specific, to follow up more, and to catch employees doing something right. But who is telling our bosses to do the same thing?"

Here is an example cited by one participant. "The district manager calls a meeting of my management team and stands there pounding the table. He berates everyone about the condition of the store and sermonizes about poor attitudes and the need to instill motivation; yet he never mentions to the team that he is impressed with the reduction in customer complaints, the low shrinkage, or the increase in sales."

We heard this complaint so many times that we invited one group of managers to write a scenario that demonstrates how their bosses should behave when they call a team meeting after an inspection of the premises. After they were satisfied with the scenario, we arranged for them to videotape it. Next, we sent the tape to headquarters so the "bosses" could see it (we put a disclaimer on the front saying that the managers played the roles under our direction). We would like to say that all bosses saw it and immediately changed their behaviors. Alas, that was the last we saw or heard of the videotape.

Supervisors, of course, are influenced by the ABCs just as employees are. And like employees, they also can be influenced by the ABC approach. For example, we have counseled managers in how to use prompts and suggestions to their bosses (A) to redirect or produce appropriate feedback behaviors. We have demonstrated how employees can provide positive statements as consequences (C) when the boss gives feedback with specific suggestions or directions or positive reinforcement to workers for improvements in outcomes. Therefore, we have one practical answer to the question "How do we encourage those managers to use the behavior-centered approach?" *Use the ABC approach to promote the use of the ABC approach.*

Our simple principle in the previous paragraph is, unfortunately, rarely followed. Usually the CEO, the head of personnel, or the plant manager schedules other managers, supervisors, directors, and foremen for a behavior-centered workshop. We would like to say that the antecedent of training is sufficient, but, as was seen throughout this book, it is not. In fact, even when the trainees are overwhelmingly enthusiastic about the material presented, very few report using the procedures 6, 12, 24, or 36 months after the workshop.[1] These results are even more disappointing when considered in light of statements made by the participants during or right after the training workshops: "Wow"; "Right on"; "This is exactly what I need"; and "I know exactly what to do when I get back to work."

We do know how to influence managers to adopt behavior practices. However, before we discuss that issue, we will first examine the types of behaviors characteristic of effective and ineffective managers and supervisors. Research tells us that effective managers spend more time monitoring the specific behaviors of their employees. Therefore, if managers want supervisors to use the ABCs, managers must follow up with the supervisors to see that they are performing as expected.

Supervisory Behavior

Much has been written about how supervisors should supervise employees, but most of it is speculation and little is based upon hard data. To collect data about effective supervision, we first need a system that helps us understand the "what" and "when" of supervision; in other words, what antecedents and consequences should we use in different situations? We need "reasonable taxonomies of what leaders and followers actually do when they interact."[2]

The Operant Supervisory Taxonomy and Index (OSTI) is one such system.[3] Based on operant conditioning, the OSTI examines three categories of supervisory behaviors: (a) performance antecedents—instructions about worker's performance, (b) performance monitors—collecting information about worker's performance, and (c) performance consequences—indicating to the worker that the supervisor has information on performance. When the following four categories are added, the OSTI covers every behavior of a supervisor: (a) references to the supervisor's own performance, (b) references to work (but not performance), (c) nonwork related statements, and (d) solitary behavior (not involved with employees).[4]

Field tests of the OSTI established the reliability of observations in two very different settings (see note 3). One was in a theater department of a university where 7 managers of a musical production were observed for an extended period of time (189 observations). Conducted in a bank, the second study involved the performance of 20 managers who worked in branch administration, data processing, loan administration, and personnel. Management ranged from the vice-president to the lowest level of teller supervisor (440 observations). Not only was the OSTI successful in discriminating among all managers—that is, it yielded unique profiles of management styles for each—but it also showed that, across time, the work-related behavior of managers in the theater declined as solitary behavior increased.

Table 13-1 shows the average percentage of time the managers in each setting spent in each supervisory category. As can be seen in that table, different patterns of supervisory behavior were found in the two settings. Whereas the theater managers spent over one-fourth of the time supervising others (antecedents, monitors, and consequences), the bank managers spent only one-sixth of their time involved in these activities. Such differences may reflect different requirements of employees and their tasks in those settings.

Now for the obvious next question about the OSTI—do behavioral observations recorded using the OSTI categories distinguish between more- and less-effective managers? Ideally, we need to identify such classes of managers by outcomes such as quantity or quality of production, net profits, or absenteeism and safety records of their employees. Then the research question becomes, "In similar settings, can we identify managers whose employees regularly produce superior outcomes and those whose employees regularly produce unsatisfactory outcomes?" Although that study has not been done yet, the question was partially answered by asking upper-level management to identify effective and marginally effective managers in the company.[5] Unfortunately, a more objective index of effectiveness was not used because of organizational constraints such as different sizes and functions of the departments managed. The findings in that study are discussed in Application 13-1.

The results suggest that there are some real differences in behaviors between those managers judged by their bosses to be effective and those judged to be marginally effective. Of course, constraints placed on the research may have distorted the findings somewhat. For example, all 24 managers knew they were being studied even though they did not know when they would be

TABLE 13-1

Percentage of Time Engaged in OSTI Categories

Category	Theater Managers	Bank Managers
Consequences	5.3	4.9
Monitors	11.3	4.3
Antecedents	11.1	5.8
Work-Related	32.2	23.2
Non-Work-Related	2.8	2.7
Own Performance	—	3.9
Solitary	37.3	55.0

The division vice-presidents in a large midwestern medical insurance firm were asked to identify a group of effective managers and another group of marginally effective managers. Based on these ratings, the top 28% and bottom 28%, 14 managers each, were selected as representative of effective and marginally effective groups.

Next, observers trained in the use of the OSTI observed each of the 28 managers across twenty 30-minute periods from October through April. Observers did not know in which classification (effective or marginally effective) the individual managers belonged, and the managers did not know when they were to be observed.

The results of the study showed that the two groups were almost identical in the amount of time they devoted to interacting with employees, discussing work, talking about performance-related matters, delivering antecedents, and providing performance consequences. The major differences were that the effective managers spent close to 50% more time collecting employee performance information, and more often actually sampled the work of the employees instead of asking the employee or asking somebody else about the employees' performance. In other words, don't ask. Go look.

observed. If we are aware of being observed, we may behave as we think we should, not as we usually behave with employees, spouses, and children.

Implementation Suggestions

The applications throughout this book support our assertion that manager behaviors affect employee behaviors that contribute to organizational goals. But how do we encourage managers to display those behaviors more often? What can higher-level management do to get first-line supervisors to use behavior-management procedures? First, if we want them to use antecedent, monitoring, and consequence behaviors, we should use them also, a message we frequently stress with parents. If you want your children to act politely, you should model politeness around the home. If we want them to carry their dirty plates from the table to the dishwasher, we should do the same. Following that rule, the consultants at a large rehabilitation center in Tennessee tried to increase supervisors' use of behavioral procedures when working with rehabilitation clients in their workshops and vocational classes.[6] Application 13-2 shows what happened.

APPLICATION 13-2
They Must Be Serious About This Stuff!

In 1983, the executive director of the rehabilitation centers of the state of Tennessee reopened a large comprehensive rehabilitation center which had been closed because of bureaucratic infighting, legal problems, staff-client dissatisfaction, etc.[7] Prior to opening the center, he arranged for the behavior-centered consultants to train and consult with management and employees in regard to the ABC approach to management and supervision of employees and clients. All management levels and employees were first given a 3-day training workshop on the behavior-centered approach. Managers and supervisors were also taught how to give follow-up training as new employees came on board.

Next, the consultants placed an expert on the use of these procedures in one department to model the correct use of the procedures of rehabilitation clients. These demonstrations occurred 5 days a week for 3 weeks and then 3 days a week for 6 weeks. Next the model was moved to Department Two where he modeled and consulted with supervisors and employees at first 1 day a week and then for 4 hours a week. After 6 weeks, he was moved to Department Three, which was responsible for vocational training in a number of areas, including sheet metal, secretarial, drafting, small engine repair, upholstery, etc. Supervisors and instructors met with him to see the ABC approach applied to their areas.

After modeling the approach within a department, middle-level managers were taught how to monitor the applications of ABC on a weekly basis. Weekly, on random days, each foreman and staff member was visited for approximately 10 to 15 minutes by the manager to inquire about the utilization of ABC that week.

Data were collected by randomly sampling two staff from each department every 3 weeks to obtain their reports of utilization of behavioral procedures with staff and clients. In addition, every behavioral plan written across the 18 months of the study was collected. Those included names, objectives, specific behaviors targeted, type of intervention, and graphs of progress.

Figures 13-1 and 13-2 show the change in procedures and plans as modeling and then supervisory modeling was introduced in the departments. Modeling by itself had little effect, but supervisory monitoring of utilization did produce improvement.

FIGURE 13-1

Average Number of Procedures
Reported in Interviews

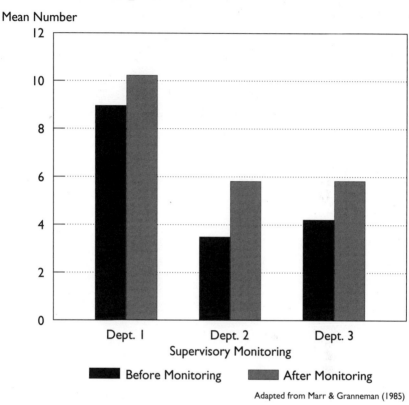

Mean Number

Adapted from Marr & Granneman (1985)

   Notice how little the demonstrations of the behavioral procedures affected utilization. Prior to the modeling, every supervisor had attended at least one 3-day workshop on the applications of behavioral approaches to modify the behaviors of the vocational rehabilitation trainees. Also, prior to the modeling phase, every supervisor had heard the director state that this is the way it's going to be; that is, the center was going to base its rehabilitation and training efforts on the ABC model.

   The plan was for staff to target specific behaviors of clients such as increasing productions skills, decreasing errors, decreasing tardiness, and increasing the wearing of appropriate work clothes and shoes. They would use antecedent

FIGURE 13-2

Total Behavioral Plans Written per Period

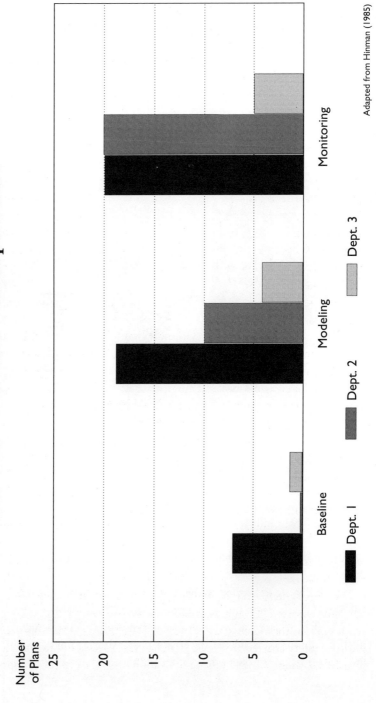

Adapted from Hinman (1985)

techniques such as stimulus control, clearly stated objectives and directions, and training. They were going to reinforce improvement, success, and effort. But, even though an expert modeled use of the procedures and answered questions, those supervisors who had cheered the plan, had testified to its need, and had given the highest grades to the training did not systematically use the techniques until their own supervisors followed up on the application of the procedures.

In most organizations, the middle-level supervisor would not know whether the first-line supervisors were actually using the ABC procedures unless direct monitoring of those supervisors was done. Periodic and frequent visits to the area of responsibility of the first-line supervisors would allow verification of the use of antecedents and consequences (see Application 13-1: "Don't Ask, Go Look"). Positive reinforcement in cases where applications are observed, and prompting and directing their use when they have not been used, will soon produce the correct supervisory behaviors, just as these procedures have been shown to be successful with other behaviors of employees.

Making such institutional changes requires commitment and follow-up from the top on down. In an interesting study of methods to produce change in a large rehabilitation organization, three outside consultants and their assistants interviewed all of the 300 employees using the ABC format: (B) What behaviors of you or others keeps you from doing your job better? (C) What are the consequences of those behaviors? (A) What do you believe causes that problem or prevents you from correcting the problem?[8]

Based on employee reports, over 100 recommendations for change were made to the supervisor of the institution. He then directed that committees of three or more be formed to study, reject, or act on each recommendation. In addition, he participated in many of the committee meetings to make sure that the only thing decided was not when the next meeting would occur. Next, he prompted monitoring by asking for a written report from each committee on its decisions and progress. The institution renewed itself because the director (a) allowed his staff to be interviewed by, and to complain to, a group of "outsiders" and (b) followed up with procedures to correct problems and monitor progress.

A more structured procedure used by upper-level managers was seen in the study reported in Application 9-3. Supervisors were trained, directed, and reinforced for the systematic application of behavior-centered procedures to improve safety and reduce accidents. The great success of the intervention as measured by net savings to the organization of $55,000 across 6 months was attributed to the application of the ABC procedures from the upper-level management, vice-president of manufacturing and president of the company, through the middle-level management, director and directors of departments, down to the front-line supervisors.[9] Table 13-2 shows examples of how the specific behaviors of different levels of supervisors were described.

It is also important to note that the supervisors were not just told to review the progress weekly with the workers in their units. They were trained in how to do this. Managers modeled the correct method of gathering the workers around the safety progress charts, giving positive feedback, and even how to make a "big deal" over success in meeting subgoals. Furthermore, supervisors were given written instructions and informal feedback on their performance.

As Table 13-2 shows, everybody was involved. Enthusiasm for the program ranged from the president to the employees. The president of corporate headquarters was so impressed with the safety outcomes that he disseminated details of the methods throughout the company and expanded the program to other parts of the plant.

Implementation via Management Antecedent Behaviors

Whether action starts at the level of the CEO, corporate president, operations vice-president, plant manager, or division director, we will refer to that person as the behavior-centered leader (BCL) to illustrate the approach. The BCL must first call together those people who report to him or her. He must clearly describe his expectations that the ABC procedures are to be used in management at all levels. If the BCL does not target an outcome such as safety, production, quality of product, or shrinkage, he should ask his managers to suggest an outcome that will be changed using ABC.

Following selection of an outcome, managers are to call their department heads or supervisors together and ask them for suggestions about how to achieve the outcome. The supervisors are also directed to obtain suggestions from their employees. The BCL needs to set a specific time table and method for getting feedback on suggestions from managers and supervisors. The BCL doesn't wait for the suggestions to roll in, but monitors on a weekly or even daily basis, what is happening, giving reinforcement or taking corrective action as appropriate. When delays occur, the BCL must communicate that they are unacceptable and that he expects action.

Once that feedback is taking place, he should initiate action, being sure to clarify who, what, where, and when in specific terms. Training of managers at all levels may be needed in how to specify targeted behaviors, how to train supervisors or employees, and how to teach supervisors to be positive.

TABLE 13-2

Specific Antecedent and Consequence Behaviors

Director	Manager	Front-line Supervisor
Includes safety performance as an objective in manager's MBO	Encourages suggestions by supervisors and workers that may improve safety	Encourages workers to suggest ways to improve safety within their departments
Prepares and maintains safety performance chart for v.p. of safety department	Includes safety performance as an objective in supervisor's MBO	Spots opportunities for improved safety which employee reviews with managers
Monthly reinforces one supervisor selected by manager for superior safety performance of section	Provides director with weekly safety performance updates	Gives positive feedback to employees during weekly meetings
Selects department to receive quarterly Best Safety Performance Award	Reinforces supervisors whose units meet or exceed goal	Reinforces individual employees for safe performance

Knowledgeable and capable persons within the organization may be available to train, or outside consultants who specialize in the behavior-centered approach might be invited to train and consult at any or all levels. The chain of A-B-C from upper levels of management down through the ranks to the employee is illustrated in Figure 13-3. Monitoring and follow-up are essential.

FIGURE 13-3

Managing Managers
ABC Activities From Top to Bottom

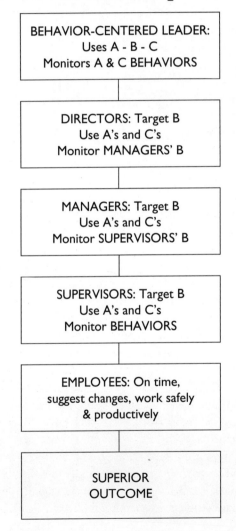

BEHAVIOR-CENTERED LEADER:
Uses A - B - C
Monitors A & C BEHAVIORS

DIRECTORS: Target B
Use A's and C's
Monitor MANAGERS' B

MANAGERS: Target B
Use A's and C's
Monitor SUPERVISORS' B

SUPERVISORS: Target B
Use A's and C's
Monitor BEHAVIORS

EMPLOYEES: On time,
suggest changes, work safely
& productively

SUPERIOR
OUTCOME

Implementation via Management Consequence Behaviors

Figure 13-3 illustrates why the chain of management is not just a passive diagram of authority but a set of active behavioral links. Notice how the BCL reinforces the directors and managers for specific management behaviors. By monitoring their actions, the BCL is able to reinforce goal setting, training, planning, directing, and reinforcing of behaviors in others.

Monitoring behaviors is important and also needs to be reinforced. A number of years ago, teachers in one school were asked to identify the most serious behavioral problems in their classrooms.[10] The teachers were then asked to direct and train their assistants to reinforce the problem children when they were doing the right thing, for example, on-task behavior, following directions, etc. After 3 weeks, the teachers were asked to reinforce their assistants for reinforcing the children. Notice the effect of this consequence to the aides *on the children's behavior* in Figure 13-4. "Why do the children improve even more in this second phase?" we ask the managers in our behavior-centered workshops. "Because people do more of those behaviors for which they receive reinforcement," they reply. The aides received reinforcement for reinforcing the children and increased their frequency of reinforcement.

Summary

Throughout the book, we have shown how the behavior-centered approach changes the behavior of employees and increases the effectiveness of an organization. Applications have identified ABC strategies that affect productivity, safety, health, absenteeism, and net profit. Research with the Operant Taxonomy of Supervisory Behaviors has indicated that effective managers devote a greater amount of time to directly monitoring employees' behaviors. Similarly, the services of a large rehabilitation center improved when supervisory monitoring began on a regular basis after staff had been trained to use and consultants had modeled the appropriate use of the ABC procedures. And yet, supervisors complain that upper- and mid-level management fails to apply the behavior-centered techniques in their management of managers. What can be done about the implementation problem?

Managers can learn to manage managers more effectively, but first they must learn to identify specific outcomes and the behaviors required to achieve those outcomes. Then they must use appropriate antecedent and consequence behaviors up and down the management ladder to influence managers to use behavior-centered strategies. As each level of management prompts and reinforces those below, it must, in turn, be prompted and reinforced by those

FIGURE 13-4

Chaining the Reinforcement Effect

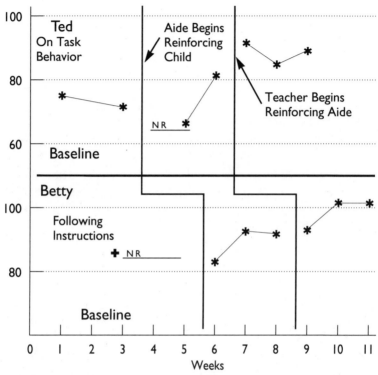

NR: No Record this week
Adapted from study by Marr, Everett, Allegretti, Cochran, & Fitzgerald (1980)

above. Antecedents and consequences are needed at all organizational levels to forge active links in a chain that can significantly improve outcomes in business, industry, and human-service delivery organizations.

NOTES

1. Marr & Greenwood (1979).
2. Campbell (1971), p. 234.
3. Komaki, Zlotnick, & Jensen (1986).

4. Subdivisions and definitions of each of the seven categories are provided in Komaki, Zlotnick, & Jensen (1986).

5. Komaki (1986).

6. Marr & Granneman (1985); Hinman (1985).

7. Sharrer (1985).

8. Marr, Roessler, & Greenwood (1976).

9. Sulzer-Azaroff et al. (1990).

10. Marr, Everett, Allegretti, Cochran, & Fitzgerald (1980).

Appendix

Proving It With Hard Data the Easy Way

The question asked by many managers is "Will behavior-centered management work in my department, store, plant, or center?" In this book, we have presented convincing evidence that the behavior-centered approach is an effective method for changing work behaviors. We have also presented evidence that modifying work behaviors changes the outcomes of production, tardiness, safety, health, sales, and even employee satisfaction. But will those methods be as effective in your setting? Although the ABC procedures have been thoroughly researched, there is always the concern that changes in settings or people could change the results.

How can you test the ABC method in your setting with your people to convince you, your boss, your employees, or even your stockholders that the behavior-centered management procedures are effective? The answer is simple: Work behaviors or the products of those behaviors must change when the ABC procedures are initiated. With that as our goal, we turn to some easy methods of demonstrating the effectiveness of the interventions.

First, a target behavior or product of that behavior must be selected. If you choose a target behavior, it should be performance-related. That is, it should be a behavior that has an effect on the outcome. Sometimes it is easier to target a product of the behavior. For example, if we want to increase production in the bakery, we can target mixing the ingredients (behavior) or placing the dough in the pans (behavior); or we can choose to target the number of loaves of bread baked (product of behavior). The applications presented in this book sometimes targeted behaviors and sometimes targeted products of those behaviors.

Table A-1 shows the various targets of some of those applications. Sometimes the behaviors that the manager wanted to modify were closely related to the products measured, and sometimes they were not. For example, the number of orders of fresh fish dinners is closely related to whether or not the waitresses suggested fresh fish, but the work capacity of firefighters, which was measured in Application 10-3, was not closely related to the targeted behavior of exercising.

TABLE A-1

Behaviors (B) and Products (P) Measured in Applications

Measure	Application	Target Behavior
B	9-4	Styrene exposure behaviors of four different types
B	8-1	Punctuality: Measured the number of employees late per day and graphed the percentage of employees present
B	4-3	Selling to include conversing with, assisting, or showing merchandise to customers, as well as ringing up sales or filling out charge slips
P	2-2	Theft: Measured by subtracting the number of sales plus the number of items on hand from the number of items there prior to intervention
P	4-6	Driving: Measured odometer on vehicles daily and verified readings of odometers eight times per month
P	4-1	Suggesting fresh fish entrees to the restaurant customers: measured percentage of fresh fish orders on the restaurant bills

Regardless of whether the behavior or a product of that behavior was selected, the target could be reliably measured. Managers did not select "work ethic," "work attitude," or "motivation" of employees, but instead measured something that was directly observable. If two or more persons went out into the plant or store to measure the targeted behavior or product, would they come back with the same number?

Easy Ways to Measure

Whatever is targeted, it should be easy to measure. Managers are too busy to spend a lot of time trying to take elaborate or complex measures. Some easy ways to take measurements are frequency counts, interval counts, time-sample counts, and duration measurement.

Frequency counts. How many days a week was he late? How many customers did he wait on during the day? How many parts that he painted had a flaw? We get the answer to each of these questions by taking a frequency count. The frequency can be converted into a percentage measure by dividing the frequency observed by the total number possible. Of the 5 days this week, he was late twice, 40%. Of the 80 employees in the department, 60 were wearing goggles, 75%.

It is not necessary to observe the person during the whole day to get a reliable measure. During the first 15 minutes or during the last 15 minutes of her shift, how many customers did she greet? As long as we take our counts during the same period every day, we can compare her performance during the baseline phase with that after we have initiated the intervention.

Duration. How many total minutes was he late coming to work, returning from breaks, and returning from lunch? How long does it take him to complete the report once he has received it? In each case, we are taking a duration measure.

Interval and time-sample recording. If we break the workday into eight 1-hour intervals, or if we break the 1 hour into six 10-minute intervals, we can use interval or time-sample measures. In interval recording, we are only concerned with whether or not he performed the behavior at any time during an interval, not how many times he did it. In time-sample recording, we are only concerned with whether or not she was performing the target behavior *at the end of the interval.*

Table A-2 illustrates the different types of measures as applied to the problem of an employee who spends too much time talking and not enough time working. Connie works on the assembly line but often leaves her workstation to socialize with other workers or talks to others while at her workstation. When she does this, she either is not there putting the three gaskets on the product or she is careless with their placement, and the product must be rejected by quality-control inspectors. The manager targets her socialization at and away from her workstation.

Although the frequency count shows a higher number of socializing incidents than the interval or time sample method, it has two disadvantages. If Connie had left her workstation to talk with Betty (B) for a half hour during the 2-hour observation period and had worked the remainder of the time, the frequency would have been 1 and would not have reflected accurately the lost

TABLE A-2

Measures of Connie's Social Behavior

Time	Activity	Frequency	Interval	Time Sample	Duration
1:00	Working (W)				
1:05	W				
1:10	W & talking to A	1			
1:15	Walks over to A while talking		1	1	
End of Interval					
Continues Talk					10 min.
1:20	Returns to work				
1:25	W & talking to B	1			
1:30	W		1	0	5 min.
End of Interval					
1:35	W				
1:36	Walks over to C	1			
1:40	Returns to work				
1:45	W		1	0	4 min.
End of Interval					
1:50	W				
1:52	W & talking to C	1			
1:55	W & talking to A	1			
2:00	W & still talking to A		1	1	
End of Interval					

Time	Activity				
2:05	Walks over to A				
2:10	Returns to work				
2:12	Walks over to A and talks	1			18 min.
2:15			1	1	
	End of Interval				
2:20	Returns to work				8 min.
2:25	W		0	0	
2:30	W				
	End of Interval				
2:35	W				
2:38	Talking to A	1			
2:40	Talking to B	1			
2:45	Walks over to C	1	1	1	12 min.
	End of Interval				
2:50	Returns to W	1			
2:55	W & talking to A		1	1	5 min.
3:00	W & talking to A				
	End of Interval				
Total		10	7	5	62 min.
Total Time to Make Observations		120 Min.	71 Min.	16 Sec.	120 Min.

production time. Secondly, the frequency count would have required the manager, or somebody else, to observe her during the full 2 hours. Although the duration measure is the most sensitive measure for this type of problem, it also would require 2 hours of observation.

The interval count only requires a "yes" or "no" for a 15-minute period. It does not require a count of how many times she socialized during the 15-minute period, only whether she did it at all during the targeted period of time. Once she had started to talk to somebody during the interval, the observer records a "yes," and then doesn't have to observe her for the rest of the interval. However, in this illustration, it still required a total of 71 minutes of observation. Thus, the interval measure requires more personnel resources than the time-sample method. The time sample only requires the manager to look at Connie at the end of each of the 15-minute periods to see whether or not she is talking. It misses some of the occasions when Connie talks, but it only requires 16 seconds of observation across the 2 hours, assuming that it takes only 2 seconds at the end of each of the 15-minute intervals to determine whether Connie is talking or not. Remember, we do not have to have an exact measure of the severity of the problem, but we do need a reliable measure that can be compared across periods or groups.

Research Designs in ABC Applications

In order to demonstrate the effectiveness of their interventions, the authors of the studies cited in the applications used one of several types of research designs. The simplest of the traditional designs incorporates an experimental group and a control group. The experimental group receives the treatment or intervention and the control group does not. The treatment is referred to as the *independent variable,* and the measure of its effectiveness is referred to as the *dependent variable.*

This type of comparison of experimental and control groups was illustrated in Application 5-1 where retail clerks in the experimental group were reinforced for retail behaviors while those in the control group were not. Figure 5-1 shows the improvement in retail behaviors and the decrease in idle behaviors that occurred in the experimental group that did not occur in the control group. Similarly, Application 6-1 described the use of an experimental/control group design when quality circles were introduced in one division of a manufacturing plant. There the graph shown in Figure 6-1 revealed the increase in productivity of the experimental group of machine operators while the control group did not change. The major criticism of that study was that the quality-circle group members were volunteers and the control-group members were not. Another illustration of the traditional experimental/-control-group design was shown in Application 8-1 where one group of employees who had frequently been tardy were given weekly bonuses for being on time. The control-group employees were not given the bonuses during the 77 weeks of the study and showed no change in tardiness.

Rather than the traditional experimental/control-group approach, most of our applications use research designs that are commonly called single-subject designs; for example, the *reversal replication designs* and *multiple baseline designs*. In both designs, we are trying to learn whether (a) the treatment or intervention is affecting the targeted employee outcomes and (b) specific employee behaviors are changing as expected.

In the *reversal-replication design,* we first collect data on the dependent variable for a period of time to determine how often the behavior occurs before the intervention begins. This period of no treatment is called the *baseline* period. When the *intervention* begins, we compare the change in behavior (if any) to the behavior during the baseline period. Next, we remove the intervention and continue to measure the behavior (*reversal*—return to baseline conditions). Finally, we reintroduce the intervention (*replication*) to see if it again has the effect on the behavior. This type of design was seen in Application 4-1 where first the percentage of fresh fish sold by each waitress was determined from the bills paid by the customers at the cash register. Then during the first intervention period, the manager offered an incentive so the waitresses would suggest fresh fish at the time orders were placed. Even though there was a 30% increase in fresh fish sold, the manager removed the incentive for a week, the reversal or return to baseline period, and then reintroduced the incentive to determine whether or not the incentive was the factor causing the improvement in sales (It was!). Reversal designs are convincing because we can see the change in our dependent variable (behavior or product of behavior) as we introduce the treatment, remove it, and reintroduce it. If we didn't repeat the introduction of the intervention, we couldn't be sure whether the change in our dependent variable was due to the intervention, a change in the weather, or a rumor about a pay raise.

Multiple Baseline Designs

Another way to determine whether or not our intervention causes the change in behavior is through the use of a multiple baseline design. A multiple baseline can be across different behaviors of the same person, the same behaviors across different departments (Figure 4-3), or even the same behaviors across different workers (Figure 7-1). For example, after collecting baseline data in two departments, we begin an intervention on a certain date in only one of those departments. At a later date we start the intervention in the second department. This delay allows us to see if the change in behavior that occurs is due to the intervention or something else in the plant that may have occurred at the same time; for example, installation of Muzak or a rumored or actual pay increase.

Application A-1 describes the use of a multiple baseline design to show the effect of a token economy on lost-time accidents in open-pit mines. In each mine, a baseline period allowed the measurement of the lost-time accidents (frequency) and the number of days lost due to each accident (severity) before the behavioral intervention was begun. The baseline measurement period included those years when extensive training on safety was an on-going activity.[1] If the procedure had only been used in one mine, we would not be sure whether the changes that took place were due to the token economy, some new company policy, or a change in union contracts. But when the change in lost-time accidents occurred in both mines only when the token economy was

---

APPLICATION A-I

Money for Mining but Stamps for Safety

In this study, a token economy was used to treat the safety problems at two dangerous open-pit mines located in Wyoming and Arizona. Prior to the behavioral intervention, the yearly average number of days lost from work due to on-the-job injuries was approximately eight times the national average (for all mines) at one of the mines and approximately three times the national average at the second mine.

Data were collected on number of days lost because of an injury, number of lost-time injuries, and direct costs of injuries (compensation insurance, medical costs, and costs of equipment repair or replacement).

Prior to intervention, extensive safety training on hazard identification, correction, and avoidance was given, including use and maintenance of personal protective equipment. Safety training was on-going, and employees were encouraged to notify supervisors of hazardous conditions.

One month before intervention, all workers who had not had a lost-time injury for the 2 previous years at the Shirley Basin uranium mine (1 year at Navajo coal mine) received 10,000 trading stamps which could be exchanged at neighboring redemption stores that carried several hundred items of merchandise. When the

continued on next page

continued from previous page
token economy was begun, workers received stamps at the end of each month if they had not suffered a lost-time injury that required a physician's care during the month. The number of stamps depended upon the safety hazards of the job, 300–700 stamps. In addition, all workers managed by a common supervisor received 200–800 stamps if no one under that supervisor had received a lost-time injury that month. Employee safety suggestions adopted by the mines on the basis of recommendations from a committee that included workers also earned from 500 to 25,000 stamps. A response cost in stamps was also instituted. Missed days because of an injury cost the person anywhere from 1 to 6 months' worth of stamps and cost the group 1 month. Damaged equipment cost 1 month of stamps for each $2,000 in damage costs.

The results of this intervention at each mine are shown in Figure A-1 and A-2. As can be seen, the token economy interventions at the mines produced dramatic improvements in number of injuries and number of days lost. Cost of injuries per year at each mine declined by over a quarter million dollars. Cost ratios (dollars saved over dollars spent on token economies) ranged from 18 to 28 at the uranium mine and from 13 to 21 at the coal mine. Injuries during the previous 10 years were about one-fourth the national average at the Shirley Basin mine and about one-twelfth at the Navajo mine.

How important were the tokens for the employees? The local union at one mine requested the program be put into the contract with the company and, when the stamps were left out of pay envelopes, one wife called and demanded her husband's stamps and another drove 50 miles to get "her" stamps.

initiated, we can be fairly certain that the change was due to the token economy. Note that if the token economy had been initiated in both mines at the same time and the same degrees in accidents had occurred, we could not attribute the changes to the token economy because they may have been due to a change in national safety laws or union activity common to both sites.

The validity of the conclusions drawn by the researchers depends upon replication. The more often the researcher has replicated (repeated) the treatment and the effects on behavior and outcomes, the more confidence that we can have in the results. We should also note that the more similar the setting of an application is to the actual setting in which the manager plans to intervene, the more likely the manager will achieve outcomes similar to those in the application.

FIGURE A-1

Effects of a Token Economy on Days Lost for Work-Related Injuries

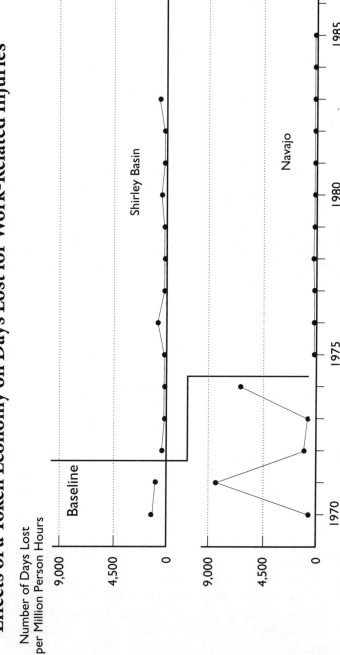

The yearly number of days lost from work, per million person hours worked, because of work-related injuries.

Fox, Hopkins, & Anger (1987)

FIGURE A-2

Effects of a Token Economy on Number of Lost-Time Injuries

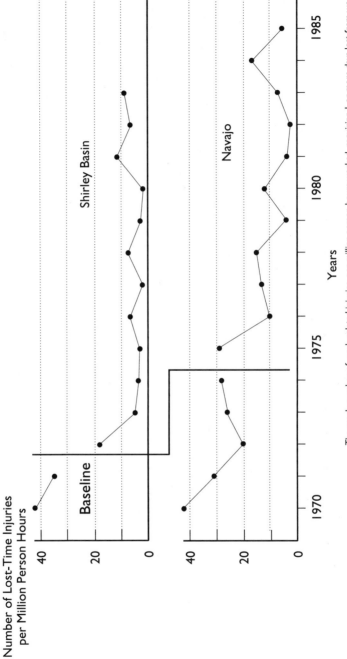

Number of Lost-Time Injuries
per Million Person Hours

The yearly number of work-related injuries, per million person hours worked, requiring 1 or more days lost from work.

Fox, Hopkins, & Anger (1987)

NOTE

1. Fox, Hopkins, & Anger (1987).

Bibliography

Adler, T. (1991). Studies sniff out fragrance effects. *APA Monitor, 22,* pp. 5, 18.

Allenspech, H. (1972). Flexible working time: Its development and application in Switzerland. *Occupational Psychology, 46*(4), 209–215.

Anderson, D. C., Crowell, C., Hantula, D., & Siroky, L. (1988). Task clarification and individual performance posting for improving cleaning in a student-managed university bar. *Journal of Organizational Behavior Management, 9*(2), 73–90.

Anderson, D. C., Crowell, C., Sucec, J., Gilligan, K. D., & Wikoff, M. (1983). Behavior management of client contacts in a real estate brokerage: Getting agents to sell more. *Journal of Organizational Behavior Management, 4*(2), 67–95.

Andrasik, F., & McNamara, J. R. (1977). Optimizing staff performance in an institutional behavior change system: A pilot study. *Behavior Modification, 1*(2), 235–248.

Bandura, A. (1986). *Social foundations of thought and action: A social-cognitive theory.* Englewood Cliffs, NJ: Prentice-Hall.

Barra, R. J. (1983). *Putting quality circles to work.* New York: McGraw-Hill.

Beckman, A. R., & Marr, J. N. (1988). Effects of goal setting, feedback and reinforcement to increase suggestive selling. Unpublished manuscript, University of Arkansas, Fayetteville.

Beer, M., & Walton, E. (1990). Developing the competitive organization: Interventions and strategies. *American Psychologist, 45*(2), 154–161.

Bem, D. J. (1968). Attitudes as self-descriptions: Another look at the attitude behavior link. In G. Breenwald, T. C. Brock, & T. M. Ostrom (Eds.), *Psychological Foundations of Attitudes,* 197–215. New York: Academic Press.

Bingham, E., Niemeer, R. W., & Reid, J. B. (1976). Multiple factors in carcinogenesis. In V. Saffioti & J. K. Wagoner (Eds.), Occupational carcinogenesis, *Annals of the New York Academy of Sciences, 271,* 14–21.

Black, J. L. (1978). *Shoplifting control through feedback to sales personnel.* Unpublished doctoral dissertation, University of North Carolina, Greensboro.

Blanchard, K., & Lorber, R. (1981). *The one minute manager.* New York: Morrow.

Blanchard, K., & Lorber, R. (1984). *Putting the one minute manager to work.* New York: Morrow.

Bowne, D. W., Russell, M. L., Morgan, M. A., Optenberg, S., & Clarke, A. (1984). Reduced disability and health care costs in an industrial fitness program. *Journal of Occupational Medicine, 26*(11), 809–816.

Broedling, L. A., & Hubb, K. H. (1983). *Productivity enhancement in the navy using behavioral science approaches.* Paper presented at the annual meeting of the American Psychological Association, Anaheim, CA.

Brown, P. (1982). *Managing behaviors on the job.* New York: Wiley.

Cady, L. D., Thomas, P. C., & Karwasky, R. J. (1985). Program for increasing health and physical fitness of firefighters. *Journal of Occupational Medicine, 27*(2), 110–114.

Campbell, J. P. (1971). Personnel training and development. *Annual Review of Psychology, 22,* 565–602.

Carter, N., Hansson, L., Holmberg, B., & Melin, L. (1979). Shoplifting reduction through the use of specific signs. *Journal of Organizational Behavior Management, 2,* 73–84.

Carter, N., & Holmberg, B. (1992). Theft reduction through product identification. *Journal of Organizational Behavior Management, 13*(1), 129–135.

Chhokar, J. S., & Wallin, J. A. (1984). A field study of the effect of feedback frequency on performance. *Journal of Applied Psychology, 69,* 524–530.

Christenson, G. M., & Kiefhaber, A. (1988). Highlights of the national survey of work-site health promotion activities. *Health Values, 12*(2), 29–33.

Close, D. W., Irvin, L. K., Prehm, H. J., & Taylor, V. E. (1978). Systematic correction procedures in vocational-skill training of severely retarded individuals. *American Journal of Mental Deficiency, 83,* 270–275.

Conrad, C. C. (1987). Who comes to work-site wellness programs? A preliminary review. *Journal of Occupational Medicine, 29*(4), 317–320.

Cox, M. H., Shephard, R. J., & Corey, P. (1981). Influence of an employee fitness pro-gramme upon fitness, productivity and absenteeism. *Ergonomics, 24,* 795–806.

Crites, J. (1976). A comprehensive model of career development in early adulthood. *Journal of Vocational Behavior, 9,* 105–118.

Crites, J. (1982). Measurement of career development. In B. Bolton & R. Roessler (Eds.), *Symposium on applied research methodology* (pp. 1–8). Fayetteville: Arkansas Research and Training Center in Vocational Rehabilitation.

Cuvo, A. J., Jacobi, E., & Sipko, R. (1981). Teaching laundry skills to mentally retarded adults. *Education and Training of the Mentally Retarded, 16,* 54–64.

Daniels, A. C., & Rosen, T. H. (1986). *Performance management* (2nd ed.). Tucker, GA: Performance Management Publications, Inc.

Daniels, A. C., & Rosen, T. H. (1986). *Performance management* (rev. 2nd ed.). Tucker, GA: Performance Management Publications, Inc.

DeFrank, R., & Ivancevich, J. (1986). Job loss: An individual level review and model. *Journal of Vocational Behavior, 28,* 1–20.

Dember, W. (1991). Cited by T. Adler in Studies sniff out fragrance effects. *APA Monitor, 22,* pp. 5, 18.

Dierks, W., & McNally, K. (1987). An Arkansas bank is putting B. F. Skinner's theory into practice with surprising success. *Personnel Administrator* (March), 61–65.

D'Zurilla, T. (1986). *Problem-solving therapy.* New York: Springer.

Everly, G. S., & Feldman, R. H. L. (1984). *Occupational health promotion.* New York: Wiley.

Exline, R., & Messick, D. (1967). The effects of dependency and social reinforcement upon visual behavior during an interview. *British Journal of Social and Clinical Psychology, 6,* 256–266.

Fein, M. (1970) *Wage incentive plans.* Norcross, GA: American Institute of Industrial Engineers.

Fellner, D. J., & Sulzer-Azaroff, B. (1984). A behavioral analysis of goal setting. *Journal of Organizational Behavior Management, 6,* 33–51.

Ferster, C. B., & Skinner, B. F. (1957). *Schedules of reinforcement.* New York: Appleton-Century-Crofts.

Festinger, L. (1957). *A theory of cognitive dissonance.* Stanford, CA: Stanford University Press.

Fischbach, T. J., Dacey, E. W., Sestito, J. P., & Green, J. H. (1986). *Occupational characteristics of disabled workers,* 1975–1976 (DHHS NIOSH Publication No. 86–106). Washington, DC: U.S. Government Printing Office.

Fisher, M. S. (1981). Work teams: A case study. *Personnel Journal, 60,* 42–45.

Forsyth, D. R. (1987). *Social psychology.* Monterey, CA: Brooks/Cole.

Foss, G., Daniels, A. C., & Rosen, T. H. (1986). *Performance management* (2nd ed.). Tucker, GA: Performance Management Publications, Inc.

Foss, G., & Peterson, S. (1981). Social-interpersonal skills relevant to job tenure for mentally retarded adults. *Mental Retardation, 19*(3), 103–106.

Fox, D. K., Hopkins, B. L., & Anger, W. K. (1987). The long-term effects of a token economy on safety performance in open-pit mining. *Journal of Applied Behavior Analysis, 20,* 215–224.

Foxx, R. M., & Bechtel, D. R. (1982). Overcorrection. In M. Hersen, R. M. Eisler, & P. M. Miller (Eds.), *Progress in behavior modification,* Vol. 13 (pp. 227–288). New York: Academic Press.

Foxx, R. M., & Hake, D. F. (1977). Gasoline conservation: A procedure for measuring and reducing the driving of college students. *Journal of Applied Behavior Analysis, 10,* 61–74.

Frayne, C., & Latham, G. (1987). Application of social learning theory to employee self-management of attendance. *Journal of Applied Psychology, 72*(3), 387–392.

Frisch, C. J., & Dickinson, A. M. (1990). Work productivity as a function of the percentage of monetary incentives to base pay. *Journal of Organizational Behavior Management, 7*(1),13–33.

Ganster, D. C., Mayes, B. T., Sime, W. E., & Tharp, G. D. (1982). Managing organization stress: A field experiment. *Journal of Applied Psychology, 67*(5), 533–542.

Gebhardt, D. L., & Crump, C. E. (1990). Employee fitness and wellness programs in the workplace. *American Psychologist, 45,* 2, 262–272.

Gibbs, J. O., Mulvaney, D., Henes, C., & Reed, R. W. (1985). Work-site health promotion: Five-year trend in employee health care costs. *Journal of Occupational Medicine, 27,* 11, 826–830.

Ginnett, R. C. (1983). *Productivity enhancement in the air force using behavioral science techniques.* Presented at the American Psychological Association, Anaheim.

Glasgow, R. E., & Terborg, J. R. (1988). Occupational health promotion programs to reduce cardiovascular risk. *Journal of Counsulting and Clinical Psychology, 56,* 365–373.

Gold, M., & Barclay, C. R. (1973). The learning of difficult visual discrimination by the moderately and severely retarded. *Mental Retardation, 11,* 9–11.

Goldstein, J. L. (1980). Training in work organizations. *Annual Review of Psychology, 31,* 229–272.

Golembiewski, R. T., Yeager, S. J., & Hilles, R. (1976). Some attitudinal and behavior consequences of a flextime installation: One avenue for expressing central organization design values. In R. H. Kilmann, L. R. Pondy, & D. P. Slevin (Eds.), *Management of organization design* (Vol. 2). New York: North-Holland.

Guthrie, G. M., Guthrie, H. A., Fernandez, T. L., & Estrara, N. D. (1982). Cultural influences and reinforcement strategies. *Behavior Therapy, 13,* 624–637.

Guzzo, R. A., & Bandy, J. (1983). *A guide to worker productivity experiments in the United States, 1976–1981.* New York: Pergamon Press.

Hackman, J. R., & Oldham, G. R. (1975). *Work redesign.* Reading, MA: Addison-Wesley.

Hake, D. F., & Foxx, R. M. (1978). Promoting gasoline conservation: The effects of a reinforcement schedule, a leader, and self-recording. *Behavior Modification, 2*(3), 339–370.

Hall, R., & Hall, M. (1980a). *How to negotiate a behavioral contract.* Austin, TX: Pro-Ed.

Hall, R., & Hall, M. (1980b). *How to use time out.* Austin, TX: Pro-Ed.

Hammer, T. H., & Turk, J. M. (1987). Organizational determinants of leader behavior and authority. *Journal of Applied Psychology, 72*(4), 674–682.

Hatfield, M. O. (1990). Stress and the American worker. *American Psychologist, 45,* 10, 1162–1164.

Haupt, E. J., Van Kirk, M. J., & Terraciano, T. (1975). An inexpensive fading procedure to decrease errors and increase retention of number facts. In E. Ramp & G. Semb (Eds.), *Behavior analysis: Areas of research and application.* Englewood Cliffs, NJ: Prentice-Hall.

Hellriegel, D., & Slocum, J. W., Jr. (1979). *Organizational behavior.* St. Paul, MN: West Publishing Co.

Henderson, M., & Argyle, M. (1986). The informal rules of working relationships. *Journal of Occupational Behavior, 7,* 259–275.

Hermann, J. A., De Montes, A. I., Dominguez, F. M., & Hopkins, B. L. (1973). Effects of bonuses for punctuality on the tardiness of industrial workers. *Journal of Applied Behavior Analysis, 6,* 563–570.

Heward, W. L. (1978). Operant conditioning of a .300 hitter? The effects of reinforcement on the offensive efficiency of a barnstorming baseball team. *Behavior Modification, 2,* 25–40.

Hinman, S. (1985). Coordination of treatments across service delivery sections: Behavior change plans. In J. N. Marr (Chair), *Consultant and supervisory practices to promote utilization of behavioral interventions in rehabilitation.* Symposium, Association for Behavior Analysis, Columbus, OH.

Hinman, S., & Marr, J. N. (1989). Overcorrection behavior analysis to decrease the loss of personal property. *Rehabilitation Psychology, 34*(1), 33–42.

Hogan, R., & Morrison, J. (1990). Reported in conference on "Work and well-being: An agenda for the 90's." American Psychological Association, Boston.

Hogan, R., Raskin, R., & Fazzini, D. (1990). The dark side of charisma. In K. E. Clark & M. B. Clark (Eds.), *Measures of leadership.* Greensborough, NC: The Center for Creative Leadership.

Hopkins, B. L., Conard, R. J., Dangel, R. F., Fitch, H. G., Smith, M. J., & Anger, W. K. (1986). Behavioral technology for reducing occupational exposures to styrene. *Journal of Applied Behavior Analysis, 19*(1), 3–11.

Hughes, C., & Rusch, F. (1989). Teaching supported employees with mental retardation to solve problems. *Journal of Applied Behavior Analysis, 22*(4), 365–372.

Hughes, R. L., Rosenbach, W. E., & Clover, W. H. (1983). Team development in an intact, ongoing work group: A quasi-field experiment. *Group & Organizational Studies, 8,* 161–186.

Iacocca, L. (1984). *Iacocca: An autobiography.* New York: Bantam Books.

Ilgen, D. R. (1990). Health issues at work: Opportunities for industrial/organizational psychology. *American Psychologist, 45,* 252–261.

Ilgen, D. R., & Moore, C. (1987). Types and choices of performance feedback. *Journal of Applied Psychology, 72*(3), 401–406.

Irvin, L. K. (1976). General utility of easy to hard discrimination training procedures with the severely retarded. *Education and Training of the Mentally Retarded, 11,* 247–250.

Iwata, B., & Bailey, J. (1974). Reward versus cost token systems: An analysis of the effects on students and teacher. *Journal of Applied Behavior Analysis, 7,* 567–576.

Jackson, T., & Vitberg, A. (1987). Career development, Part 2: Challenges for the organization. *Personnel, 64*(3), 68–72.

Johns, G., & Nicholson, N. (1982). The meanings of absence: New strategies for theory and research. In B. M. Staw & L. L. Cummings (Eds.), *Research in Organizational Behavior, 4,* 127–172.

Johnson, B., & Cuvo, A. (1981). Teaching mentally retarded adults to cook. *Behavior Modification, 5,* 187–202.

Johnson, C. M., & Masotti, R. M. (1990). Suggestive selling by waitstaff in family-style restaurants: An experiment and multisetting observations. *Journal of Organizational Behavior Management, 11,* 35–54.

Jones, S. C. (1973). Self- and interpersonal evaluations: Esteem theories versus consistency theories. *Psychological Bulletin, 79,* 185–199.

Kalderen, E. (1980). Teknikens roll i det snatteriforhindrande arbetet [The role of technical innovations in shoplifting prevention] *Report from conference on shoplifting,* March 13, 1980 (pp. 57–62). Stockholm: Brottsforebyggande Radet.

Kanfer, F., & Gaelick-Buys, L. (1991). Self-management methods. In F. Kanfer & A. Goldstein (Eds.), *Helping people change* (pp. 305–360). New York: Pergamon.

Kaplan, L. H., & Burch-Minakan, L. (1985). Reach out for health: A corporation's approach to health promotion. Special issue: Health promotion. *American Journal of Occupational Therapy,* 777–780.

Katzell, R. A., & Guzzo, R. A. (1983). Psychological approaches to productivity improvement. *American Psychologist, 38,* 468–472.

Katzell, R. A., & Thompson, D. (1990). Work motivation: Theory and practice. *American Psychologist, 45*(2), 144–153.

Kazdin, A. E. (1972). Response cost: The removal of conditioned reinforcers for therapeutic change. *Behavior Therapy, 3,* 533–546.

Kazdin, A. E. (1984). *Behavior modification in applied settings.* Homewood, IL: Dorsey.

Kazdin, A. E., & Bootzin, R. R. (1972). The token economy: An evaluative review. *Journal of Applied Behavior Analysis, 5,* 343–372.

Kim, J. S., & Hamner, W. C. (1976). Effect of performance feedback and goal setting on productivity and satisfaction in an organizational setting. *Journal of Applied Psychology, 61*(1), 48–57.

King, B. T., Lau, W. W., & Sinuko, H. W. (Eds.) (1983). *Productivity programs and research in U.S. government agencies.* Washington, DC: Smithsonian Institution.

Knight, J. L., & Salvendy, G. (1981). Effects of task feedback and stringency of external pacing on mental load and work performance. *Ergonomics, 24,* 757–764.

Komaki, J. (1977). Alternative evaluation strategies in work settings. *Journal of Organizational Behavior Management, 1,* 53–77.

Komaki, J. (1986). Toward effective supervision: An operant analysis and comparison of managers at work. *Journal of Applied Psychology, 71*(2), 270–279.

Komaki, J., Barwick, K. D., & Scott, L. R. (1978). A behavioral approach to occupational safety: Pinpointing and reinforcing safe performance in a food manufacturing plant. *Journal of Applied Psychology, 63,* 434–35.

Komaki, J., Waddell, W. M., & Pearce, M. D. (1977). The applied behavior analysis approach and individual employees: Improving performance in two small businesses. *Organizational Behavior and Human Performance, 19,* 337–352.

Komaki, J., Zlotnick, S., & Jensen, M. (1986). Development of an operant-based taxonomy and observational index of supervisory behavior. *Journal of Applied Psychology, 71*(2), 260–269.

Koretz, G. (1988). Economic trends. *Business Week,* 3062, 14.

Korman, A. K., Glickman, A. S., & Frey, R. L. (1981). More is not better: Two failures of incentive theory. *Journal of Applied Psychology, 66*(2), 255–259.

Latham, G., & Frayne, C. (1989). Self-management training for increasing job attendance: A follow-up and replication. *Journal of Applied Psychology, 74*(3), 411–416.

Leigh, J. P., & Lust, J. (1988). Determinants of employee tardiness. *Work and Occupations, 15*(1), 78–95.

Locke, E. A. (1982). Employee motivation: A discussion. *Journal of Contemporary Business, 11,* 71–81.

Locke, E. A., Saari, L. M., Shaw, K. N., & Latham, G. P. (1981). Goalsetting and task performance: 1969–1980. *Psychological Bulletin, 90,* 125–152.

Lublin, J. S. (1980, September 17). On-the-job stress leads many workers to file and win compensation awards. *Wall Street Journal.*

Luthans, F., & Kreitner, R. (1985). *Organizational behavior modification and beyond.* Glenview, IL: Scott, Foresman.

Luthans, F., & Lyman, D. (1973). Training supervisors to use organizational behavior modification. *Personnel,* September–October, 38–44.

Luthans, F., Paul, R., & Baker, D. (1981). An experimental analysis of the impact of contingent reinforncement on salespersons' performance behavior. *Journal of Applied Psychology, 66*(3), 314–323.

Mahoney, D. (1976). Factors affecting the success of the mentally retarded in employment. *Australian Journal of Mental Retardation, 4,* 38–51.

Mann, T., & Silverman, R. (producers); Rosenberg, S. (director). (1980). *Brubaker* [Film]. Twentieth-Century Fox Film Corporation.

Marholin, D., & Gray, D. (1976). Effects of group response-cost procedures on cash shortages in a small business. *Journal of Applied Behavior Analysis, 9,* 25–30.

Marks, M., Mirvis, P., Hackett, E., & Grady, J. (1986). Employee participation in a quality circle program: Impact on quality of work life, productivity, and absenteeism. *Journal of Applied Psychology, 71*(1), 61–69.

Marr, J. N. (1985). Rationale and method for modifiying staff behaviors. In J. N. Marr (Chair), *Consultant and supervisory practices to promote utilization of behavioral interventions in rehabilitation.* Symposium, Association for Behavior Analysis, Columbus, OH.

Marr, J. N., Everett, F., Allegretti, C. L., Cochran, W., & Fitzgerald, J. A. (1980). Chaining the reinforcement effect from teacher through aide to child. Paper presented at a meeting of the Association of Behavior Analysis, Chicago, IL.

Marr, J. N., & Granneman, B. D. (1985). Utilization of behavioral interventions by staff. In J. N. Marr (Chair), *Consultant and supervisory practices to promote utilization of behavioral interventions in rehabilitation.* Symposium, Association for Behavior Analysis, Columbus, OH.

Marr, J. N., & Granneman, B. D. (1988). Over-correction behavior analysis to reduce dormitory key losses. Unpublished manuscript, University of Arkansas, Fayetteville.

Marr, J. N., Granneman, B. D., Hinman, S., Ferritor, D., & Sharrer, J. (1985). *Consultant and supervisory practices to promote utilization of behavioral interventions in rehabilitation.* Symposium, Association for Behavior Analysis, Columbus, OH.

Marr, J. N., & Greenwood, R. (1979). Utilization of behavioral knowledge from short-term workshops. *Evaluation and the Health Professions, 4,* 455–462.

Marr, J. N., Hinman, S., & Bush, R. (1979). Reduction of imaginary truck driving behavior by reducing the truck. Presented at the Fifth Annual Western Regional Conference on Humanistic Approaches in Behavior Modification. Las Vegas, NV.

Marr, J. N., Lilliston, L., & Zelhardt, P. (1974). The use of a token economy to teach the token economy. *Journal of Professional Psychology,* 440–445.

Marr, J. N., Roessler, R. T., & Greenwood, R. (1976). *Behavioral assessment of staff problems.* Symposium, International Association of Psychosocial Rehabilitation Services, Miami, FL.

Marr, J. N., & Roessler, R. T. (1986). *Behavior management in work settings.* Fayetteville: Arkansas Research and Training Center in Vocational Rehabilitation.

Martin, G., & Pear, J. (1992). *Behavior modification: What is it and how to do it.* Englewood Cliffs, NJ: Prentice-Hall.

Mathews, R., Whang, P., & Fawcett, S. (1980). Development and validation of an occupational skills assessment instrument. *Behavioral Assessment, 2,* 71–85.

McCuddy, M., & Griggs, M. (1984). Goal setting and feedback in the management of a professional department: A case study. *Journal of Organizational Behavior Management, 6*(1), 53–64.

McKelvey, R., Engen, T., & Peck, M. (1973). Performance efficiency and injury avoidance as function of positive and negative incentives. *Journal of Safety Research, 8,* 23–32.

McNees, M. P., Egli, D. S., Marshall, R. S., Schnelle, J. F., & Risley, T. R. (1976). Shoplifting prevention: Providing information through signs. *Journal of Applied Behavior Analysis, 9,* 399–405.

McNees, M. P., Gilliam, S. W., Schnelle, J. F., & Risley, T. R. (1979). Controlling employee theft through time and product identification. *Journal of Organizational Behavior Management, 2,* 113–119.

McNees, M. P., Kennon, M., Schnelle, J. F., Kirchner, R. E., & Thomas, M. M. (1980). An experimental analysis of a program to reduce retail theft. *American Journal of Community Psychology, 8,* 379–385.

McSweeny, A. J. (1978). Effects of response cost on the behavior of a million persons: Charging for directory assistance in Cincinnati. *Journal of Applied Behavior Analysis, 11,* 47–51.

Meichenbaum, D. (1983). Teaching thinking: A cognitive-behavioral perspective. In J. Segal, S. Chapman, & R. Glaser (Eds.), *Thinking and learning skills* (Vol. 2). Hilsdale, NJ: Earlbaum.

Miller, L. (1978). *Behavior management: The new science of managing people at work.* New York: John Wiley & Sons.

Miller, B. W., & Phillip, R. C. (1986). Team building on a deadline. *Training and Development Journal, 40,* 54–57.

Mirvis, P. H., & Lawler, E. E. (1984). Accounting for the quality of work life. *Journal of Occupational Behavior, 5,* 197–212.

Mullen, T., & Marr, J. N. (1993). Signs to reduce theft in drugstores. Paper presented at the Association for Behavior Analysis, Chicago, IL.

Narayanan, V. K., & Nath, R. (1982). A field test of some attitudinal and behavioral consequences of flextime. *Journal of Applied Psychology, 67*(2), 214–218.

National Institute for Occupational Safety and Health. (1983). *Program of the National Institute for Occupational Safety and Health: Program plan by program areas for fiscal year 1983* (DHHS Publication No. NIOSH 83–102). Washington, DC: U.S. Government Printing Office.

National Institute for Occupational Safety and Health. (1985). Prevention of work-related musculoskeletal injuries. In *Proposed national strategies for the prevention of leading work-related diseases and injuries* (Pt. 1, NTIS No. PB87–114740, 17–34). Cincinnati, OH: Association of Public Health.

National Institute for Occupational Safety and Health. (1985). *Proposed national strategies for the prevention of leading work-related diseases and injuries* (Pt. 1, NTIS No. PB87–114740). Cincinnati, OH: Association of Public Health.

National Institute for Occupational Safety and Health. (1988). *Proposed national strategies for the prevention of leading work-related diseases and injuries* (Pt. 2, NTIS No. PB89–130348). Cincinnati, OH: Association of Public Health.

National Institute for Occupational Safety and Health. (1988). Prevention to reduce neurotic disorders in the U.S. workplace. In *Proposed national strategies for the prevention of leading work-related diseases and injuries.* Cincinnati, OH: Association of Public Health.

Nemeroff, C., & Karoly, P. (1991). Operant methods. In F. Kanfer & A. Goldstein (Eds.), *Helping people change* (pp. 305–360). New York: Pergamon.

Newman, J. E., & Beehr, T. A. (1979). Personal and organizational strategies for handling job stress: A review of research and opinion. *Personnel Psychology, 32,* 1–43.

Nicholas, J. M. (1982). The comparative impact of organization development interventions on hard criteria measures. *Academic Management Review, 7,* 531–542.

Nordstrom, R., Hall, R. V., Lorenzi, P., & Delquadri, J. (1988). Organizational behavior modification in the public sector: Three field experiments. *Journal of Organizational Behavior Management, 9*(2), 91–112.

Oetting, G., & Miller, C. (1977). Work and the disadvantaged: Work adjustment hierarchy. *Personnel and Guidance Journal, 56,* 29–35.

Offerman, L., & Gowing, M. (1990). Organizations of the future: Changes and challenges. *American Psychologist, 45*(2), 95–102.

Oliver, L. W., van Rihn, P., & Babin, N. (1983). *Productivity improvement efforts in army organizations.* Presented at a meeting of the American Psychological Association, Anaheim, CA.

O'Reilly, C. A., & Puffer, S. M. (1989). The impact of rewards and punishments in a social context: A laboratory and field experiment. *Journal of Occupational Psychology, 62*(1), 41–53.

Orpen, C. (1981). Effect of flexible working hours on employee satisfaction and performance: A field experiment. *Journal of Applied Psychology, 66*(1), 113–115.

Overs, R. (1964). The interaction of vocational counseling with the economic system. *American Journal of Economics and Sociology, 23*, 213–222.

Owen, J. D. (1976). Flextime: Some problems and solutions. *Industrial and Labor Relations Review, 29*, 152–160.

Parasuraman, R. (1991). Cited by T. Adler in Studies sniff out fragrance effects. *APA Monitor, 22*, pp. 5, 18.

Paul, C. F., & Gross, A. C. (1981). Increasing productivity and morale in a municipality: Effects of organizational development. *Journal of Applied Behavioral Science, 17*, 54–78.

Pedolino, E., & Gamboa, V. U. (1974). Behavior modification and absenteeism: Intervention in one industrial setting. *Journal of Applied Psychology, 59*, 694–698.

Pennar, K. (1988, June 6). The productivity paradox. *Business Week, 3055*, pp. 100–102.

Perry, N. J. (1988, December 19). Here come richer, riskier pay plans. *Fortune*, pp. 51–58.

Peterson, S. (1981). Social-interpersonal skills relevant to job tenure for mentally retarded adults. *Mental Retardation, 19*, 103–106.

Polankoff, P. L., & O'Rourke, P. F. (1987). Managed care applications for workers' compensation. In *Business and Health*. Washington, DC: Washington Business Group on Health.

Pritchard, R. D., Hollenback, J., & De Leo, P. J. (1980). The effects of continuous and partial schedules of reinforcement on effort, performance, and satisfaction. *Organizational Behavior Human Performance, 25*, 336–353.

Pritchard, R. D., Jones, S. D., Roth, P. L., Stuebing, K. K., & Ekeberg, S. E. (1988). Effects of group feedback, goal setting, and incentives on organizational productivity. *Journal of Applied Psychology, 73*, 337–358.

Reid, D. H., Schuh-Wear, C. L., & Brannon, M. E. (1978). Use of a group contingency to decrease staff absenteeism in a state institution. *Behavior Modification, 2*(2), 251–266.

Rettig, E. B. (1975). How to reduce costly "mis-takes" in a steak house. *Work Performance, 2*, 4–8.

Rodin, J., & Salovey, P. (1989). Health psychology. *Annual Review of Psychology, 40*, 533–579.

Rosenberg, R. D., & Rosenstein, E. (1980). Participation and productivity: An empirical study. *Industrial and Labor Relations Review, 33*, 355–367.

Ross, A. S., & White, S. (1987). Shoplifting, impaired driving, and refusing the breathalyzer: On seeing one's name in a public place. *Evaluation Review, 11*, 254–260.

Ross, L. (1977). The intuitive psychologist and his shortcomings: Distortions in the attribution process. In L. Berkowitz (Ed.), *Advances in experimental psychology* (Vol. 10). New York: Academic Press.

Saari, L. M., & Latham, G. P. (1982). Employee reactions to a continuous and variable ratio reinforcement schedule involving a monetary incentive. *Journal of Applied Psychology, 67*(4), 506–508.

Sarason, I., & Sarason, B. (1981). Teaching cognitive and social skills to high school students. *Journal of Consulting and Clinical Psychology, 49*(6), 908–918.

Sauter, S. L., Murphy, L. R., & Hurrell, J. J., Jr. (1990). Prevention of work-related psychological disorders: A national strategy proposed by the National Institute for Occupational Safety and Health. *American Psychologist, 45*(10), 1146–1156.

Schneider, B. (1975). Organizational climates: An essay. *Personnel Psychology, 28*, 447–479.

Schneider, B. (1985). Organizational behavior. *Annual Review of Psychology, 36*, 573–611. Palo Alto, CA: Annual Reviews, Inc.

Selz, N., Jones, J., & Ashley, W. (1980). *Functional capacities for adapting to the world of work.* Columbus: National Center for Research in Vocational Education, Ohio State University.

Sharrer, J. (1985). The administration perspective on behavior change: Management of consultation. In J. N. Marr (Chair), *Consultant and supervisory practices to promote utilization of behavioral interventions in rehabilitation.* Symposium, Association for Behavior Analysis, Columbus, OH.

Sheridan, J. H. (1972). Who didn't show up today? *Industry Week, 174,* 30–35.

Shippee, G., & Gregory, W. L. (1982). Public commitment and energy conservation. *American Journal of Community Psychology, 10,* 81–93.

Shrauger, J. S. (1975). Responses to evaluation as a function of initial self-perceptions. *Psychological Bulletin, 82,* 581–596.

Skinner, B. F. (1953). *Science and human behavior.* New York: Free Press.

Skinner, B. F. (1969). *Contingencies of reinforcement.* New York: Appleton-Century-Crofts.

Skinner, B. F. (1974). *About behaviorism.* New York: Knopff.

Smith, F. J. (1977). Work attitudes as predictors of attendance on a specific day. *Journal of Applied Psychology, 62,* 16–19.

Smith, T. (1981). Employer concerns in hiring mentally retarded persons. *Rehabilitation Counseling Bulletin, 24,* 316–318.

Smulder, P. G. W. (1980). Comments on employee absence/attendance as a dependent variable. *Journal of Applied Psychology, 65,* 368–371.

Social Security Bulletin. (1989). Annual statistical supplement, 1989 (DHHS Publication No. 13–11700). Baltimore, MD: U.S. Government Printing Office.

Spencer, D., & Steers, R. (1981). Performance as a moderator of the job satisfaction-turnover relationship. *Journal of Applied Psychology, 66*(4), 511–514.

Spielger, M. D., & Agigian, H. (1977). *The community training center: An educational-behavioral systems model for rehabilitating psychiatric patients.* New York: Brunner/Mazel.

Srebalus, D., Marinelli, R., & Messing, J. (1982). *Career development: Concepts and procedures.* Monterey, CA: Brooks/Cole.

Starr, B. M. (1980). The consequences of turnover. *Journal of Occupational Behavior, 1,* 253–273.

State of Michigan. (1987). *Report on worker's compensation: Annual report for 1986.* Lansing, MI.

Staw, B. M. (1980). The consequences of turnover. *Journal of Occupational Behavior, 1,* 253–273.

Sterns, H. L., & Doverspike, D. (1989). Aging and the training and learning process in organizations. In I. L. Goldstein (Ed.), *Training and development in work organizations: Frontiers of industrial and organizational psychology* (pp. 299–332). San Francisco, CA: Jossey Bass.

Stumpf, S. (1984). Adult career development: Individuals and organizational factors. In N. Gysbers and Associates (Eds.), *Designing careers* (pp. 190–215). San Francisco, CA: Jossey Bass.

Sulzer-Azaroff, B., Loafman, B., Merante, R. J., & Hlavacek, A. C. (1990). Improving occupational safety in a large industrial plant: A systematic replication. *Journal of Organizational Behavior Management, 11*(1) 99–120.

Sundstrom, E., De Meuse, K. P., & Futrell, D. (1990). Work teams: Applications and effectiveness. *American Psychologist, 45*(2), 120–133.

Switzer, E. B., Deal, T. E., & Bailey, J. S. (1977). The reduction of stealing in second graders using a group contingency. *Journal of Applied Behavior Analysis, 10,* 267–272.

Thurber, S., & Snow, M. (1980). Signs may prompt antisocial behavior. *The Journal of Social Psychology, 112,* 309–310.

Tjosvold, D. (1984). Effects of leader warmth and directiveness on subordinate performance on a subsequent task. *Journal of Applied Psychology, 69*(3), 422–427.

U.S. Bureau of the Census. (1990). Statistical abstract of the United States: 1990 (110th ed.). Washington, DC: Author.

Van Houten, R. (1984). Setting up performance feed-back systems in the classroom. In W. Heward, T. Heron, D. Hill, & J. Trap-Porter (Eds.), *Focus on behavior analysis in education* (pp. 114–125). Columbus, OH: Charles Merrill.

Van Houten, R., & Nau, P. A. (1983) Feedback interventions and driving speed: A parametric and comparative analysis. *Journal of Applied Behavior Analysis, 16,* 253–81.

Verhave, T. (1966). The pigeon as quality-control inspector. *American Psychologist, 21,* 109–115.

Wacker, D. P., & Berg, W. K. (1983). Effects of picture prompts on the acquisition of complex vocational tasks by mentally retarded adolescents. *Journal of Applied Behavior Analysis, 16,* 417–433.

Wallin, J. A., & Johnson, R. D. (1976). The positive reinforcement approach to controlling employee absenteeism. *Personnel Journal,* August, 390–392.

Walton, R. E. (1976). Innovative restructuring of work. In J. M. Rosow (Ed.), *The worker and the job* (pp. 145–178). Englewood Cliffs, NJ: Prentice-Hall.

Weitzel, W., Schwarzkopf, A., & Peach, B. (1989). The influence of employee perceptions of customer service on retail store sales. *Journal of Retailing, 65*(1), 27–39.

Wikoff, M., Anderson, D. C., & Crowell, C. R. (1983). Behavior management in a factory setting: Increasing work efficiency. *Journal of Organizational Behavior Management, 4,* 97–127.

Wilk, L. A., & Redmon, W. K. (1990). A daily-adjusted goal-setting and feedback procedure for improving productivity in a university admissions department. *Journal of Organizational Behavior Management, 7*(1), 55–75.

Winkler, R. C. (1970). Management of chronic psychiatric patients by a token reinforcement system. *Journal of Applied Behavior Analysis, 3,* 47–55.

Yagi, J. (1991) Cited by T. Adler in Studies sniff out fragrance effects. *APA Monitor, 22,* pp. 5, 18.

Zimmerman J., Overpeck, C., Eisenberg, H., & Garlick, B. (1969). Operant conditioning in a sheltered workshop. *Rehabilitation Literature, 30*(11), 326–333.

Zohar, D., & Fussfeld, N. (1981). Modifying earplug wearing behavior by behavior modification techniques: An emperical evaluation. *Journal of Organizational Behavior Management, 3,* 41–52.

Index